A NEW KIND OF MONSTER

TIMOTHY APPLEBY

A NEW KIND OF MONSTER

THE SECRET LIFE AND SHOCKING TRUE CRIMES OF AN OFFICER . . . AND A MURDERER

BROADWAY PAPERBACKS
NEW YORK

Library of Congress Cataloging-in-Publication Data is available upon
request.

ISBN 978-0-307-88872-3
eISBN 978-0-307-88873-0

Printed in the United States of America

Cover design by James Iacobelli
Cover photographs: © Glenn Davy/All Canada Photos/Corbis (house);
© Walter B. McKenzie/Getty Images (soldier)

10 9 8 7 6 5 4 3 2 1

First U.S. Edition

CONTENTS

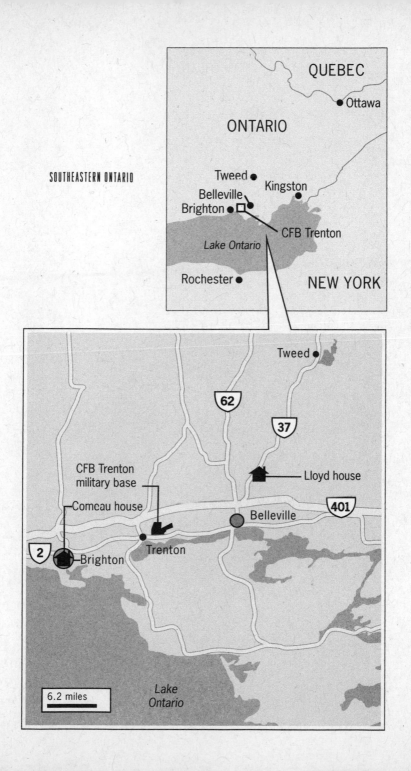

SOUTHEASTERN ONTARIO

QUEBEC

Ottawa

ONTARIO

Tweed

Kingston

Belleville

Brighton

CFB Trenton

Lake Ontario

Rochester

NEW YORK

Tweed

62

37

CFB Trenton
military base

Lloyd house

401

Comeau house

Belleville

2

Brighton

Trenton

6.2 miles

Lake
Ontario

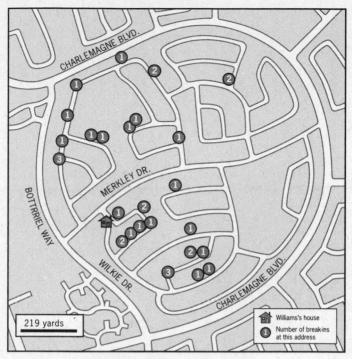

Crime sites in Orleans neighborhood, Ottawa.

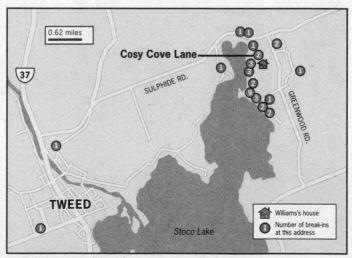

Crime sites in Tweed.

A NEW KIND OF MONSTER

INTRODUCTION

He looked like a haunted man, marched into court every day in handcuffs and ankle shackles, a burly police officer on each arm. Clean-shaven and neatly groomed, still a colonel in the Canadian air force, Russell Williams wore a dark jacket and slightly mismatched pants, brown shoes and a pale, open-necked shirt, no tie allowed. The dozen other cops always stared at him hard as he was led to the glass-walled prisoner's box a few minutes before the proceedings began, and so did everyone else in the packed courtroom. But he never glared back. He would stand for a moment to have the cuffs removed, his eyes averted, and then meekly sit down.

At age forty-seven, Williams remained a muscular figure, six foot two, 180 pounds. He'd kept fit inside his cramped cell at Quinte Detention Centre over the past eight months with a rigorous push-ups regimen. And during his four-day guilty plea and sentencing in Belleville, two hours east of Toronto, there was always concern among court officials that he might suddenly try to bolt or lunge for a weapon of some kind. What did he have to lose? He would never walk the streets again, and he'd already made an imaginative attempt to kill himself while in custody. But he never did step out of line—he always behaved.

He resembled a husk of a human being, a forlorn portrait in misery and disgrace, the first colonel in the history of the Canadian Armed Forces—and there have been more than 16,000 of them—to be charged with murder. Many killers have dead, lizard-like eyes, indicative of a lifelong indifference to the suffering they have wrought. But Williams's eyes were alive, bright with torment. A couple of times during the proceedings he wept, and from three yards away his grief seemed genuine, though he was surely sniffling as much for himself as for anyone else. Mostly he just gazed at the courtroom floor, as though deeply ashamed of who he was.

And he *was* ashamed. The most closely guarded secret of the Russ Williams story is the fact that along with the tsunami of evidence of unspeakable crimes that police found on his home computer, there was also child pornography. And that was the one offense to which he refused to plead guilty. Murder, rape and bizarre sexual assaults, scores of terrifying, fetish-driven home invasions—he was ready to admit to all of that, in a series of confessions that were mostly truthful, although sprinkled with self-serving evasions. But he was not willing to acknowledge downloading child pornography from the Internet, and during the pretrial negotiations he'd been adamant: child porn charges would be a deal-breaker. If they were laid, there would be no guilty pleas on the murder and sexual assault charges. Instead, everything would go to trial—an outcome that neither the prosecution nor the defense was eager to force.

As he sat in the prisoner's box, flanked by two officers of the Ontario Provincial Police (OPP), Williams would occasionally take a sideways peek at the courtroom, or glance up at the two flat TV screens at the front of the room where the photo exhibits provided a glimpse into his secret world of horror.

Here he was: the formerly proud commander of the country's most important air base, the popular career soldier with top-level military-security clearance, the crackerjack pilot who'd once flown a Polaris Airbus to London to bring Queen Elizabeth and Prince Philip to Canada for a royal visit. Here he was, via the damning photographic evidence: in the bedroom of a teenage girl whose home he had invaded in the dead of night while everyone was away. His lean, naked frame was stretched out on her neatly made bed as he leered confidently into the expensive Sony camera he'd carefully set up. One arm was draped around a large white stuffed animal; his other hand gripped his erect penis as he masturbated into the girl's underwear.

Dozens of similar pictures were shown, excruciating close-ups of the killer's genitalia and his face as he posed in his stolen trophies, gaze unflinching. Many were unnerving to look at—spectators in the courtroom often averted their eyes—and his computer hard drives had held thousands of such images, adroitly concealed within folders and subfolders. And this was not the worst of it. Not by far. These were just the pictures of himself and his lingerie keepsakes, and the least offensive of them were released to the public as court exhibits, chiefly pictures showing Williams modeling some of the 1,400-plus items he admitted stealing. Not screened in court, because they were deemed too disturbing, were the long, grotesquely choreographed videos of the bondage, rape and deaths of the two women he had killed, spectacles of numbing violence and cruelty in which he was scriptwriter, director and star. He had taken scores of still pictures as well.

Now he was nearing the end of the line. Early each October morning outside the ornate Belleville courthouse, police dogs barked in the darkness as squads of cops waited, preparing to hustle Williams inside, behind a black canvas screen that shielded him from the television cameras. Reporters began lining up at five in the morning for a spot in the 153-seat courtroom, and an overflow room with a videolink one floor down held many more spectators. Curiosity in Belleville and the environs was intense as the last scenes in this horrifying saga of murder and sexual obsession were played out.

But there was nobody there in court for Williams as the curtain came down: no family, no members of the military, not a single ally save his well-paid Ottawa lawyers. Russ Williams had become a toxic commodity because he had betrayed every-thing and everyone: his country, the armed forces, his wife, his parents, his few friends, the many people who had admired him and loyally worked under him during his sterling 23-year career. A few days after his conviction on all eighty-eight charges, he was formally stripped of his rank and medals; later his uniform was burned in an incinerator at the air base he had once commanded, and the two medals were shredded. Williams will serve his life sentence in an isolated prison cell the size of a small bathroom, under 24-hour camera surveillance. His chances of parole are around zero, and he will almost certainly die in that claustrophobic cell in Kingston Penitentiary, or in one very much like it.

And for what?

In large part the answer was up there on the big TV screens, as Hastings County Crown attorney Lee Burgess and colleagues read in the lengthy agreed statement of facts that accompanied Williams's guilty pleas to two counts of first-degree murder, two of sexual assault, two of unlawful confinement, and eighty-two home break-ins. It was all about sex—sexual fantasy, sexual obses-sion and sexual control, taken to a homicidal level that most people in the courtroom could barely comprehend. The other motivations were strong but secondary: the power he wielded over his victims, and the thrill of taking ever more risks in the belief that he was smart enough to stay ahead of any pursuit.

The detectives who took his detailed confessions had had to look no further than his two homes to find most of the physical evidence they sought. Williams had not only stored and carefully itemized the spoils of his obsessive break-ins, a collection of stolen women's underwear so extensive that twice he had had to take some of it to fields outside Ottawa and burn it. Along with the videos and thousands of still photos of himself, he had also documented everything in copious typed notes, describing each one of the crimes to which he was now willing to plead guilty.

Other serial killers have kept diaries too, and it was plain that for practical purposes he *was* a serial killer. The strict definition of the term as used by the FBI and the RCMP is that he or she has claimed at least three lives, and Williams killed two people. Yet there is no doubt whatever among justice officials close to the investigation that he would have murdered again had he not been caught, and would have continued to kill. And he all but said so himself.

As well, it was evident that he had long been a sexual deviant, and now here he was: a stalker and cunning sex killer who had been commanding 8 Wing/CFB Trenton, Canada's most important air base, the air force's operational hub.

How was that even conceivable?

In thirty years of writing about crime in Canada and conflict abroad, I thought I'd seen every kind of killer. But Russell Williams did not resemble any of them, and in one way he seemed the scariest of all, because so many different people who'd dealt with him had respected him and liked him so much. Throughout his long military career he'd been almost universally seen as a smart, decent guy, a stickler for organization and a bit awkward socially, but also generous and very often kind. What had changed him into the monster now before the court? Or had everybody just been fooled all along? It was suggested, and the analogy was not entirely fanciful, that he resembled a Jekyll-and-Hyde character: by day, an exemplary, upstanding citizen; by night, transformed into a loathsome, terrifying predator.

Eight months had now elapsed since Williams had been charged with murder, and it was becoming increasingly evident that no additional cases were likely to be laid at his door, suggesting he had unleashed his instincts unusually late in life. And if so, then why? What was the trigger? That was what everyone was asking, and none more so than the people who had known him—or had thought they did. And nobody, it seemed, had an answer.

1

A VILLAGE UNDER SIEGE

Neatly dressed in casual clothes, the tall, lean man didn't have a lot to say as he patiently waited his turn in the barber's chair that Saturday morning. Saturdays are often a busy time for Tweed barber Reg Coté, a fixture on the village main street for thirty years, and in that regard October 3, 2009, was no different. Longtime customers, mostly middle-aged, stop in for a sixteen-dollar haircut and a chat with whomever is there, including the agreeable Coté, a good talker and listener whose Quebec accent remains strong. There's no red-and-white striped barber's pole outside his shop, but there's a makeshift one inside, and his salon resembles the traditional model: an informal, walk-in business with a single barber's chair and an L-shaped seating arrangement, where men who know each other can catch up on local developments, good and bad.

But this was no ordinary Saturday morning in Tweed. The usually tranquil village was struggling to make sense of an unusual piece of local news. Two days earlier, under the headline "Public Safety Concern," provincial police at nearby Madoc had issued an unsettling press release:

The Ontario Provincial Police (OPP), Central Hastings detachment are investigating two break-ins that occurred, in which a male suspect entered the home while the residents were sleeping. On September 17 and again on September 30, 2009, both in the early hours of the morning, an unknown male entered Tweed residences. During both separate incidents, the suspect struck the female victim, tied her to a chair and took photos of her. The suspect then fled the scene. The OPP want to remind everyone to ensure all doors and windows are secured and to practice personal safety. Please report any suspicious activity to the police immediately by calling 911. OPP officers are following up leads to identify the suspect. If anyone has information about these incidents, they are asked to call the Central Hastings OPP.

Some particulars were missing from the release. Nothing conveyed the fact that the attacks had been sexual in nature, and that after being blindfolded and tied to chairs, both women had had their clothes cut off before nude photo sessions began. Nor that the home invasions had lasted hours, and that they had occurred within a few hundred yards of each other, on adjoining roads on the rural outskirts of town.

A half hour's drive north of Belleville, Tweed lies roughly midway between Toronto and Ottawa. Once a bustling way station on the Toronto–Montreal rail line, these days Tweed is a laid-back community of about 1,600, with three times that number in the greater area. Yet it is also a fairly worldly place, home to many retirees, and most households have access to the usual modern telecommunications devices. So word of the twin assaults spread quickly.

Already, out-of-town undercover officers had been spotted— faces not familiar in Tweed—in unmarked cars and in at least one instance peering out the windows of someone's borrowed house. In undercover surveillance, a good rule of thumb is that the smaller the venue, the harder it is to remain unseen. And it hadn't taken long for some of Coté's more astute customers to notice that something unusual was afoot in the Cosy Cove Lane area, a few minutes' drive from Victoria Street, the main thoroughfare.

So on this Saturday morning, the barbershop conversation consisted of little else but the mystery intruder and what he might do next. "Suddenly there's people coming into the shop and talking about all this," Coté recalls. And as he clipped and snipped, Coté was not the only person in the shop paying close attention to the discussion. So too was the tall man with the brush cut waiting to get a quick trim.

The chatter was laced with rebukes for the police. Why hadn't they put out the full story? And why hadn't they issued an alert after the first home invasion, on September 17? Why did they wait for the guy to strike again?

It was an issue that would become a sore point in Tweed, although there was a certain logic to the information gaps. Police investigating serious crimes routinely withhold details that can only be known by the perpetrator, such as the caliber of a gun or the quantity of cash stolen in a robbery. In this instance, more-over, investigators were navigating a fine line between warning the public and trying not to trigger panic—and an instant media blizzard—which is what might well have happened if all the bizarre details had become known. As well, an undercover operation was supposed to be under way. What's more, there had initially been a credibility issue with one of the two women who'd been attacked.

But that's not how many people in Tweed saw things, at least not at the time, as the talk buzzed in Coté's barbershop that morning. And as it did, most of his customers very likely had little idea who the tall, well-dressed man might be as he sat there quietly listening. But Coté knew, because he was one of his regulars; he'd been cutting his hair for several months. He was Colonel Russell Williams, forty-six, wing commander of the sprawling

8 Wing/CFB Trenton air base, a 45-minute drive southwest of Tweed, and for several years a resident of the short, winding road named Cosy Cove Lane.

Rich in history and folklore, perched on the edge of Stoco Lake, Tweed feels different from many small Ontario towns, perhaps a bit more sophisticated. A dwindling handful of dairy and cattle farmers still make a living in the hills outside town, and nineteenth-century brick buildings line Victoria Street. Along with its numerous retirees are many others who have exchanged big-city stresses for a smaller paycheck and a more low-key lifestyle. Tweed is the former home of Patrick LeSage, the retired judge who presided over the sensational Paul Bernardo murder trial in 1995. Provincial Liberal cabinet minister Leona Dombrowsky is a lifelong Tweedite too. It's a place where plenty of people still go to church, patriotism and small-c conservatism run deep, and some of the newer arrivals in town will tell you it can take years before you are accepted by the old guard. Yet Park Place Motel owner and Indian expatriate Neil Patel says that during his four-plus years in mostly white Tweed he has yet to encounter a racial slur. Nor has he once had to call police to deal with unruly guests at his well-run hostelry, tucked on the shoreline beach of Stoco Lake at the entrance to town.

Now, almost overnight, the comforting sense of security had evaporated. No one had the least idea of the identity of the Tweed Creeper, as he became known. But it didn't look as if he lived very far away. Tweed residents began locking their doors and many started keeping a loaded gun at hand.

"My mom didn't really want me walking anywhere, and when I walked to the bus stop in the morning, it was dark in the morning back then, so I was always looking over my shoulder, and

I was really scared at night," says Ruth, a Tweed teenager who would learn months later, to her great horror, that her home had been broken into and robbed of underwear by the same intruder who had attacked the two women. "It was hard to sleep. I was thinking that someone was going to come in my house. I always woke up in the middle of the night, at like two in the morning, because that's when all this stuff happens."

Amid the speculation and rumor, the police were working with full reports of the two bizarre attacks, which had occurred on adjacent roads connected by a wooded footpath. The first victim, known as Jane Doe, was a young mother in her early twenties who had been asleep in her recently rented lakeside cottage with her weeks-old baby; her spouse, a truck driver, was away, working up north for Ontario Hydro. In an account that police initially seemed to doubt because it sounded so improbable, she told them the intruder came inside, probably through an unlocked door, and woke her. He then struck her—hard—before blindfolding her, tying her to a chair and taking out his camera for a lengthy nude photo session. When he was finished, he fled into the night. There was no sexual penetration or sexual assault in any usual sense. She never saw the attacker's face. Her baby was left unharmed, and did not waken.

A report form was filled out, but there was little follow-up at first. The investigating Madoc OPP officers wondered briefly whether the attack—if it had even taken place—might have been the work of the woman's spouse, but they swiftly discounted that possibility. And the cops' problem was not merely that their rural and small-town experience had left them unprepared for a strange case like this, which seemed to belong in the pages of a big-city tabloid. It was also that the intruder, whoever he might be, had left behind nothing that could be traced—no items of clothing, no fingerprints and no samples of DNA.

Moreover, fairly or not, the young woman had a reputation for being erratic, and perhaps in this case she was possessed of an overactive imagination. Among the few Tweed residents who heard of the incident, there was the quiet suggestion that she might be suffering from postpartum depression.

Then, thirteen days later, the second attack took place.

A former accountant and telemarketer, and mother of three, 46-year-old Laurie Massicotte lived alone in her lakeside cottage on nearby Cosy Cove Lane. She recounted in an interview what happened.

As she often did, she had fallen asleep under a blanket on her living room couch, watching late night television. And the TV was still on when she woke, finding herself under assault from a man she could not see. The blanket was over her head and he was repeatedly punching her in the head and face. For many long minutes he kept his hands tightly on her throat—she feared she was going to be throttled—and as he did so, he warned her not to resist or to try to look at him.

The intruder had entered her home through an unlocked window at the back of the house, out of sight from the road. He told her that a robbery was under way, that he had accomplices who were in the house and that his job was to control her. With Massicotte's head still under the blanket, the man reached underneath and blindfolded her with a strip of pillowcase material he had sliced up. A second strip was used to bind her hands behind her back.

What followed was more than three hours of terror. "After he got my blindfold on me, he stood up, obviously, and he barked at me, 'Are you looking at me?' And I said, 'Oh no, God no.'" It was the wise thing to say. "You don't want to see me," was his reply. The robbery story was a ruse, and though she didn't realize it until later, there were no accomplices. Instead, the invader made her sit on the couch and, with the blindfold still on, he tied her up with a kind of harness he had fashioned from another pillowcase. He then stripped her naked by cutting off her clothes, wielding the blade with great precision. "It didn't leave a scratch on me," she said. Then the photo session began. The assailant took dozens of photographs, directing Massicotte as he obtained shots from numerous angles. She could hear the camera clicking.

But before any photos were taken, something curious took place. She told her attacker that her head was throbbing from the blows and that she needed some aspirin. Still in her blindfold, she was led to the bathroom and given two before being returned to the couch. "He was patting my head after he brought me back to the couch. As we were walking, he was rubbing my head softly, and he was apologizing, saying, 'Sorry for that,'" she recounts. "He was sorry for punching me in the head."

The intruder made many other conciliatory gestures, constantly reassuring Massicotte that if she cooperated he would not kill her. In a tone she is sure he deliberately kept low so as to disguise his voice, he called her "Laurie" many times, made small talk and said she seemed like "a nice person." Only fleetingly did he touch her sexually, and when she protested he stopped.

Her worst moment came near the end, after he had ordered her, still naked and in her harness, to strike a particularly obscene pose. He said he was leaving to make sure "the others" had got away but that he would be back in ten minutes to collect his camera gear. She heard the sound of a zipper. "And I thought that's where the gun was coming from, and he told me no, it was just his camera bag. I thought for sure he had a gun, I started fussing real bad. He told me, 'No, Laurie, I don't have a gun,' and he let me feel the camera strap on my face, to let me know it was only a camera."

He finally departed at around four-thirty. He had to leave by then, he told her a couple of times, and by coincidence or not, a couple of doors down from Laurie Massicotte's house lived a man who left home for work each morning at 4:45. Half an hour later she managed to struggle free, calm down somewhat and call 911. Within ten minutes two uniformed officers from the Madoc OPP detachment were at her door, soon followed by plainclothes detectives, a big forensics truck, a canine unit and a phalanx of other police who fanned out and began scouring the woodland that surrounds Cosy Cove Lane.

One thing that particularly puzzled the police who investigated this incident—different police officers were handling the first one—was that her assailant had been so oddly considerate of her, even as he tormented her, as if he was doing something he somehow had to do but wished he didn't.

A year later, Massicotte remained thoroughly traumatized by what she was put through. "I was terrorized to death. I'm still in shock. I'm lucky that I have my inside protectors and my inside strength," she says. "I still live it, minute by minute, but I get through it. He let me live, but it went on for three hours."

Massicotte's distress that day did not end when the police showed up at her door. Her teenage twin daughters were not living with her, and even as she was being questioned by detectives, they were learning of their mother's ordeal via a string of lightning-fast text messages being relayed around their Belleville high school, messages that depicted the assault as being even worse than it was. "My daughters found out through texting on the playground, in grade twelve. It trickled down and my daughter is trying to figure out where the heck this all came from. And by the time it got to my daughter, it was saying I had been raped and brutalized, tied up and raped. She was so angry and upset, and she didn't know if any of it was true."

Nor was anyone else in Tweed sure what to make of it all. Within days, news of the two home invasions was all over the village, and the victims' identities and addresses became widely known as well. And as the details seeped out, the fear level began to soar.

"With the second attack, things just blew up in town," Coté the barber remembers. "Usually doors were unlocked and now they were all locked. In this small community I would say probably 70 percent of the people have guns, if not more, and I know a lot of guys taught their wives and girlfriends how to shoot because of this, and I know a lot of people who were keeping guns under their beds."

Some Tweed residents, including reeve Jo-Anne Albert, had heard only a few sketchy details about the first attack. The home invasion targeting Massicotte, however, dispatched a shock wave. "That changed everything. That changed how the people in Tweed live, and we will never go back to how we were—at least I hope we don't," says Albert, an affable schoolteacher-turned-politician who has lived in Tweed for close to forty years and probably knows it as well as anyone. "It took away the innocence of a small town, I really believe that. "

Yet even as alarm bells began ringing, a parallel crime wave was under way in Tweed, and this one was largely unseen. Over the previous two years, dozens of peculiar house burglaries had been taking place, almost all in the same Cosy Cove Lane neighborhood where the two women were assaulted. These were not run-of-the-mill break-ins, which usually target cash and valuables that quickly get sold for a fraction of their value. Rather, they were the work of a single-minded sex fetishist whose sole quarry was women's underwear of all types: panties, bras, girdles, thongs, swimsuits. In a couple of instances, bathrobes and shoes were taken too. Entry to the homes had been gained in a variety of ways, often involving no more than walking through an unlocked door. And where there was forced entry, the most common means of access was a picked lock rather than a smashed window or jimmied-open door. In almost every instance, no one was home at the time, indicating that the intruder had done considerable reconnaissance before breaking in.

But almost no one in Tweed knew anything about this. In all, there were forty-five such burglaries in the area over a two-year period, many of them repeat trips to earlier targets (one residence was hit nine times). But almost all went unnoticed, or else they were not reported, possibly in some cases out of embarrassment. Police had been apprised of just one, and there was no mention of stolen underwear. Of course, no one in Tweed could have imagined that a similar wave of break-ins was simultaneously taking place in the Ottawa suburb of Orleans, 125 miles away.

To say that Russ Williams kept a low profile in Tweed, his adopted home for several years, would be an understatement. To call him near invisible would be more accurate, and this was in keeping with virtually every other facet of his nonmilitary life. He was occasionally seen at a convenience store or gas station, but for most of Tweed, Williams simply didn't exist. He was never spotted in the liquor store or at taverns. He didn't buy groceries in the big IGA Food Market. He never stopped off to grab a quick sandwich or coffee in the Gateway restaurant or the By the Way Internet café, two hubs of local activity on Victoria Street.

Perhaps most striking of all, he was unknown at the Tim Hortons outlet at the Sulphide Road cutoff on the outskirts of town, which led up to his nearby home on Cosy Cove Lane. Williams was not much of a coffee drinker, usually preferring tea. Nonetheless, his avoidance of Timmy's seems odd, to say the least. Ubiquitous across the nation, the famed Canadian coffee-and-doughnut chain holds a semi-iconic status in the military; it even has a presence at the Canadian Forces base in

Kandahar, Afghanistan, which Williams had several times visited. As well, the Tim Hortons coffee shop at Sulphide Road served as a meet-and-greet point in Tweed for local residents and busloads of Canadian troops heading to Afghanistan from the big army base in Petawawa, north of Ottawa—the site of their last cup of home-brewed coffee before going off to war. The ritual got started in 2008, the year before Williams assumed command of 8 Wing. Students from St. Carthagh Catholic School gathered to salute the soldiers at Timmy's, where each was handed a gift card. Then the troops made a second stop at the Legion Hall on the high street, where they were hailed by students from the S.H. Connor and Tweed-Hungerford senior schools.

Given the role the coffee shop played in the community and its links with the military, it might have been expected that the 8 Wing base commander living just up the road would be a regular visitor. But as far as is known, he never stopped by there. "When this all came down, it was a real shocker, because we had no idea he lived up on Cosy Cove," says a longtime employee. "No idea at all. We'd never heard of the guy until this. When we did, we freaked."

So if Williams was anxious to avoid the people of Tweed, why would he get his hair cut in the relatively exposed environment of Reg Coté's small barbershop? There seem to have been two compelling reasons, one being intelligence gathering.

"He would come in here, and he's far from being a stupid man, so he would get information here," Coté said later. "It's easy to get information in a barbershop—ask a question, listen to what everybody has to say. He would always be listening more than talking. So after the second girl [was attacked], of course he's in here, sitting here waiting for a haircut, hearing all the talk, so he knew right away there was undercover cops."

Coté recalls Williams as a taciturn customer, always courteous. "I talked to the guy a lot. He didn't say much at first, but eventually he started talking more. The first time he came in here I figured he'd never come back—he didn't say much, wouldn't talk to me. But he always listened. What you hear in a barber's shop is not always true, but the way I figure it, he thought he was never going to get caught. And so maybe he started doing things more out in the open than before."

Williams never made any mention of the two home invasions, as far as Coté can recall. "He was way too smart for that."

In one otherwise casual barbershop conversation that would take on some significance later, Williams did make inquiries about one of his next-door neighbors on Cosy Cove Lane, Larry Jones. "I remember Russell asking me if I knew Larry Jones, and the way he asked me was as if he didn't know, although by then he'd been coming in here for a long time," Coté says. "He asked me what's he like and I said, 'Well, yeah,' and we were talking about it. I've heard so many things about Larry since I've been in Tweed . . ." So, too, had many other people in the village, and not all the gossip about Jones was friendly.

All the talk about police surveillance that October Saturday morning may have given Williams a scare, because three weeks would elapse before there was another of the lingerie raids he had been stealthily committing in Tweed for two years—a relatively long gap in the pattern. But if he had been rattled, his caution didn't last. His next target, on October 24, was a house on Sulphide Road, just down the road from his Cosy Cove Lane cottage, close to the Tim Hortons. That was to be the last break-in in Williams's immediate neighborhood; two more Tweed homes would be burgled in the first week of November, but both were off his usual beaten path.

And there was a second explanation for Williams's regular visits to Coté's shop for a quick trim. The obvious alternative to having his hair cut in Tweed would have been to do what other 8 Wing personnel did: stop in at the Trenton air base's own barbershop, on the south side of the property, a thirty-second walk from Williams's office at command headquarters. But doing so would have exposed him to the one thing he was anxious to evade, in Tweed, in Trenton and everywhere else: conversation and scrutiny. No less than its civilian counterpart, a military barbershop and its relatively informal atmosphere is an excellent place to catch up with news and rumors, and perhaps ask a polite question or two of the customer in the chair, even if he is the base commander. The barbershop on the base has closed its doors since Williams was there, but when it was open there would usually be three or four people getting a haircut at the same time.

One of the defining characteristics of Williams's extremely busy seven-month spell as the leader of 8 Wing was his concerted effort to spend as little of his free time as possible on the base, or in the company of other senior officers. He didn't live there, he was rarely seen in the officers' mess, and he became more and more reliant for communication on his BlackBerry, which he used to receive and dispatch a steady stream of messages. At the same time, a big part of a wing commander's duties consists of being in the public eye, especially at busy 8 Wing, where the pace was often hectic. Williams attended plenty of official functions, to have his photo snapped and to speak a few words to a reporter from *Contact*, the base's excellent weekly newspaper. But there were many others that he skipped, sending a junior officer to stand in for him instead.

Only after he was arrested did questions begin to surface as to why he had been so aloof, although some people did think it odd at the time. One of those people was retired army lieutenant-general Jack Vance—General Jack as he is known, a greatly respected figure in Tweed, and a former vice chief of staff of the Canadian Armed Forces. Now seventy-seven, Vance remains sharp of mind, and he knows a thing or two about watching for bad apples within the military: before he became vice chief, he oversaw personnel operations for the entire armed forces for five years. No screening system could have detected Williams's latent criminal instincts, he believes—not within the armed forces and not in any of the other major public-oriented professions, such as the judiciary, the medical world or the Church. Yet Vance has come to believe that Williams's day-to-day behavior could have drawn more scrutiny that it did.

"The thing I notice about him is this: Base commander basically means being there all the time. Why on earth would he not live there? There was a house for him. He would finish a very good day's work in Trenton and jump in his car, or go to this particular bar in Belleville, instead of going to the officers' mess. It was as if he was shunning his own officers, because he wanted to get away from them. More to the point, psychologically he wasn't there—he wasn't committed. And it was kind of a shame his wife wasn't there too, because there's a really important job for the wife of a base commander . . . I would have thought that somebody of a more senior rank might have noticed all that."

In Tweed, by contrast, there was very little for anyone to notice.

Williams lived a highly compartmentalized existence, and off-duty in the civilian world he barely registered as a member of the community, a consistent pattern during his entire 23-year career with the military. He had very few close friends, he belonged to no social clubs or volunteer organizations, he never attended church as far as is known, and he had no children. He was a computer whiz, easily able to keep pace with the advances of the information age, but his expertise was largely confined to his professional life—and to his macabre, sex-drenched secret life. No blogs or chat rooms or social media websites show any sign of him.

In Tweed, moreover, which has long had close ties to the Trenton base, something else cloaked him. Among the handful of Tweedites who were aware of Williams, such as next-door neighbors who would wave or occasionally exchange greetings, his prestigious position as commander of the 8 Wing base lent him a natural aura of mysterious authority—perfect cover for his clandestine night life. This, after all, was someone who had been entrusted with top-secret information, had flown prime ministers and royalty around the world, and dealt regularly with people at the top levels of government. A couple who lived next door to Williams and his wife, Mary Elizabeth Harriman, on Cosy Cove Lane, Monique and Ron Murdoch, knew them a little better than most, occasionally socializing with them and playing cards, and at least once Ron Murdoch went out ice fishing on Stoco Lake with Williams.

But the Murdochs were very much in the minority. The few people in Tweed who did brush shoulders with Williams encountered a courteous, distant figure, invariably calm and polite. He and Harriman, an executive director of the Ottawa-based Heart and Stroke Foundation of Canada, had purchased the big cottage at 62 Cosy Cove Lane in August 2004, two months after he was promoted to lieutenant-colonel and took the helm of the Trenton 8 Wing air base's 437 ("Husky") Transport Squadron—the same base he would later command in its entirety after reaching full colonel five years later. They paid $178,000 for the blue-gray frame bungalow on the edge of Stoco Lake, the longtime residence of an elderly couple who could no longer take care of it. It was a second home for Williams and Harriman, their main residence being a handsome house in the eastern Ottawa suburb of Orleans that they had bought brand new.

After Williams was transferred away from 437 Squadron, the cottage on Cosy Cove Lane remained as a weekend getaway spot. Then, with his promotion in July 2009 to full colonel and commander of the 8 Wing base, he was back at work in Trenton and back living in Tweed, an easy 45-minute commute down Highway 37 and then along the busy 401.

The cottage's commanding view of Stoco Lake was impressive, the building itself less so. A glimpse inside after it had been searched and ripped apart by police following Williams's arrest showed thin gray paneling on the walls, cheap ceiling tiles and Formica countertops. Furnishings included a battered beige carpet, an ancient wooden crate-turned-table that had once contained dummy bombs, a green-and-white striped couch, an old piano, a heavy ceiling fan and various floor lamps. Down below was an unfinished basement, and in the adjoining garage was the man of the house's favorite recreational toy: a sixteen-foot Lowe bow rider with a big Evinrude outboard to power it on his many fishing trips. On the sloping back lawn, facing the lake and the boat dock, was a large ornamental wishing well.

Harriman's name adorned the mailbox along with that of Williams, but over the years she had visited Cosy Cove Lane only intermittently, and to the people of Tweed she was, if possible, an even more remote figure than her husband. Certainly there was no reason to believe either of them was connected even in the slightest to the twin break-ins that had taken place in September. Nor were there any other suspects in sight. And that's where things stood a few weeks later, when amid the simmering fear and alarm the police investigation took a huge wrong turn.

October 29, 2009, was a Thursday, two days before Halloween, and it was around one-thirty in the afternoon when Larry

Jones's universe began crashing in around him. He was returning to his Cosy Cove Lane home empty-handed from a par-
tridge hunt, dressed in his customary camouflage gear, his small
dog, Wes, by his side. What happened then, he says, "was like
the end of the world." At sixty-five, Jones was a lifelong Tweed
resident, a vigorous, talkative figure, and not a universally popular one. Now he was about to become a pariah, shunned by
almost everyone he knew.

Jones has lived on Cosy Cove Lane for much of his life. His
house was one of twenty-one mostly winterized residences
dotted along the road, nestled comfortably on the Stoco Lake
shoreline, and it sat immediately next door to the cottage belong-
ing to Williams and Harriman. Jones and his wife, Bonnie, had
lived at their place for thirteen years. Retired from his job as a
surveyor with the Ministry of Natural Resources, Jones was and
is endlessly busy: onetime head of the Stoco Lake ratepayers
association; a Legion member; trail warden for the snowmobile
club, with authority to dispense fines to scofflaws; occasional
manager of the sports arena; local handyman.

Some people in Tweed say unhesitatingly that they don't much
care for Jones. Many years earlier, the police had become involved
in some minor domestic trouble at the Jones household, and he
was once shot in the hand by an angry neighbor. Ask around
Tweed about Jones and you will hear complaints that he has long
had a reputation for being overbearing and abrasive.

Yet domestic stability is also a hallmark of Jones's life. A
grandfather, and married to the same woman for more than
forty years, Jones has had plenty of disagreements with neighbors, but he has never been arrested and his violations of the law,
he says, can be summed up by a single speeding ticket. Along
with his wife, treasurer for the Municipality of Centre Hastings,
his numerous friends include many police officers.

But there was nothing friendly about the small army of Ontario Provincial Police officers who were waiting for him as he pulled his Jeep up in his driveway that October afternoon. They didn't tell him right away why they were there. In all, there were twenty or more cops standing around his house, including plainclothes police, two or three to a car. Jones's first thought was that he had been broken into.

"Oh no, sir, it's way worse than that," was the reply. "But we can't tell you right now." Jones soon gleaned that they wanted to talk to him about the two home invasions that had occurred nearby a few weeks earlier, one just a few doors down from the Jones home.

This was not Jones's first encounter with the police in connection with the attacks. A few hours after the September 30 assault, as tracker dogs and armed police scoured the woods, uniformed officers went door to door, canvassing neighbors. Had they heard or noticed anything suspicious overnight? Had any strangers been spotted in the neighborhood recently? And as they made their way along Cosy Cove Lane, Jones saw them knock at number 62, immediately next door to his house. It belonged to Williams, the air force officer who had bought it five years earlier and after some time away was now living there again while he ran the 8 Wing/CFB Trenton air base. Not that he was seen a great deal; he usually did the commute back and forth to Trenton when it was dark, while on weekends he would generally head back to Ottawa to be with Harriman.

Jones recalls that September 30 morning vividly. "They walked on to Russ Williams's place there, knocked on the door and waited for a few minutes. Then I walked out and met them. One of them went to another neighbor and the young cop stayed here and talked to me and asked me if I'd heard anything that morning or seen anything.

"And he said, 'Who lives next door there?' and I said, 'Russ Williams,' and he said, 'Yeah, I see that on the mailbox. Same name as the commander of CFB Trenton.' And I said, 'No, that *is* the Russ Williams of CFB Trenton, that's him,' and he said, 'Oh, really, you're not kidding. Well then, I guess we don't have to look at him.'"

The police canvass moved on.

Now, almost a month later, here they were again. A glance at the search warrants the police had brought with them showed Jones just how ominous things were. The warrants stated that the police were seeking, among other things: computer digital storage devices; women's underwear, including black and purple La Senza brassieres and thong underwear with the logo of a poodle; two baby blankets; pornographic photos and videos; a pair of white shoes; zip ties. The cops crowded into Jones's house, examining and seizing a wide range of items: a laptop, a DVD reader, a CD reader, USB sticks, memory sticks. Also scooped up were his hunting knife, his work boots—around a hundred items in all.

Incredulous and stunned, Jones found himself in a squad car being read his rights on the way to the Madoc OPP detachment for interrogation. "We've been investigating you for three weeks, sir. We know all about you," he recounts one of the cops telling him. "We got a really good tip, sir. That's why we're here."

At the police station, Jones managed after some difficulty to call Bonnie at her workplace to tell her he'd been detained for questioning in the sex assaults. Her initial reaction was to tell him to quit fooling around. Then she realized it was all deadly serious. "It was unbelievable," she said later.

The next few hours were the worst of Larry Jones's life.

The OPP is a formidable organization, made up of close to six thousand uniformed officers, plus civilians and auxiliaries, serving a province of more than 12 million people. Part of its hub in

Orillia, in central Ontario, is its cerebral, highly specialized Behavioural Sciences and Analysis Services unit. And one of those experts was on hand now, in charge of interrogating Jones, to whom it was made plain he was squarely in the police sights.

How did he break into the two houses? he was asked. Did he have a key? (In both instances there had been no signs of forced entry.) What was going through his mind when he was doing this? Other, more personal questions were asked: As a child, had he been molested or beaten? What were his sexual interests? Police also listed for him the charges he would be facing if he was, indeed, the masked intruder. And one particularly loaded line of inquiry remains seared into his memory. Paraphrased, it went like this: "If you were the person who broke into Laurie Massicotte's house on September 30, and tied her up and sexually assaulted her—if you were—would you be guilty?"

Three times Jones was asked that question, and three times he refused to answer it because of the way it was framed. Instead, he kept repeating his unequivocal denial. "I said, 'No, I wasn't there.'"

Other, peripheral issues surfaced in the interrogation. Many years earlier, he and Bonnie had had a rowdy altercation that had briefly drawn police attention. The couple ended up apologizing to each other, but now that incident was revived—as indicative of Jones's unstable temperament, it was suggested.

During the search of Jones's home, half a dozen ancient copies of *Penthouse* magazine had been unearthed, the most recent dating back to 1981. Pornography on the premises, eh? went the line of questioning. What's the significance of that? Jones told them there was none.

In the course of the questioning, he also learned why the police had turned their attention on him. A few years back he'd stopped by Laurie Massicotte's house to look at some floor-tile work she'd had done. After that she'd dropped by his house several times, unasked and never staying for long. But the acquaintanceship would end up being unfortunate for Jones. A week or two after she was assaulted, Massicotte had called police to tell them that although she was blindfolded and never saw her attacker's face, she now believed she recognized his voice, and that it was the voice of Jones.

Confronted with the police suspicions, Jones denied everything, his mind reeling as he insisted once again that a dreadful mistake had been made. But along with protesting his innocence, Jones also did the smart thing. Instead of clamming up in a panic and perhaps calling a lawyer (who would assuredly have instructed him to stop talking immediately), he willingly gave the cops everything they wanted, except a confession: a DNA sample, extracted from a saliva swab; fingerprints; palm prints. Later he took a polygraph test and passed it with flying colors. Why not? he reasoned. He had nothing to hide.

Nor did his physique match that of the assailant, described by Massicotte as apparently a young man. And so, early that evening, badly shaken after three hours of interrogation, Jones was allowed to go home. The police weren't completely through with him, though. Even after it was made clear to him that he was probably in the clear, the OPP detective heading the Massicotte investigation, Constable Russ Alexander (later to take a key role in Williams's arrest), continued to ask neighbors if they'd ever been bothered by him, Jones says. Had they ever seen him peeking through their windows? Notice anything else suspicious about Jones?

The day after Jones was picked up for questioning and then released, Massicotte recalls, "Russ Alexander phones me up and says, 'We searched Larry Jones's house. However, we didn't find anything.'" She asked the detective about Jones's status. "Let's put it this way: he's certainly a person of interest," was Alexander's response, she says. Police also remained suspicious of Jones's son, Greg, and asked him to take a polygraph, which on the advice of his father he declined to do.

But the damage had already been done. No crime, murder included, engenders the fear and social disgust that instantly attaches to a person suspected of a sex crime, wrongly or not. Some defense lawyers will tell you they would rather have a client convicted of bank robbery or drug dealing than acquitted of a sex offense, because of the lasting opprobrium.

So it was with Jones, and so it would remain until Williams was arrested. "My heart broke for Larry and his wife, because I know their grandchildren, they're the same age as mine," says Jo-Anne Albert, the reeve. "Kids are cruel. Parents are going to talk at home and not care that the kids are listening. They have four [grandchildren] up there in school, and for them it was a bad time."

Jones himself says the experience was devastating. "Nobody came for two or three months. I was all by myself, except for my very close friends. They've all come back now, but I can tell you, this was very scary."

Back home after his long inquisition at the Madoc OPP detachment, Jones now had to deal with the unpleasant reality that the source of his troubles was Massicotte, who, while not a close friend, was someone he'd known for years. Later—after Williams was arrested—she apologized profusely, Jones says. "She says to me, 'Larry, I'm so sorry. I didn't really want to phone the police and tell them it was you.'"

So why *did* Massicotte make that fateful call? She says today it was a combination of confusion and being urged by a friend to pick up the phone and give the police Jones's name. The friend was one Jonas Kelly, a man related to Jones through marriage and who didn't much like him. "I was told by Jonas Kelly what to do.

He told me to phone my detective and tell them that I recognized the voice," she says. "When I phoned them to tell them I thought I recognized the person's voice, I didn't even want to say who it was, I was so scared. But then they came right out and asked me. The detective suggested to me it wasn't Larry, it was his son Greg. And I said, 'No, Larry.' And he said, 'Oh, Laurie, do you think you could come down to the station right away and give us a statement.'"

So she did. Police picked up Larry Jones the same day. There was no other evidence against him.

Jones now believes that Massicotte was unstable and therefore easily influenced by Jonas Kelly. As for Massicotte, she was not reluctant to speak out about her ordeal. After Williams was arrested, she gave several interviews to the media in which she excoriated the OPP for not having issued a warning after the first attack.

Most remarkable, however, was her willingness to forgive her attacker. "I'm not in the judgment department, but I'm in the forgiveness department, and I feel everybody has a God-given right to forgive," she says. "He let me live. It was like he didn't want to kill me. I always look at the good in people. I can't speak for any of the others, I can only forgive him for what he did to me, and now he has to live the rest of his life [in a prison cell]. I despise him, but I can forgive him, because of the simple fact that he let me live, and that's what I wanted most. And I have to be able to forgive to move on."

News that Jones had been picked up and questioned at length about the twin attacks spread swiftly through Tweed. And it reached Williams too. Jones knows that, because even though it never occurred to him at the time that the colonel might be the real predator, he was anxious to learn how widely word of his troubles with police had spread. So, through a mutual friend, he asked a civilian Trenton air base staffer who knew Williams well whether the colonel had by any chance mentioned that Jones—his next-door neighbor—was a prime suspect in the unsolved attacks. The subject had indeed come up, and Williams's response was curiously casual, Jones recounts. He seemed to have heard something about Jones being detained and questioned but appeared entirely unperturbed. "Get out of town. Larry Jones wouldn't do something like that," was how Williams's response was relayed back to Jones.

Jones chatted briefly to Williams several times after that, talking about nothing very much, and the matter was never raised. "He could have asked me what was going on, but he didn't," Jones says. "He carried on like nothing had happened."

In hindsight, two other incidents—one before Jones was taken in for questioning and one after—took on a distinctly sinister bent in Jones's mind.

Few visitors ever came to the Williams home, and Jones remembers the day in July 2009 when his neighbor took over as base commander. The commander had laid on a big party on his back lawn. Tables were set up, the grass was newly mowed, a portable toilet was rented. "I thought he was expecting a hundred people from the way it was all set up," Jones says. But none of the neighbors on Cosy Cove Lane were invited, and not many others showed up either—perhaps fifteen in all.

Given the absence of cordiality, Jones was a little surprised by a conversation he had with Williams in September 2009, the same month the two women were attacked in their homes. Dressed in his camouflage gear, Jones was heading out to shoot a few grouse, and was just loading his shotgun into his truck when his next-door neighbor wandered over. Uncharacteristically inquisitive, Williams wondered where Jones's hunting camp was. Jones told him it was about six miles away, in the thick forest that lines each side of Cary Road, an isolated gravel road southeast of Tweed village. At first the colonel wasn't sure where exactly that was. Jones gave further directions. Williams responded, "Ah, yes," and there the conversation ended.

Initially Jones didn't give the encounter much thought, even after a friend of his spotted Williams in the area a few weeks later, on foot, staring off into the distance and appearing lost. But when Williams was arrested, the exchange rushed back to haunt Jones. A few hours after Williams was charged, the body of his second murder victim, Jessica Lloyd, was located. It lay in the woods about a mile from Jones's hunting camp, some forty feet in from Cary Road, half concealed among a pile of rocks.

Was Williams trying to frame Jones? A second mysterious incident suggests that perhaps he was. On the same night that Lloyd was kidnapped, January 28–29, 2010, Jones says someone broke into his garage, across Cosy Cove Lane from his house, where he keeps his boats and snowmobiles. Curiously, however, only three items appeared to be missing: a blue cigarette lighter, a pair of work gloves and an old coat that his dog, Wes, a West Highland terrier, was fond of sleeping upon. What happened to those items remains a mystery. Jones wonders if Williams could have taken the items with the idea of using them to frame him for a crime, but he concedes he may never know.

As for what he went through with the OPP, Jones takes a charitable view. "Half of those guys are friends of ours, we've played hockey together—my niece and my nephew are both OPP officers. So all this wasn't their fault. They just weren't trained for an investigation of this magnitude."

———

Tweed settled down a bit in the next few weeks, but the tension lingered. Residents pitched in to knit a giant scarf in support of Canada's athletes at the Vancouver Olympics, as the We Believe campaign sponsored by the Chamber of Commerce took hold. "Tweed was at its best, prouder and stronger, because people felt as though they were finally involved in something that brought them together," remembers Lisa Ford, who with her husband operates the By the Way coffee shop on Victoria Street.

Then two things happened. Midway through November in the rural outskirts of Belleville about midway up Highway 37 as you head towards Tweed, there was a break-in at the house of an artist and music teacher whose husband was away. The intruder took some sex toys and underwear. And, terrifyingly, he left a taunting message on the woman's home computer, suggesting he had been in the house at the same time she was on the previous evening, hiding in an upstairs linen closet.

Few people in Tweed heard about the burglary, and the Belleville police who investigated it seemed to know nothing about the two earlier sex attacks around Cosy Cove Lane.

About a week later, there came word of what sounded like a domestic-related homicide in Brighton, just west of Trenton along Highway 401, an hour's drive from Tweed. A flight attendant attached to CFB Trenton had been found murdered in her home, where she lived alone. Provincial police from Northumberland County took charge of the case and urged local residents to stay calm. "There are no present issues with regard to public safety," an OPP officer said on November 30, five days after Corporal Marie-France Comeau's asphyxiated, bloodied body was discovered in her bedroom, wrapped in a duvet.

To the residents of Tweed, there was no special reason to make any connection between the events in their community and either of these incidents, particularly the Comeau homicide.

Brighton seemed very far away. And for the handful who did hear about what had occurred, the least likely person to be in any way involved would probably have been the pleasant, seldom-seen military figure who had arrived in Canada from England more than four decades earlier.

A-TOWN

David Russell Williams was born into a world of middle-class privilege, filled with high achievers. Later in life he would tell friends he didn't remember much about his early childhood, and whether that's true or not, he rarely spoke about it, even when pressed. After his arrest, when it became clear that his extraordinary cruelty and violence had been directed exclusively at women, observers looked to his roots for possible clues as to what might have fostered his rage, and some were there to be found.

Deep River has long been one of the jewels of the upper Ottawa Valley, the lush, green Laurentian Mountains on the northern Quebec shore of the Ottawa River providing a spectacular backdrop. Tucked into the river's south shoreline, all but invisible from the nearby Trans-Canada Highway that links it to the Chalk River Research Laboratories ten miles down the road, the small town was the first place in Canada that Williams called home. He was a few weeks shy of five when he, his British-born parents and his younger brother, Harvey, arrived there more than forty years ago, riding a wave of incoming scientists, technicians and their families attracted by high-paying jobs and what in many ways was an idyllic existence.

Affluent and remote, a white-collar oasis of Ph.D.-toting intellectuals plunked down in a rugged northern landscape,

Deep River was by any yardstick unusual. Naturally, much has changed since then. The trees that dot Deep River's neat, curvy residential streets are thicker and taller. The many sailboats that used to be moored off the Deep River Yacht and Tennis Club— the town's social hub during the two years that Williams lived there—have largely been replaced by houseboats.

The small downtown core looks different too, reconfigured after a big fire tore through it in 1998, destroying the landmark Giant Tiger store and half a dozen other businesses. No longer an all-white enclave, there is a growing immigrant population, mostly from Asia. And the town's relationship with Atomic Energy Canada Limited, the Crown corporation tasked with managing the country's nuclear program, has also evolved. Deep River has always been called A-Town—A for atomic—and is still joined at the hip to Chalk River, with AECL remaining by far the area's principal employer. But no longer does the corporation own the big, comfortable houses in which the scientists and their families lived.

"They used to own everything. It was a company town. You pretty much had to work at Atomic Energy to keep a house," says realtor Jim Hickey, who has lived in Deep River since 1945. Hickey and his family spent their first few years in rented accommodation. "And my father would warn me to keep the grass cut, because there was a shortage of housing, the implication being that we'd better keep it cut or we might lose it. I was twelve when he died, and I remember one of the [AECL] employment officers coming to the house with his wife and telling my mother, 'When this guy's old enough to work, send him in to see me.'"

But Deep River's current population of around 4,400—7,600 in the greater Deep River area—hasn't changed much, nor have the town's attractions. Waves lap at the golden beaches, a magnet for family picnics, just a few minutes' walk from the downtown. Sunrises over the river are legendary, and a short drive away is the eastern edge of Algonquin Park. Stroll around Deep River and you will be hard put to see a piece of litter. Serious crime barely exists. In 2009, the ten-officer police force recorded 199 occurrences, two-thirds involving theft or other property crime. Residential neighborhoods don't have sidewalks, because everybody knows to drive slowly and safely.

"People who come here for the first time call this God's Country," enthuses Karen Bigras, deli manager at Fleury's Super-Valu, the anchor retail outlet in the small downtown. Bigras moved to Deep River in 1969, when she was four, a year after the Williams family arrived, and she recalls a very happy childhood. "I absolutely loved it. We didn't have to worry about anything, we were allowed to ride our bicycles and walk on the road, we didn't have any fears. All the kids went to playgrounds, and there was always things to do outside: camp days, arts and crafts. The word *bored* didn't exist when we were children. I don't know anybody who didn't have a wonderful childhood here. A lot of the people I went to school with have moved back here to raise their children."

But it was not the town's agreeable environment and lifestyle that brought the Williams family to Deep River. Rather, it was Chalk River's cutting-edge lab facilities, whose jobs lured scientists from around the world, principally from Britain. The Chalk River Laboratories were the sole raison d'être for Deep River, as they are today. Chalk River remains the source of more than one-third of the world's—and almost all of North America's—supply of medical diagnostic isotopes, a safe radioactive material used chiefly to diagnose illness.

The atomic theme is ubiquitous in the town. Numerous schools and streets are named after pioneers of Canada's nuclear development, a stylized atom logo adorns city stationery, and A-power has long had a place within the local culture. A 1950s rock band called themselves Phil Rowe and the Atomic Five, and there was a men's basketball team named the Neutrons.

This was the milieu to which the Williams family transplanted themselves, six years after Canada's first nuclear power plant, the CANDU prototype, went online near the Chalk River Labs. And for a four-year-old boy uprooted from the English Midlands, moving there must have been a grand adventure.

Williams was born on March 7, 1963, in the small town of Bromsgrove in Worcestershire, southwest of Birmingham, where both his parents attended university after marrying in Wales the year before. Russell's father, Cedric David Williams—Dave was the forename he used all his life—had emerged from his studies as a skilled metallurgist. In an era when most Britons could readily immigrate to Canada if they chose, opportunity beckoned in the shape of a job offer from AECL. So, in early 1968, the Williams family—Dave, Christine, Russell and Harvey—packed their bags and launched their rather strange new life.

Constructed amid great secrecy and built in part by German prisoners of war, the Chalk River Nuclear Research Laboratories were created in 1944 by the federal government as part of the nuclear Manhattan Project, which created the A-bomb. The basic idea, enthusiastically promoted by Winston Churchill, was that U.S. and British know-how would fuse with Canadian uranium, all in a suitably isolated location. Deep River was the company town built to house the scientists and their families who poured in.

To this day the myth persists that Chalk River was the source of the plutonium in the atomic bombs dropped on Hiroshima and Nagasaki in 1945. In fact, the war had ended by the time the first Chalk River nuclear activity began. Nonetheless, it remained for many years a highly enigmatic enterprise. Both Deep River and Chalk River were patrolled by armed guards, with access to either place controlled by military checkpoints. Deliberately placed upwind and upriver from Chalk River to avoid possible fallout from its reactors, Deep River sits between the Trans-Canada Highway and the Ottawa River, about 125 miles northwest of Ottawa and a 45-minute drive from the big Petawawa army base.

Everything in Deep River was meticulously planned—so much so that years before the Williams family arrived, its critics mocked it as sterile, artificial and oppressive. In a jaundiced and now-famous article in *Maclean's* magazine in 1958, author Peter Newman painted a picture of a community that could sometimes be stifling, likening Deep River to "a utopian attempt to create a happy environment where all is ordered for the best." The writer quoted a poem penned by a resident that mocked Deep River's entrenched sense of good order:

> *Although the town is trim and neat,*
> *With cozy houses on every street,*
> *Though saying so is indiscreet,*
> *I hate it.*

But the poet was assuredly in the minority among the mostly urban-educated professionals who lived in and around Deep River. Writing in 1970 as Deep River marked its twenty-fifth anniversary, visiting *Globe and Mail* reporter Rudy Platiel marveled at what he called "a town with few parallels." He noted the energetic volunteerism, the busy library, the enthusiasm at the weekly newspaper, and the scores of clubs and social groups— everything from yachting and drama to track and field, curling, bridge and a symphony orchestra whose conductor doubled as a neutron physicist. "This town is clubbed to death, always has been," according to Hickey the realtor. "Access to the big city didn't used to be what it is today, and people made do with what they had."

In short, Dave Williams and his family had arrived in a small town with a sophisticated urban feel to it, full of skilled professionals with high expectations. The work was steady, the money was good, and home was a big three-bedroom duplex on Le Caron Street that the Williamses bought in March 1968, the same month Russell turned five.

An elderly English-born widow who lived in the other half of the duplex at the time and is still in Deep River today remembers his parents as standoffish and aloof. Russell, however, was a lively, friendly little boy who would chat across the fence, sometimes in very English-oriented slang. One time he solemnly informed her that his younger brother, Harvey, had just "spent a penny" in the garden flowers, a euphemism for relieving oneself that was dated even then. Like everyone else who learned of his arrest four decades later, the former neighbor was horrified by the news. "He was a smart kid, very smart. I don't know where he went wrong, but something went wrong. I hope they throw the book at him."

No less stunned was retired teacher Erma Wesanko, who taught Williams in the kindergarten class at Deep River's T.W. Morison Public School. A snowbird, she was vacationing in Florida when she got word. "It was a tremendous shock, quite a surprise. His name rang bells when I heard it, and when I saw his picture I absolutely remembered him as this little blond boy I had known. I could just picture him. He was a quiet little boy. I can't remember him being tremendously outgoing. He was just a normal little boy, very attractive, gorgeous really. It's just a very sad story. It hurts me terribly to think about how this could happen to someone."

Wesanko remembers her teaching days in the community with great fondness. "Deep River was such a great place for children, a safe town with all kinds of activities and all kinds of things to do."

But beneath the smooth veneer of familial stability was an undercurrent of turbulence, barely concealed then and today widely acknowledged: a permissive 1960s sexual ethos was flourishing in the community. "It was like Peyton Place [the New England town in the classic novel about the sordid secrets that lie beneath a placid exterior], quite a little den of iniquity. People were trading partners and sleeping with one another's wives," says retired schoolteacher Dianne Murphy, who also taught at Morison when Williams attended.

Many marriages ruptured, "and a lot of people stayed with their new partners," Murphy remembers. "They had what they called the Key Club, and quite a few people participated. A lot of the professionals would have been involved, more than the techies. The population was heavily loaded with British immigrants, and there was a certain kind of class system that was incorporated into this town. Some neighborhoods were designed exclusively for the professionals, others were for the tech people."

Karen Bigras, too, recalls the Key Club, a conduit for wife swapping. A participant would go to a party at the club with his or her spouse and then leave with someone else's partner. Bigras first heard about these goings-on when she was seven. "You put your keys in a hat. My parents were shocked and horrified when they found out about it. They had been asked to join."

Retired family therapist Peter Addison, who spent six years as chief counselor at the Deep River high school, knew both of

Williams's parents and tried unsuccessfully to help them when their marriage faltered. "It was an exciting time, it was all happening, this nuclear thing was going to be their salvation," he says of the Deep River residents. But Addison also recalls a social milieu that was "neurotic as hell," in which sexual experimentation seemed to blend with an adherence to conventional middle-class values. "It was a strange society. None of that free-spirited stuff was as free-spirited as it appeared to outsiders. The parents were pretty traditional. Some of them didn't understand why kids would have a choice about what they wanted to do. I remember arguing with parents when kids would want to drop Latin or something. It would be, 'No, they can't do that.'"

Some who lived in Deep River at the time remember Williams's father, David, as a loud, authoritarian figure who would insult his wife in front of others and insisted on having his way. Neither parent was overtly affectionate, several people said; both seemed preoccupied with their busy lives. "Russell's mother would come down to the [Yacht and Tennis] Club and leave him on his own to play on the waterfront," remembers a former resident who was a few years older than Russell and knew the family. "Frankly, the teenagers at the club really did not like the father at all. He became the subject of many pranks. He had a quick, sharp temper and was easily provoked."

How much impact any of this had on Williams's psyche and how much it shaped his future life is subject for speculation. What is certain is that his home life was soon going to change radically.

Living on Birch Street a couple of blocks from the Williams house was another family drawn to Deep River by the Chalk River project: Jerry and Marilynn Sovka and their three young children. An Alberta-born nuclear physicist, the son of Czech immigrants, Jerry Sovka was educated at the Massachusetts

Institute of Technology and he too had attended the University of Birmingham, on a scholarship, which is where he may have first met Christine Williams. "Jerry Sovka was very much involved with the Yacht and Tennis Club—and many other things," says retired AECL electrical engineer Bill Bishop, who has lived in Deep River since 1967. "He was a very social person, maybe too much so. He was a ladies' man, he liked women, he had an air about him. He was a real hustler."

The Williamses and Sovkas were close, and nowhere more so than at the Deep River Yacht and Tennis Club, the epicentre of social life where live rock bands often played on Saturday nights. The club also had a reputation as a "meet market." (Some people had a less genteel term: the Deep River Twat and Penis Club.) "The Brits brought—I won't say peculiarities—but they brought a freer kind of attitude," opines another long-ago Deep River resident, who spoke on condition of anonymity. "If you went to a dance, you didn't just dance with your wife, you danced with three or four other partners . . . It was socially accepted in Britain, probably an offshoot from the postwar years. It was pre-Woodstock, but the acceptable threshold was steadily winding its way down. It was just a very fluid marital scene in some circles. I don't know what was going on behind closed doors, but at the yacht club dances, for example, they were definitely pushing the envelope."

Peter Addison recalls the yacht club well, and recounts crewing with both David Williams and Jerry Sovka. "Sometimes I'd be the assistant—I was the first mate and they were the captains. David was a tough captain when we were sailing together. Usually they had separate boats, but occasionally they sailed together." And even in a community brimming with high achievers, both men stood out. "David was one of the top nuclear metallurgists, and you don't get to that level unless there's a certain part of your personality that's able to be obsessive," Addison says. "He and Jerry in their respective fields were among the top people in the world at the time, and that's why he was able to move wherever he wanted to, because he was in demand. And he was competitive—anyone at that level is competitive. I remember that from when we skied together a couple of times in Quebec, he and I and another buddy. He was interested in music, theater and nuclear metal. And he was a hell of a good singer." He could also be extremely stubborn, Addison recalls. "I remember once he and I organized a dance for something or other, and we had a big argument about what kind of orange juice to use."

Christine Williams, as she was known then, a tall, accomplished tennis player, "was as charming as she was good-looking," in the words of another former Deep River resident. "It was always small talk, but she always had a pleasant remark to make."

Yet there was a pronounced conservative streak. Addison recalls a weekend when Christine Williams took care of his young son and daughter, aged three and four. To the surprise of both, she insisted that they change into their bathing suits in different rooms. "She was a little bit prissy, and they thought that was pretty amusing, because that was the hippie time in Canada, too, and we would sometimes go swimming without bathing suits.

"Chris was extremely attractive, yet the funny thing was, David used to put her down all the time. David was in charge. She was expected to wait on him, and everything he did was expected to be wonderful. David and Chris had a lot of marital problems, and I don't think he understood the whole thing about relationships . . . I don't think he had much connection with the kids even when he was there."

In October 1969, Christine Williams filed for divorce. In a day when a divorce application had to cite a reason for separating, hers was on grounds of adultery, stating that her husband had been having an affair with Marilynn Sovka. The application was not contested and the Williamses split up. Christine sold her husband her share of the house, gaining custody of their two sons, and the three moved out. For a short spell she and the boys lived in nearby Petawawa, home to the big army base. The former duplex neighbor recalls helping her haul the furniture down Highway 17.

Meanwhile, Jerry Sovka had filed his own divorce petition against Marilynn, also alleging adultery with Dave Williams. Both divorces were made final in February 1970, with the three Sovka children remaining with Marilynn.

With her divorce just four months old, Christine remarried in June of that year—the bridegroom being none other than Jerry Sovka, who had taken a job as a senior engineer with Ontario Hydro in Toronto. They would stay together for the next thirty years before separating—an event that would prove greatly upsetting to Williams, judging by his response, which was to sever almost all contact with his mother. At the time of her son's arrest, Nonie Sovka, as Christine Williams was now known, was living in an elegant condo on Toronto's Harbourfront, and even though she was approaching seventy, was still working as a physiotherapist at the city's acclaimed Sunnybrook Health Sciences Centre.

David Williams stayed on in Deep River for another year. A newspaper photo from February 1971 shows him singing with the local choral group, which he directed. But the romance with Marilynn Sovka—"a very nice woman," as Addison remembers her—did not last, and soon he had kindled a relationship with another woman, again married with children. She left her family to move with Williams to Germany, where he had a new job, but that relationship too soon fizzled.

The ever-peripatetic David Williams, to whom Russell would remain close for most of his life, later returned to North America, first to New York and then eventually to a position with General Electric's Nuclear Products Division, based in San Jose, California. He also became a naturalized American. At the time of Russell Williams's arrest he was employed at Wake Forest University in Winston-Salem, North Carolina, where he was editor-in-chief of the journal *Biomaterials*. Father and son never lived together after Dave and Christine divorced, but they maintained a strong bond and would often visit each other, according to people who knew them both. During his confession and in subsequent talks with police, however, Russ Williams more than once made it clear that he did not want his father to visit him behind bars.

3

A NEW LIFE

"Give me the child until he is seven and I will give you the man."

—Jesuit motto, attributed to 16th-century Roman Catholic missionary Francis
Xavier

At age seven, Russ Williams was on the move again. He and five-year-old Harvey had been uprooted once before in their lives and now they were in Toronto, a new city, with a stepfather in place of their father and a new family name, Sovka. Their mother had even changed her first name, from Christine to Nonie, her middle name.

The marriage arrangements between the two divorced couples were unusual, in that they comprised a direct exchange between the four partners: while Jerry and Nonie Sovka were raising Russell and Harvey in Scarborough, a Toronto suburb, Jerry's three children were being looked after in Deep River by their mother, Marilynn.

How much distress the upheaval caused the brothers is only a guess, because Williams rarely discussed his family history with anyone, and friends learned not to raise the topic. "It was clear to me when I met him that his parents were divorced and that it wasn't a happy thing to delve into," says Jeff Farquhar, a former University of Toronto roommate who was to become a longtime close friend.

All through his adult life, Williams would remain closer to his father than to his mother. They stayed in constant touch, often visited each other, and several times Dave Williams stayed at his son's lakeside cottage in Tweed. Back in 1970, however, it's possible that on the heels of the tumultuous breakup in Deep River the move to Toronto came as a relief to young Russell. Jerry Sovka in his thirties is remembered as being more easygoing than David Williams. Two former friends, a retired married couple in Toronto who knew the Sovkas when they lived in Scarborough, recall Jerry as funny, energetic and tolerant of his new stepsons, although, as with so many of the ambitious alumni of Chalk River, his job always came first.

The Sovkas moved several times over the next few years, migrating from North York, another of Toronto's suburbs, to Scarborough, where the brothers attended one of the Montessori elementary schools. The family rented a house, and then another one, before buying a home of their own and reselling it soon afterward. Then, in May 1975, came the purchase of a small but splendidly located bungalow, perched on the Scarborough Bluffs overlooking Lake Ontario. For $89,900, the Sovkas got a run-down property on a huge, elongated 50-by-550-foot lot. It was at 15 Lakehurst Crescent, a quiet, T-shaped cul-de-sac south of Kingston Road, in one of Scarborough's old, established neighborhoods, tucked between two pieces of wooded parkland where wildlife was often seen.

Russell and Harvey Sovka lived there for almost four years, the longest time the young brothers had lived anywhere in their lives, and the house is remembered as a cheerful place. What it lacked in size it compensated for with a big, sloping back lawn and a million-dollar view across the lake, where Jerry and Nonie

Sovka would sail, a continuing interest. The back lawn was a great venue for parties. "It was a gorgeous lot," a former family friend recalls. "I remember one party in particular that Jerry and Nonie had out on the back lawn. I could always remember it because Jimmy Connors and Bjorn Borg were playing tennis on TV, and a lot of us played tennis at the time."

On the tidy, laid-back street, the Sovka family seemed to make a good fit. "She was sophisticated, he was nice," says longtime resident Eileen Azar, who has lived on Lakehurst Crescent for thirty years and once attended a small party at the Sovkas' home. "I don't know why they invited us, we hardly knew them. They were just friendly."

Some found them less so. Living directly across from the Sovkas was Mark Brousseau, a few years older than the two brothers and today a civil servant in Toronto. He remembers the Sovka parents as aloof and distant. "They were both kind of cool to me. They never spoke to me, ever. My impression was that the mother was very controlling, not what you'd call a loving family. Everything seemed very icy cold, a very strict household. Nothing ever seemed spontaneous.

"But Russell and Harvey were nice guys. They seemed to be close, always doing things together. Russell was always polite, he would wave at me. Everything seemed kind of planned for them, and it was obvious they had money. I never went in their house, but whenever I saw them outside they always looked neat."

The interior of the old Sovka home on Lakehurst Crescent doesn't feel as cramped as it probably did back then. Retired IBM instructor Bill White and his wife Margaret live there now, and they've knocked down walls and added a kitchen skylight through which light pours in. Big poplar and black locust trees have filled up much of the big backyard, along with a gazebo-style child's playhouse. When Williams was arrested, the couple were astonished to learn that their house (worth close to $1 million these days) is his former home. "I was hoping to find some evidence, maybe some bones or a diary, " Bill White quips. "We looked everywhere. We still haven't gone through the attic."

White's sleuthing instincts are not wholly far-fetched. The twisted psychology that drives sex killers and predators can often be traced back to dark, unhappy childhoods, manifested in youthful aggression, brooding frustration with the world and—a surprisingly common phenomenon—cruelty to animals. Williams, however, told detectives during his confessions that he thought his sexual—and ultimately murderous—obsessions started relatively late in life, beginning in his twenties and thirties. True or not, nothing unusual emerges from a careful examination of his early life. As a boy, Williams was well behaved, shy and polite. As a teen, some thought him a snob, but mostly he is remembered as intelligent and self-effacing, reluctant to talk about himself or to make a big fuss about anything.

Also visible in his early teen years were signs of the rigorous self-discipline and dependability that would help shape his military future. He had an early morning newspaper route, he was always punctual, and he had no interest in drugs or booze. He was well organized, never happier than when organizing others, and he was a quick learner, provided the topic interested him. He was fastidiously hygienic and invariably well dressed, even in casual clothes, two lifelong traits.

Whatever the task, Russ Sovka would apply himself hard, mocking slackers. And that energy also shaped his twin passions, sports and music. He excelled at both, especially music, first as a pianist (an interest shared with Harvey) and then as an impressively powerful trumpet player. Jerry Sovka would sometimes join his stepsons for jam sessions. When Williams began attending Birchmount Park Collegiate Institute on Danforth Avenue in 1978, he soon distinguished himself as a jazz trumpeter, quickly rising to become a member of the senior band. Yearbook photos from that year show a serene-looking youth with a helmet of neatly coiffed hair swept across his forehead, gazing confidently at the camera. The band later made a trip to Germany. Later, at university, his love of playing and listening to music—he had an impressive knowledge of jazz—would seem to vanish overnight. From that point on, these activities would be of no interest to him.

His other great enthusiasm, however, sports and fitness, would never leave him. A diet-conscious regimen of hard jogging and other self-punishment kept him in exceptionally good shape.

At Birchmount, not everybody was enamored of the new arrival. "I know he kind of thought of himself as being better than other people," band percussionist Tony Callahan would later say. "There was an air about him, the way he talked . . . the way he would roll his eyes at you if you said something. He was condescending." Former Birchmount schoolmate Sandy Zarb, who these days lives in Pickering, east of Toronto, remembers Williams as a polite loner. "He was in my music class in grade ten or eleven. I played the flute. He was a quiet guy. He wasn't outrageous the way teenage boys can be, he was kind of serious, and he only hung around with one or two people. Russell was not an outspoken guy, or a jokester. He would talk when you talked to him. He seemed kind of shy, very aloof and very focused—to me a serious type. I didn't pay much attention to him."

In short, Russ Sovka blended in. His mother, Nonie, however, was not enthralled with Birchmount Collegiate, which had a reputation for having a tough edge and, at the time, a high dropout rate, reflective of a north–south divide at the school: the rich kids, who mostly lived south of Danforth Avenue, nearer the lake, tended to do well in school; the lower-income ones from the north side, less so. So extracurricular activities were organized for the two Williams boys by their mother, tennis lessons in particular.

Tall, slender and possessed of a beauty that would last into her old age, Nonie Sovka's aristocratic demeanor drew a mixed response. "I think she was very socially conscious, that was my impression of her," a former neighbor remembers. "Very cool—a product of the English system, very correct. They were involved in all sorts of activities, as I remember. Nice people, but cool and distant. You know—go to the right schools. She once made some crack about French, about wanting to learn French properly, and she didn't want to learn it in Quebec."

The two young brothers remained close to each other. They were well behaved and considerate, both good students, definitely not part of Scarborough's rowdy crowd. Russell would sometimes go to parties but was often a wallflower, sitting quietly to one side, perhaps chatting to a girl. No one ever saw him smoking cigarettes or pot, nor did he get drunk, which earned him a lasting reputation for sobriety. "He was always a very correct, nice young man—I always felt a bit too correct," Brousseau, the onetime neighbor, says. "A friend of mine had a big New Year's Eve party, a few blocks over. Russ was there, we were chatting a bit, and I remember how he was very kind of reserved, not a loudmouth at all. There was a young girl there that Russ liked, her name was Sara. I saw them holding hands once. I guess it was kind of a puppy romance."

The brief relationship, if it was that, stands out because Williams had so few girlfriends before he married in 1991 at age twenty-eight. Handsome and smart, he always drew attention from young women, particularly after he joined the air force. But he reciprocated almost none of it, often telling male friends that he was wary of being snared by a gold digger.

Any romance at this particular time of his life would likely have been doomed to failure anyway, because big changes were on the horizon again. At that New Year's Eve party at the end of 1978, where Russ Williams unbent his already lanky frame and danced to *The Rocky Horror Picture Show*'s "The Time Warp," a brief announcement was made by one of Russ's contemporaries, bidding Russ and his family farewell. Jerry Sovka had just accepted a new job: he was to oversee construction of a nuclear plant in South Korea.

And so, early in 1979, the Sovkas packed up again, and headed this time for the city of Pusan, located at the southeastern tip of the Korean peninsula. Also known as Busan, Pusan is South Korea's largest port and second-biggest city, and Russell and Harvey lived there for about a year, attending a school for expatriates. The ever-athletic teen took advantage of his stay to learn some martial arts and play baseball, which he quickly came to love (he was a pitcher). But it was not necessarily the happiest of times for Williams: often mistaken for an American, he told of being jeered at, and of seeing Caucasian women spat at. "Once he got spat in the face by a Korean kid who called him a Yankee, and he never got over that," Jeff Farquhar, Russ's university chum, recalls. "He learned a lot about Far East culture, he could use chopsticks, and for sure he was no Archie Bunker. Russ was definitely cosmopolitan in his approach to the world—he liked people from all walks of life. But for some reason that [incident] just did him in for Koreans generally."

Williams's year in South Korea marked the last time he and Harvey ever lived with their mother and stepfather. While the parents stayed on in Pusan, Russell and Harvey were sent back to Toronto in 1980, Russell first, with Harvey following close behind. There, they were enrolled as boarders at Upper Canada College, the elite midtown boys' school.

Since its founding in 1829, UCC has been a crucible for Canada's ruling class and high achievers. Its alumni comprise numerous lieutenant-governors, judges, premiers, Olympic athletes and Rhodes scholars, and at least forty have been inducted into the Order of Canada. Famous old boys include Michael Ignatieff, leader of the federal Liberal Party when Williams was arrested, author Robertson Davies and disgraced media baron Conrad Black, expelled from UCC for stealing and selling exam papers.

At university, Williams would speak fondly about his two years at UCC, lauding the school's structure and discipline. Then as now, UCC was two schools in one, encompassing a prep school and an upper school, grades nine to thirteen, with a total of roughly six hundred students. And while UCC ties often stretch from generation to generation, the Williams brothers went there because of its sterling reputation and because their parents could afford the fees, which were around $6,000 per year for boarders.

There were two boarding houses at UCC, Seaton's and Wedd's, where Williams lived. Both had an entrenched sports culture—volleyball, soccer, tennis, softball and squash, which Williams would play relentlessly for hours in the courts on the west side of the building, smashing ball after ball against the back wall. He was also a member of the jazz ensemble, which sometimes interacted with the drama club, providing a musical accompaniment to the well-attended plays the club put on.

Along with its success stories, UCC has had its share of scandal. In 2007 it dispatched a mass letter to all UCC graduates, staff and former staff, apologizing for a series of notorious, headline-grabbing incidents involving sexual and physical abuse that had rocked the school for years, first surfacing in the late 1990s. Five UCC staff members were charged with sex offenses, including possession of child pornography, and three were convicted. Later came a big lawsuit on behalf of eighteen former students. The school said in its letter that the crimes were the most difficult issue it had ever had to deal with, and some took place while the Williams brothers were there. There seems to be no evidence, however, that they were in any way affected, or that they even knew of the abuse.

As he matured at UCC, Russ Sovka became more confident, which some interpreted as being stuck-up. "He didn't have a lot of friends, zero social interaction. He pretty much played the trumpet and stuck to himself," a former school roommate recounts. "He completely lacked any social skills whatsoever. I just can't recall him having a single person he spent a lot of time with. In typical conversations, if there were subjects he had knowledge of, it was like he was above discussing them with you. He was creepy." A hint of that arrogance can be gleaned from his graduation message in the 1982 UCC yearbook, in which he reprised the famous remark of trumpet legend Louis Armstrong: "If you have to ask what jazz is, you'll never know."

A much less harsh assessment comes from Innes van Nostrand, who also attended UCC in the years 1980–82 and went on to become its vice-principal, a post he holds today. "Russ was a fairly quiet, very responsible guy who didn't really stand out per se, not a big extrovert. I think he was well enough liked. I would call him responsible and diligent. What teenagers are after in life is fitting in. The vast majority of them are driven by the desire to fit in, and he'd found an outlet through his music. The music program was booming at that stage, they'd brought in a couple of very dynamic music teachers, and a lot of people started getting really involved, and it was an area he did very well at."

Van Nostrand didn't immediately recognize Williams's name when the arrest took place; he always knew him as Russ Sovka. When he did make the connection, he was like just about everyone else who had ever had dealings with Williams: he was speechless, simply disbelieving that the pleasant young man he remembered stood accused not only of murder and sexual assault but of unleashing his terrifying violence on a soldier under his command. "I don't think there's anyone from [UCC] who could ever have imagined that if someone had done these kinds of crimes it would have been this guy. Some things are just stunning. I'd say this shows you can never be definitive about anyone."

Williams graduated from UCC in 1982, and the two brothers' paths then diverged. Harvey was to head for Montreal's McGill University and the beginnings of a career in medicine, while Russell enrolled at the University of Toronto's Scarborough campus. Russ's two years at UCC had passed quickly and pleasantly. "He remembered it very fondly," Jeff Farquhar says. "He said he had a lot of fun and he was very proud of his UCC ring, which he wore all through university. He seemed to have made some great relationships with teachers."

As far as is known, however, Williams didn't maintain contact with a single person he had known at UCC, nor with any of the friends he had made at Birchmount. There is an online database for UCC alumni. At the time of his arrest, it listed Russell Sovka as "lost."

One person he did stay in touch with was his stepfather, Jerry Sovka, and the contact remained occasional but steady through most of his life, with Christmas greetings exchanged only a few weeks before he was arrested. At the time, Sovka was living in Aix-en-Provence, France, and was still working in the nuclear field.

Williams's adult relationship with his mother, Nonie, was much more distant. When he was arrested in February 2010, they had largely been out of touch for several years. Neither parent was willing to be interviewed for this book. In emails, both parents asked for privacy at what Nonie Sovka called "this terrible time." Harvey Williams, now a medical doctor in Bowmanville, Ontario, issued a short statement to the many inquisitive news organizations struggling to piece together a profile of the killer colonel. In it, he attested that "a deep rift" had resulted from the 2001 separation of Jerry and Nonie Sovka. "We rarely had any contact until two years ago, when my mother and I tried to find a way to repair the family rift. We have had only minimal contact with him in the past two years."

Nonie Sovka did nonetheless attend what must have been an immensely proud occasion: the elaborate swearing-in that saw Williams take command of the 8 Wing/CFB Trenton air base in July 2009, the peak of her son's 22-year military career. Also there, sitting separately on the other side of the podium in the bright sunshine, was her long-ago husband, David Williams.

4

DRILL SERGEANT

In the fall of 1982, at the age of nineteen, Williams began a four-year arts course in politics and economics, from which he would graduate with a medium-level honors degree. As at UCC, his marks and classroom performance showed a good, competent student rather than a brilliant one. But he seems to have changed and matured at university. Conceivably his time at UCC had allowed him to loosen certain ties to his mother and stepfather, who would move from South Korea to Hawaii, where Jerry Sovka was hired as chief engineer overseeing the Canada–France–Hawaii telescope. What's clear is that for the first time in his life Williams was living independently, free from the constraints of home and boarding school.

Together with five other students, he moved into a brown-brick Scarborough College subsidized townhouse, unit C8. Former U of T roommates and staff portray a bolder, more gregarious Russ Williams, as he began calling himself (reclaiming his biological father's name), than the quiet, serious UCC student. Certainly he looked different, with a longish shag haircut and a full beard that made him resemble Swedish tennis megastar Bjorn Borg, one of his idols.

Politically, he seemed to gravitate from left to right during his four years at U of T, according to a former U of T staff member who taught Williams several classes and marked his papers. He began as a liberal and a big fan of Pierre Trudeau—who was in his final years as prime minister, long after Trudeaumania—but steadily became drawn toward the muscular conservatism of the Reagan administration, and its adventures in Grenada, Central America and the Middle East. Jeff Farquhar says he witnessed the same shift. (Later Williams became a staunch admirer of George W. Bush. A year after the 2003 invasion of Iraq, he wrote a curiously myopic thesis in defense of the mission, even as it sank into bloody chaos.)

The six housemates varied widely in their academic pursuits, but as a group they quickly bonded. In their second year, five of the six moved together into another unit, and several remained friends after that. In both years, Williams lived on the top floors of the two townhouses, at his insistence. And from the outset he was the self-appointed organizer-in-chief, a neatness fanatic. The floors and furniture were kept so squeaky-clean that visitors would remark upon it; slippers had to be worn by the roommates, shoes left by the door; chores were allocated with a rigorous in-house schedule that earned its protagonist the nickname Drill Sergeant. The first clear signs of the obsessive-compulsiveness that would define such a large part of his character were becoming evident.

He kept up links with his parents. The brothers spent Christmas of 1982 with their father, Dave, in Schenectady, N.Y., and the next year were reunited for the holidays with Jerry and Nonie Sovka in Scarborough. Twice Russell and Harvey also flew to Hawaii for Christmas visits and once Jerry Sovka's own three children joined them there; the five youngsters spent at least one summer vacation together too.

Yet Russell rarely spoke of his family and retained a strong air of loneliness, former university friends say. At the end of his first year at U of T he went on a solo cycling trip to England

and Wales with a prized ten-speed bike and his camera. He took a bad fall, hurting his hand, but before tending to the wound he photographed it, later laughing it off.

And indeed, a lighter side of his personality began to emerge. He never became a party animal, eschewing both drugs and booze except for the occasional beer, and usually heading off to bed before the other residents of C8. But he rapidly became known as an orchestrator of elaborate, often invasive practical jokes. Frequently the pranks were childish: hiding in a house-mate's closet, waiting for him to come home and settle down, and then springing out with a loud yell; saran-wrapping the top of a toilet bowl and daubing pretend cracks on a mirror; apple-pie beds, the top sheet refolded into a shallow crease so the victim's feet rammed into it as he climbed in. Others were more creative, such as gluing pennies into a door frame so the knob wouldn't turn. And in one memorable case—illustrative of a remarkable mechanical expertise that in later years made him an amateur authority on Swiss watches—Williams disassembled a front-door lock, adjusted the internal tumblers and then put it back together so it needed a different key.

He delighted in seeing a hapless victim walk into one of his traps, and was famous for unleashing his loud, braying laugh when they did. But the others in C8 pulled similar stunts, and as they recall, it was all in fun. Another time Williams organized an ad hoc group of raucous musicians wielding garbage can lids and drumsticks. His trumpet blasting, he led them on a parade through the campus to the tune of the Beatles' "Yellow Submarine."

"He was very friendly and cheerful and he had a great sense of humor," one of his former friends remembers. "At no time was there ever any suggestion that he was leading a double life, or that he had strange proclivities or tendencies, or was interested in violent porn—or porn, period."

Williams's parents may have been well off, but there was not a lot of cash around and he was frugal, always keeping close track of expenditures. After even a modest evening out, he would return home and itemize the cost down to the last cent. But he didn't mind spending money if he had to, and if he thought it was worth it. As the information age began accelerating in the early 1980s, Williams was one of the first among his peers to grasp the enormous potential of the personal computer. He bought one of the early ones, which served as word processors rather than Internet portals, along with a printer, and he mastered the technology with ease. He was quick to purchase a CD player too, when they arrived—a Sony; nothing but the best, scraping up the cash even if he couldn't really afford it.

Ever constant was his near-fanatical preoccupation with fitness—jogging, baseball, and punishing games of squash and tennis, of which he had an encyclopedic knowledge. Jeff Farquhar recounts watching Williams perform at a marathon tennis tournament in September 1982. "He played tennis that whole day, and it was a hot day, I remember, it was Indian summer. He kept winning match after match. And when he was done, he stopped like an engine without oil. Three of us guys in residence picked him up and carried him all the way up the hill to residence, and we dumped him in the bathtub and poured the water on him and shut the door.

"And he was in there groaning and screaming, with leg cramps all the way up his leg. I'd never seen anybody like that—I laughed so hard. He was a big, lanky guy [Williams stood six foot two, with a lean, muscular build of about 180 pounds that hardly changed throughout his adult life]. Oh my God, he couldn't move. I've never seen that kind of muscle fatigue in anybody."

There may have been a touch of recklessness, too. Another roommate walked into the kitchen to find Williams and a friend shooting off a BB gun, firing at objects floating in the sink, pellets ricocheting around the room. But there was no hint of malice or viciousness in anything Williams did, Farquhar insists. "He had a conscience, he always had a conscience. That's what really leaves me stunned about this whole thing [the arrest and criminal charges]. Russ always had this strong sense of right and wrong."

For all his discipline, he was also quite capable of evincing emotion. Farquhar recounts the day in January 1986 when the space shuttle *Challenger* blew up and disintegrated off the coast of Florida, killing all seven crew members—this, at a time when Williams was nearing graduation and giving serious thought to becoming a pilot. "I remember that like it was yesterday. I was the guy with the TV. I had a little fourteen-inch color screen and I brought it out to the living room for everyone to share. Russ was so horrified. I remember he came running into the house. 'Oh my God, did you hear, did you hear?' And I was saying, 'Yeah, that's really sad, really horrible.' But I'm looking at him like, wow, this reaction was almost over the top. He was really, really, really upset, just so in awe and in shock."

At around the same time, Williams experienced another, more personal upset. He had met Misa, a Japanese exchange student, toward the end of his first year at U of T and had fallen for her hard. They began seeing each other and for more than two years the tall Williams and his diminutive girlfriend were an item. By every estimate, he was devoted to her. But if the feelings were mutual, it didn't show; years later, none of Williams's former friends could recall seeing them hug or kiss.

It was not his first fling. Shortly before starting at university he had dated a woman who now lives in British Columbia. He abruptly severed the relationship, leaving her heartbroken. But with Misa it was the other way around. She told him they were through, and he took the news very badly. One former friend said it was the only time he ever saw him cry.

The rupture's long-term impact on Williams is guesswork. Certainly it became of great interest to Ontario Provincial Police detectives after he was arrested and it had become evident that every one of his dozens of horrifying crimes was directed at women.

Tracked down in Japan by *Globe and Mail* reporter Greg McArthur almost a quarter century later, Misa knew that her long-ago companion had been arrested and charged with murder and sexual assault, but she declined comment, saying she had nothing to add. "All I can say is, whatever my experience was, I don't think it will be of any use [to you]," she told McArthur. It's nonetheless clear that this was Williams's first serious romance, and probably his last until he met his future wife, Mary Elizabeth Harriman, whom he would marry in 1991.

Along with other residents of unit C8, Jeff Farquhar didn't much care for Misa, who he says seemed to have an oddly intimidating effect on the normally controlling, assertive Williams. "She ran him like a whipped horse," he says. "It was always her way or the highway, and he was always trying to acquiesce—what she wanted to do or not want to do. She always wanted to hit the books harder and didn't have a lot of time left over for Russ, so there was always an argument about finding time to do things together."

Another ex-roommate describes an incident when he needed to speak to Williams and stopped by the home of Misa, also in residence. "I knocked on the door and I was told by the other women that Russ and [Misa] were up in her room. So jokingly I said, 'Russ, put your clothes on and come down.' Well, he didn't come down and then I found out a few days later that he and his girlfriend were very upset that I had made a comment like that, which quite surprised me. I made a point of apologizing to him and to her."

The breakup with Misa sent Williams into a depression, according to Farquhar, and he struggled to achieve a reconciliation. He sent her a dozen long-stemmed roses, and would hover around places on campus where he knew she would be. But she sent the roses back, and even entreated Farquhar—by no means a friend of hers—to persuade Williams to back off. "She was getting really pissed," Farquhar says.

When it became evident to Williams that the separation was permanent, he was inconsolable. "I don't know of him dating anybody after Misa, not at all," says Farquhar. "That doesn't mean he wasn't well liked—God, I mean a lot of women liked him because he was a great guy. The only time I ever pushed him was if there was an event or an upcoming dinner at the university and you were expected to have a date. And Russ would say, 'No, not going.'"

Williams was not the only student on the Scarborough campus with some serious issues involving women. One year behind him, also pursuing an economics-related course, was a blond, fresh-faced student destined to become the most notorious sex killer of his generation. His name was Paul Bernardo, and he was convicted in 1995 on two counts of first-degree murder and multiple other charges, including two of aggravated sexual assault, in which he used a knife. So heinous were his crimes, and so numerous, that he was designated a dangerous offender, a classification that reduces parole possibilities to almost nothing.

Bernardo committed at least eleven extremely violent rapes—probably many more—and most of them occurred in the large Toronto suburb of Scarborough, generating widespread local terror and earning him his pre-arrest nickname, the Scarborough Rapist. Trial testimony from his wife and accomplice Karla

Homolka (convicted of manslaughter and released after serving out a full twelve-year prison term) strongly suggests Bernardo was responsible for a long-term pattern of sex attacks that were never solved. The first two attacks for which he was convicted took place in Scarborough on May 4 and 14, 1987, a few weeks before he graduated from U of T with a degree in commerce and economics. After Williams was arrested in February 2010, an imaginative newspaper story that garnered widespread attention amid the saturation coverage speculated on the basis of comments from an invisible police source that the two killers may have been "pals" who had partied together or had even "competed against each other."

There's not a shred of evidence to support this thesis. Williams and Bernardo graduated in different years (not both in 1987, as the story stated) and there is nothing to indicate they ever met. Toronto police swiftly examined the ostensible connection and drew a blank. So too does Farquhar, who says today that if Williams had known Bernardo, he would have been aware of Bernardo too, and he was not. The author of the newspaper article even consulted Bernardo, via his father, to see if he could recall a Russell Williams from his Scarborough university days. Bernardo (always glad of a diversion as he serves out a sentence of life imprisonment in solitary confinement) told his father he did not.

Far more credible was the possibility that Williams had committed a cold-case homicide that to this day remains unsolved: the August 1987 sex slaying in Scarborough of 21-year-old Margaret McWilliam. Williams had completed university more than a year earlier, and was by then no longer living in Toronto. Nonetheless, at first glance the links appear compelling. McWilliam was found raped and strangled to death in Warden Woods Park, about three miles from Williams's old home on Lakehurst Crescent, which Nonie and Jerry Sovka still owned at the time. (They sold it in November 1987 for $349,000.) As with Williams's two known murder victims, the cause of death was asphyxiation. And there was a possible further connection: McWilliam had moved to Toronto a year earlier after graduating from Kemptville College, south of Ottawa. But she had been raised in Deep River, the first place Williams lived after immigrating to Canada from Britain. Could their shared roots have led to an acquaintanceship? In addition, an unconfirmed report after Williams's arrest said that someone resembling a jogger had been seen fleeing the Warden Woods Park crime scene—a young man wearing a red baseball cap.

McWilliam's parents still live in Deep River, and their hopes were briefly raised that their daughter's ghastly murder almost twenty-three years earlier might finally be solved. But it was not to be. McWilliam's killer had left behind some DNA, and it does not match that of the former colonel, according to the Toronto homicide detective who heads the cold-cases section.

On leaving university in 1986, Williams was at a loss as to what to do next. Still in Scarborough, he rented the basement of a well-kept townhouse not far from the campus, and found himself a couple of part-time jobs. One was waiting tables at the Red Lobster, a seafood chain. The other was a summer position as a clerk in the university's financial services department, where he pulled another prank that can only be described as bizarre.

Long retired and now living in Britain, June Hope worked in the personnel unit across the corridor from the finance department. She remembers Williams as "a nice kid"—tall and good-looking, with a prominent jaw, a jazz aficionado who seemed lonely and "wouldn't talk about his mom and dad very much except to say they were abroad."

One morning Hope walked into her fourth-floor office, or at least tried to. What greeted her was a sea of crunched-up balls of old-style computer paper, the type that was aligned to the printer by means of a ribbon of holes along the margin. "It filled the room," Hope remembers. "I couldn't find my desk or my chair or my computer. It was all obscured by paper. I opened the door and was met by a wall of paper."

The previous night, Williams had persuaded one of the secretaries to let him into Hope's office, where he had spent hours crunching up the paper and spreading it around.

"I was gobsmacked," Hope says. "I walked in, I was just amazed." And as she stared, she turned and heard a "click" noise behind her. An amused Williams was standing there with a camera, recording her moment of astonishment. Unimpressed, she asked him if he had nothing better to do with his time, and he replied that he did not.

Very soon, however, he did. He had resolved to become a pilot.

Twenty-five years after its release, *Top Gun* may not hold a spot in the lexicon of great moviemaking. Inevitably, the pre-digital simulated air stunts look dated, redolent of a video game. Worse are the tissue-thin plot, cliché-soaked dialogue, garage-band soundtrack and endless close-ups of Tom Cruise's face, alternately cool and confident and riven with angst. "You're one of the best pilots in the Navy, what you do up there is dangerous," a wide-eyed, hard-to-get Kelly McGillis tells the morose protagonist as he nurses a drink and ponders his bleak future. "But you've got to go on. When I first met you, you were larger than life. Look at you. You're not going to be happy unless you're going Mach-2. You know that . . ."

Hackneyed or not, *Top Gun* and its only-the-best-will-do-in-the-military mantra left Williams deeply impressed. "Russ became a nut about *Top Gun*," Farquhar recalls. "We all joked about it. He was really hung up on that movie. It was a huge fascination to him back in 1986. He was fixated on it, nothing less. He could recite you the lines forward, backward. He watched that movie so many freaking times, we all teased him about it. 'Oh, there goes *Top Gun*.'

"And it went beyond a joke. He really, really soaked it up. And then, when he announced his career as a pilot, I said, 'C'mon, you've watched *Top Gun* too many times. You're going to join the air force? We don't have aircraft carriers here.' I said to him, 'You took politics and economics—why'd you bother?'"

Tom Cruise's determination to win the affections of his instructor also seemed to resonate with Williams as he struggled with his breakup with Misa. "I used to joke about that behind his back," Farquhar says. "I was thinking, 'Oh shit, he thinks this is going to win her back. He's going to show up in his F-14.'"

Shortly before graduation, it was an uncle of Farquhar's who gave Williams his first flying lesson. "My uncle liked to pat himself on the back because he taught Russ how to fly. He used to take me up in his Cessna all the time, and we'd fly over the cottage, fly down to the University of Windsor where my sister was, go out for dinner, come back. And then one day Russ was hanging around and my uncle said, 'You guys want to go out for a flight?' 'Yeah.' So we went up, Russ moved behind the controls and my uncle let him take over. And I remember my uncle commenting, 'Wow. He's a natural. He's really good at it.'

"And [Williams] met him a few more times. He'd go to the cottage and my uncle would be there and they'd talk about things that my uncle would bring up—the latest plane he'd been on down in Florida, that type of thing. And my uncle's next-door neighbor, when he moved to Burlington, was a current Air Canada pilot. I introduced Russ to him and I remember that had a huge impact on him."

Williams also took flying lessons at Toronto's Buttonville airport. And when he was accepted by the military early in 1987, he didn't hesitate. Yet in one of the other twists in the early life of Russ Williams, he came close to becoming a police officer instead. At around the same time he applied to the air force, he also applied to the RCMP, and the Mounties came calling first. "He had a telephone call from the RCMP, they'd sent him a letter accepting him, but he was still waiting for the air force and he wanted to defer," Farquhar recalls. "They said, 'No no, if we come calling for you, which we have, we don't wait for you, you're either our guy or you're not.' And he was really surprised, a little bit disappointed, but he really wanted to wait for the air force. So they said, 'Goodbye, that's it.'"

Williams's short-lived aspirations to be a police officer are worth noting, and not only because years down the road he would keep many police busy as a predator and serial killer. Like any other successful candidate, he would only have been accepted by the RCMP after rigorous screening and background checks, with particular emphasis on mental stability. A rule of thumb in police recruitment is that the best predictor of a person's future behavior is his or her past conduct, and extensive interviews with friends, current and former, are a staple in the process. But at age twenty-four, there was evidently nothing in Russ Williams's history that caused the RCMP any serious concern.

The six friends from unit C8 pursued different paths. Williams's closest friend from those first two years became a successful fundraiser with the March of Dimes, earning himself the country's highest civilian honor, the Order of Canada, only to commit suicide a few years later by jumping from a bridge onto a busy highway, an event that caused Williams great distress when he learned of it. Another, an exchange student from Hong Kong, had to abandon his expensive condominium and his Porsche and flee to Taiwan as authorities probing a shady financial deal closed in. A third former roommate became a successful lawyer, a fourth made a good living as a car dealer specializing in expensive models. The fifth ex-roommate became an investments adviser.

As for the colonel-to-be and future killer, in mid-1987 he packed a couple of suitcases and headed west for basic training at CFB Chilliwack in British Columbia. His path was set.

5

A PILOT SOARS

The Canadian Armed Forces in 1987 was an unhappy, often bewildered organization still struggling to define itself. Under Liberal defense minister Paul Hellyer, an eccentric figure who later in life became obsessed with space aliens, the three branches of the military had been integrated during the 1960s, with a unified rank structure and under a single command. On paper there was good reason for the overhaul. The army, navy and air force had long been tugging a succession of governments in competing directions. As well, there was deep concern within the Liberal Party that the military had become too independent-minded: a credible report has claimed that during the October 1962 Cuban Missile Crisis, Canada's military leaders resolved between themselves that if nuclear war erupted between the U.S.A. and the Soviet Union, they—not the government in Ottawa—would determine Canada's response.

In practice, integration was a good idea that went disastrously wrong and damaged the military for years. The restructuring was intended to consolidate and unite, but it had the opposite effect. The top-down, one-size-fits-all approach engendered wide hostility among all three branches, each of which resentfully defended its bit of turf. The result was an operational chain of command that was at best inefficient, at worst incoherent.

Now, in the mid-1980s, the end of the Cold War was stirring renewed gloomy debate about the whole purpose of the Canadian military, and whether it was even worthwhile having one. There were suggestions the armed forces should restrict themselves to doing what they did best—wearing blue helmets and keeping the peace in foreign hot spots—and leave it at that. And up ahead lay more trouble: the convulsive Somalia Affair, which in 1995 resulted in the disbanding of the Canadian Airborne Regiment, and big budget cuts that would strip large sections of the military to the bone.

Williams, the pilot-to-be, was hardly affected by any of this. On the contrary, the disorder and general malaise offered opportunity for a confident 24-year-old with exceptional organizational skills and great technical aptitude. In many ways, he was exactly the quasi-corporate breed of modern officer the politicians said they were looking for: forward-looking, an informal but committed team player, comfortable with high-tech and the mushrooming communications revolution.

From the start, he belonged to an elite. At the downtown Toronto military recruitment office where he first applied, plenty of other walk-ins said they wanted to be pilots too, and at that time only about one in ten made it to the next phase, the week-long aircrew selection process. Aircrew selection encompassed aptitude tests, a rigorous physical exam, and visual and spatial orientation tests. Recruiters also tried to assess the personalities of the applicants. Fighter-pilot potential, for example, is different from transport-pilot material. In the year Williams signed up, the elimination rate from within that aircrew recruitment pool was also about 90 percent; just one in ten was approved and went on to join the air force. So of the original intake of budding pilots, 1 percent made the cut.

"They don't just pick guys and send them up the ranks," says an air force member, still in the military, who joined the same year as Williams and went through pilot training with him at CFB Moose Jaw. "They're looked at very closely and put into very specific situations and scenarios to see how they handle it. Then they might go, 'Yeah, this person has the potential to become a good leader,' and then they develop that person, start pushing them if they're willing, and then away they go."

One mental trait is of particular interest to recruiters assessing prospective pilots: the ability in an unexpected situation or crisis to make a snap judgment and then instantly focus 100 percent on whatever needs to be done, distracted by nothing, for as long as it takes. It was a quality Williams had in spades, all his life. When he was young, his keen capacity for detail took the form of being diligent and thorough. Later, it would become compulsive and obsessive. All through his life, people marveled at his encyclopedic ability to store facts in his mind and retrieve them at will.

Once through the door, his first stop was basic training, better known as boot camp, which as an officer cadet meant a fourteen-week stint at CFB Chilliwack in south-central British Columbia. Basic training is an intense experience designed to weed out the keen-but-weak ones, which it does very well. The course is and was a blend of rudimentary military skills, such as weapons handling and first aid, together with classroom sessions on leadership fundamentals and ethical values. Above all, the emphasis is on fitness, and despite his strength and excellent physical condition, Williams found the experience grueling.

"Boot camp was brutal, absolutely horrible," recounts Farquhar, his former university friend. "In the first couple of days he remembered one guy breaking his leg, and he talked about the grind, all the running through the bushes and doing it for days on end, not getting much sleep or [much to] eat. It was a big endurance test. He said to me, 'Oh man, they're making or breaking you right there. If you can't hack the first two weeks, that's it.'"

He did hack it, and from there he was dispatched to the CFB training school in Portage la Prairie, Manitoba, for a few weeks' instruction in the basics of flying. Then it was on to CFB Moose Jaw in Saskatchewan, often referred to as 15 Wing Moose Jaw, a longtime training base for pilots. There, Williams learned to fly by mastering the Avro-manufactured Tudor jet, a big, lumbering airliner descended from the famous British Lancaster bomber.

"I remember when he was in Moose Jaw, he said this was the point that would make or break him as a pilot," Farquhar recalls. "He wanted to fly, but he was not going into helicopters—he was deathly fixed on not becoming a helicopter pilot. That was not where he wanted to be. He said helicopters were old and useless, and they were widow makers."

From day one he was a natural pilot, says the former rookie who trained alongside him, picking up the basics with an ease that impressed his instructors. His skill marked a lifelong aptitude with airplanes and many other mechanical things. Years later, Williams would master the Airbus, an extremely complicated aircraft, in just a few days.

Along with his prowess at flying and the confidence that went with it, he began to show a side of his personality that would later seem utterly at odds with his crimes, but which many of his peers observed throughout his career: a generosity, even kindness, in his dealings with younger, less experienced colleagues. "How I remember him from Moose Jaw was as this very helpful type of person," recalls the former fellow rookie. "He started out at the bottom like everyone else, but later, as a senior student, part of his job was to help the junior guys coming in. And he did—he was really nice to them. He was just a very nice guy."

———

It took Williams a little under three years to earn his wings, which is about the average. Now he was a fully qualified military pilot, and it was during the next stage in his career that it began to be apparent what a good one he really was. From Moose Jaw he returned to the training school at Portage la Prairie, this time as an instructor, with the rank of lieutenant. In those days not many pilots went straight from learning to teaching, but Williams did, and the former air force major who oversaw him explains why.

Former air force major Greg McQuaid, now retired and living in Kelowna, B.C., had about twenty instructors under his supervision, half of them freshly minted pilots, and Williams stood out. "Of the new instructors, he was one of our best, one of the top one or two. Russ was an excellent instructor, perfect, very bright. A big thing with being a flight instructor is the ability to observe and analyze errors, and determine what correct course of action would fix them, to develop a style so you could present your criticism without sounding overly critical."

His flight-instructor course under McQuaid lasted about eight weeks. Then he began teaching in a classroom setting. But most of his instruction was done in the air, typically consisting of two instruction missions a day. "Russ was in his right niche, and I would see the results in his students, who were very quick to sum up who their instructors were," McQuaid says. "They were under great pressure, so it was very important for them to get a top instructor. He was one of the more popular ones, and his students tended to have good results."

McQuaid knew Williams for two years. "I would have seen him every working day—all the kibitzing, all the rainy-day volleyball games, Friday nights in the officers' club, all that—and I found him to be sociable. I've heard others say, since [the criminal charges] came up, that they found him on the cold side. I didn't see that at all, though of course I had a different relationship than some others might. I wasn't his buddy, I was his boss. I was a major, he started out as a lieutenant, and under my tenure he became a captain. And I helped him become a captain. I wrote his personnel evaluation report. He got a shiny personnel evaluation report from me, and he earned it. He was a sharp guy, and I suspect that aided him in hiding his crimes."

Like so many others, McQuaid later looked back and wondered how well he had really known Russell Williams. "Was this always there, all subdued? Did something go off in his life? When I first heard of it, I said, 'I don't believe it, there's a mistake—there *is* a mistake.' Then, as the evidence starts coming out, you ask yourself: 'Did I miss something?'

"He was intense, no question. I recall talking to him when it seemed like he was looking at the back of your head through your eyes. But he was also cool. I've been a pilot for thirty-eight years, and a big part of my life has been screening pilots. And one of the things we look for in a pilot is the ability to remain calm and cool under pressure, and he struck me as having that ability . . . And in a sense, it turns out maybe he had it too strong."

Midway through his tour at Portage la Prairie, Williams did something that surprised his few close friends: he got married. Jeff Farquhar recalls first hearing about the bride-to-be. "I had tripped out to Winnipeg and we were driving along number 1 highway toward Moose Jaw when he brought it up. He said, 'Hey, I've got a girlfriend . . . I met her in Calgary.'"

Williams was marrying someone whose long professional career and pleasant, self-effacing personality would complement his own. After his arrest, some people who knew the couple casually said the union looked to be less a marriage of great affection than one of convenience, and one that seemed to work extremely well. But others said there was a genuinely strong bond between husband and wife, and certainly Williams's palpable distress about her during his police confession suggests that.

Mary Elizabeth Harriman was an only child, five years older than her husband, and after marrying Williams she retained her maiden name. When they met, she had a University of Guelph bachelor's degree in applied science, specializing in nutrition, and had just completed an MBA in adult education at St. Frances Xavier University in Antigonish, Nova Scotia. Now she was working with the Dairy Nutrition Council of Alberta, part of a lifelong commitment to health-related causes. She went on to join the Ottawa-based Heart and Stroke Foundation, for whom she would work for many years, rising to the prestigious position of associate executive director, the post she held when her husband was arrested. The federal government's lobbying database, which keeps track of how corporations and associations try to influence policy, shows that she had by then spent more than ten years pressing for tougher government action in combating smoking, trans fats in foods and childhood obesity.

Before getting married, Williams and Harriman shared a rented apartment in Portage la Prairie, listed in the phone directory under both of their names. Then, one day before they married, they paid $75,000 for a detached home on Wilkinson Crescent. The small, nondenominational wedding ceremony took place at the Winnipeg Art Gallery on June 1, 1991.

Williams was twenty-eight, Harriman thirty-three. Both sets of parents attended, as did the onetime girlfriend Williams had dated before going to U of T. Farquhar was the master of ceremonies, a favor Williams reciprocated at Farquhar's own wedding four years later. "It was nice, a little less formal than I was used to," he recalls. "About eighteen people were there, I think, but I didn't really know her at all. I really met her on the date of the wedding."

The topic of children came up that day, Farquhar says. "I remember slapping him on the back after they'd taken their vows and saying, 'Are we going to see a bunch of little Williamses running around?' And he said, 'Ah no, Jeff. We've discussed this and it's just not in the cards.'" Another wedding guest asked Williams the same question and got the same answer. The world was too unstable a place to bring any more children into it, he said glibly. More likely, he simply wasn't interested. "Russ was never hugely child-oriented. He was good when kids were around, but he would only tolerate them so far," says Farquhar.

Harriman's father, Frederick, was a former military man and Second World War veteran who later became a geologist with a mining company in the small northern Ontario town of Madsen, where he met his future wife, Irene, and where Mary Elizabeth was raised. Williams warmed to both his in-laws, and was happy to school Fred Harriman in the use of computers. Both the older Harrimans have since died, but after Williams and their daughter bought a home in Orleans in 1995, Fred and Irene were for several years occasional visitors.

Back at Portage la Prairie, Williams's two-year stint as a pilot trainer was nearing its end. And as it did so, there came a strange glimpse of the low-key but unmistakably narcissistic facet of his personality that ultimately would have such a bearing on his hideous life of crime: his love of taking pictures of himself, and of being a showman.

The occasion was in 1992. A much-admired, now-obsolete air force demonstration team nicknamed "Musket Gold" was to perform its final air show, flying four bright-yellow, single-engine CT-134 Beech Musketeers that were soon to be taken out of service. McQuaid, Williams's boss, handpicked him to be one of the four pilots, and the Musketeers, as they were dubbed, spent weeks training for the team's swan song. The exercise went off flawlessly and Williams added a special touch. He brought along a VHS video camera and filmed himself inside the cockpit, smiling widely against a backdrop of the other Musketeers wheeling and maneuvering their planes high up in the sky. He edited the footage and added a soundtrack, the eerie song "Exile" by the Irish artist Enya, featured in the 1991 movie *L.A. Story*. The other pilots were given copies of the video as mementos.

The air show was a huge personal success for him, and he was promoted to captain soon after. His two years at Portage la Prairie were a natural springboard for the next phase in the steady upward trajectory of his career: electronic war games, played high above the Atlantic ocean.

In July 1992, Williams and Harriman sold their home for a small profit and headed for Canadian Forces Base Shearwater in Nova Scotia. Harriman took a job with a provincial nutritional-awareness program. Located on the eastern shore of Halifax Harbour, CFB Shearwater was home to the 434 Combat Support Squadron, and one of the smallest air bases in the country. Williams's new mission was at the controls of one of the base's three CC-144 Challenger jets, small, versatile planes designed primarily for electronic warfare and coastal patrol work.

This might have been the moment he'd been waiting for since his repeated viewings of *Top Gun* at university. In much the same way police training works, the exercises involved deploying against a simulated enemy. The squadron also had a couple of T-33s, a 1950s single-engine plane that resembles a missile and which played the role of intruder. The two types of planes feigned combat, the Challenger trying to disrupt the enemy's communications system as the planes soared and swooped around each other.

Williams and Harriman spent three uneventful years in the community, which they later told friends they viewed as a backwater. But for both, it was also a stepping stone. Harriman's work with Nova Scotia's nutrition program opened the door to her job with the Heart and Stroke Foundation, while for Williams, opportunity beckoned in the form of a spot with the highly prestigious 412 Squadron in Ottawa, known as the VIP squadron.

In those days, the CC-144 Challenger in which he had circled and swooped in the skies above Shearwater performed double duty. As well as being a reconnaissance and electronic-warfare plane, it was a people mover and business jet, and the plane of choice for 412 Squadron. Then as now, the squadron provided transport for important government officials, high-ranking military members and foreign dignitaries visiting Canada. As well, the squadron provides support for Canadian Forces missions at home and abroad, including medevac flights. Though technically under the command of 8 Wing/CFB Trenton, the squadron is based in Ottawa, and for the next six years, still a captain, Williams's primary task was to fly assorted VIPs back and forth. He later said it was a job and a responsibility he really enjoyed. Plaques from appreciative clients—Governor General Roméo LeBlanc, Prime Minister Jean Chrétien, Deputy Prime Minister Sheila Copps—hung on the walls of his upstairs office in the shiny new house in Orleans, an east Ottawa suburb, that he and Harriman purchased in August 1995 for $165,000.

The house was at the end of Wilkie Drive in Fallingbrook, one of Orleans's newer districts, a tidy middle-class enclave of parks and curved streets, home to commuters and their families and to many members of the military and the RCMP, active and retired. It's a very civil, friendly sort of place, where neighbors live separate lives but gladly help out when someone needs an errand run or a car jump-started. George White moved to Wilkie Drive at around the same time as Williams and Harriman, and as a retired air force mechanic with a son in the military, he might have expected some sort of deeper bond to develop. But it never did.

"We met very easily, and because we were both air force we had a common background, we knew what to discuss and what not to discuss," White says. "We talked a lot about the technical stuff. I understood the systems—the engines, the hydraulics, the air conditioning, and the functionality of all that. So it would be casual technical talk—landing speed, takeoff speed, cruise speed, duration, fuel flow, that kind of stuff. We both understood all the acronyms. Russ, of course, was flying VIPs in the Challenger, and he was sharp, very thorough. No matter whether it was cleaning and washing his car or flying an airplane, he had a mental checklist and everything was to perfection.

"But always, always, he was so guarded in all his conversations. He never once slipped or opened up. He would smile but he wouldn't joke. You'd never hear a joke from him. I can still picture him standing there talking. He would hesitate and look you right in the eye and give you a definitive answer."

Harriman and Williams kept their house on Wilkie Drive for fourteen years, the longest he lived anywhere in his life, and the two became familiar figures to their immediate neighbors. Their cars—Harriman drove a BMW, Williams his Nissan Pathfinder— would pull up in the driveway at day's end, and the couple were invariably pleasant to their neighbors, who were always glad to see them. Sometimes after one of his daily runs a perspiring Williams would grab a Gatorade, amble over and exchange a few words with whoever was around. Occasionally the couple would take Williams's much-prized bow rider for a spin together; he would fish, she would read.

Pleasant as they always were with their neighbors, however, Williams and Harriman kept very much to themselves. Visitors to the couple's home were few and far between, and not once in all those years were any of the Wilkie Gang (as the half dozen residents clustered near the top end of the street called themselves) invited inside for a drink or a meal. Living directly across the street was retired government employee and bus driver Shirley Fraser, who had a key to their house and would stop in when they were away, which was often, to keep an eye on things and feed Curio, their peculiarly bad-tempered cat. Fraser talked to Harriman enough to know a few things about her: that she was a keen golfer, would often go to a nearby gym and was fond of antique furniture. But the chitchat only went so far. "You never heard a word about what she was doing at work," Fraser says. "All I knew was that she worked for the Heart and Stroke Foundation. They were both very, very private."

Shock waves rolled up and down Wilkie Drive when Williams was arrested. Fraser wept when she heard he was accused of murder and sexual assault, and she initially assumed some dreadful mistake had been made. "It's one of those things you just can't fathom." A few weeks later, as happened in Tweed, Williams's former neighbors were further shaken when he was charged with scores of fetish-driven break-ins.

George White was just as amazed. Less than a year earlier, in July 2009, he had been invited to the handover ceremony at 8 Wing/CFB Trenton, where Williams formally took charge of the sprawling base. "I talked to Russ's secretary [who had been assigned to him] in Trenton just prior to him getting there, and she wanted to know all about him. 'What's he like?' I said I had nothing bad to say about Russ. I praised him and said he's a wonderful man to work with, I've never seen him other than being friendly. You're going to love this guy—he's today's base commander, not yesterday's, he's a new generation, cordial, friendly.

"I put him up on a pedestal. He just wasn't one to flaunt it. When he got a promotion, I'd see his uniform and say, 'Russ, you got a raise in pay,' And he'd say, 'Yeah, yeah.' When he got promoted to lieutenant-colonel and took over the 437 [Transport] Squadron, I said, 'Russ, if you keep on like this, you're going to be Chief of Defence Staff,' and he'd just nod. Russ never bragged about anything, he did things by the book, and that's why he was so successful at going up that military ladder."

In one peculiar footnote to Williams's years on Wilkie Drive, remarkable only because he later began breaking into so many nearby homes himself, his own house was burgled. The thief gained entry by prying open a basement window at the side of the house. All that was taken, Williams said later, was his leather aircrew briefcase, containing charts, maps, airport details and emergency procedures for different types of aircraft. It would have had no value to anyone else and was later found, intact, beside a sports field not far away. Williams and Harriman installed security bars on the basement windows, and then an alarm system. What seemed slightly odd, in hindsight, was that Williams mentioned the burglary at all. Normally he never said anything about himself, least of all to complain.

"None of us knew that he had a brother," George White said after the arrest. "He had talents none of us even knew about, like his music. Neither of them really opened up about everyday things, and looking at things in hindsight, every answer— everything—was a guarded response. He would never, never, be spontaneous in his conversation, there was no flow, everything was a really calculated response. I always thought that was because of the work he did, and the kind of training he'd had, where everything is so structured."

Williams spent more than four years with the VIP squadron, then reached for the next rung in the air force ladder. In November 1999, he was promoted to major and appointed Director General Military Careers, the career director for military pilots of multiengine airplanes. Mostly a desk job, it entailed assessing and in large part determining the futures of the senior air force military pilots—majors, captains, lieutenants—who flew the Canadian Forces' big planes. That's when transport pilot Major Garrett Lawless, now attached to the Portage la Prairie CF training school, first heard about Williams. Later, Lawless worked directly under him, getting to know him perhaps as well as anybody did, and growing to like him very much.

"The job he had with Military Careers was to manage who's going where, and who's getting posted to what place, to make sure that the big-picture requirements of the service were being met," Lawless says. "We all talk about his time as a career manager, when he handled everybody's files, because it was like the guy had a photographic memory. He knew intimate details of every individual pilot in the multiengine group, and that would be hundreds of files. He would also remember if people found excuses to not take postings, he would know exactly what the professional background was of basically every pilot in the group. It was very impressive how much information he just carried around in his head.

"He expected everybody to be totally dedicated to the operation, so some people who got wounded from the decisions that he made do hold some ill will for him. But you would not find anybody—save for his victims—who would have a personal issue with him. He had no tolerance for personal excuses. If someone didn't want to do something for a personal reason—their dog died, or their aunt was sick, whatever—he had no time for that. But you'll never find anybody to say his decisions were unfair."

So after knowing Williams fairly well for several years and flying with him many times, was there anything at all, any possible clue, that in hindsight seems to hold significance? "No, I really wish there was. The emotional turmoil I went through following the revelation would have been easier if I'd been able to look back and think, 'Oh, that's what was going on.' But there was nothing. He was always socially distant, did not engage in a lot of small talk—office gossip, joking around, that kind of stuff. Whenever you were talking to him, you would be talking about something that mattered."

Two accomplishments distinguished Williams's time with Military Careers, both of which greatly endeared him to many of the younger officers. One was that he opened up and expedited the promotions process, which in the air force had for years lagged behind that of the army and the navy. Second, he ended the stranglehold that certain entrenched cliques had acquired on the transfers process, whereby they got continuously recycled through the plum jobs with the most sought-after aircraft.

Now, however, came a phase in his career that showed some of his limitations. In August 2003, Williams became a student once again. The Master of Defence Studies research project was part of the military's Command and Staff Course, and Williams chose as his topic the U.S. invasion of Iraq earlier that year, an attack he termed "the first political and military action of its kind." Grandly titled "Managing an Asymmetric World—a Case for Preventive War," the 57-page thesis he wrote would earn him the military graduate degree he needed to reach the rank of lieutenant-colonel. A project of this type, undertaken by Williams at the Canadian Forces College in Toronto, is not a master's degree as such; rather, it confers on the student an in-house credential. The results are revealing, displaying an author plainly anxious to show he was a man of the world. What comes across most strongly, however, is a mental rigidity that places a premium on raw power and muscularity—control—while selectively seeing what it chooses to see.

Five months after the Bush administration unleashed its onslaught on Iraq, a roiling global debate was under way over where the mission was headed. Iraq was on fire. With minimal resistance to the invaders, Saddam Hussein's ramshackle, vastly outgunned police state had swiftly fractured and sunk into the chaos widely predicted by the war's foes. Now a brutal insurgency was taking hold, marked by death squads, daily bombings, the plundering of billions of dollars' worth of foreign aid, the collapse of the country's infrastructure and, above all, enormous civilian suffering. Iraqis were beginning to flee their neighborhoods, cities and homeland in the hundreds of thousands.

You would not know any of this from the stiff, antiseptic essay Major Williams crafted. At age forty, Williams had never visited the Middle East. Nor had he been in combat. And nor, until now, had he posed as an authority on the pros and cons of preventive war. Williams's essay begins with a flourish, quoting in its first paragraph George W. Bush's address to the world on March 19, 2003, as the U.S. invasion was launched. Williams wrote, "The President explained that the threat posed by Iraq was too great to ignore, adding 'We will meet that threat now, with our Army, Air Force, Navy, Coast Guard and Marines so that we do not have to meet it later with armies of fire fighters and police and doctors in the streets of our cities.'"

It all smacked of the "domino theory" that had defined U.S. policy in Vietnam a generation earlier—if we don't fight them over there, we'll be fighting them in California—and was not a view widely held among Canadian politicians, nor the country's

military leaders. The Afghanistan mission yes, the consensus
went, because al-Qaeda's nest of leaders lived there and had to be
crushed. But Iraq was another matter, and not merely because
Canada's forces were already stretched to the limit in Afghanistan.
Years before President Obama articulated the same argument on
the campaign trail, there was apprehension in Canadian military
circles that the Iraq war would divert energy and resources from,
and ultimately undermine, the Afghan effort, which clearly it did.

Williams, however, seemed to harbor no such doubts. After
dwelling at length on the distinction between preventive war and
preemptive war (a preemptive strike takes place quickly, in response
to a sudden threat; a preventive war is planned over time), he concluded that both can be justified, even when most of the world dis-
agrees. It was an argument that had been spelled out a year earlier
in a landmark White House policy statement, "The National
Security Strategy of the United States of America," which laid the
philosophical underpinnings for the Iraq adventure. Repeatedly
Williams's thesis approvingly quotes that declaration, along with
another heavily favored source, a bellicose speech Bush had delivered to West Point military cadets in the fall of 2002.

His paper thus emerges as enthusiastic approval for the
"might is right" logic nurtured by Bush and his inner circle.
Similar praise is heaped on the other event Williams offers in
support of preventive military action: Israel's much-criticized
destruction of Iraq's Osirak nuclear reactor in 1981. Absent,
however, despite the author's nine months of toil, is any fresh
information or insight. Instead, sprinkled with the use of the
royal "we," Williams's thesis essentially rehashes other authors'
material. "Preventive war is a subject that can evoke a great deal
of emotion from those who choose to argue its merits or short-
comings," he wrote in his turgid introduction.

It is an issue that demands examination from several directions. Most pundits limit the scope of their arguments, typically addressing one or two of the several important elements. In order to more fully develop this paper's position, we shall draw upon the inputs of a variety of writers to present both sides of various aspects of the issue, allowing a more complete assessment of the utility of preventive war . . .

More troubling than the prose, however, is the tunnel vision. Before the invasion, Iraq was portrayed by neocon hawks—Williams was evidently among them—as a sinister, well-oiled battle machine that had committed mass atrocities before and, given the chance, would do so again in a heartbeat. Those who actually visited Iraq in the run-up to the war, and talked to its frightened people, saw something altogether different: a shabby, bankrupt gangster state that had been on its knees for years and, exceedingly mindful of how the Kuwait debacle had played out twelve years earlier, was now frantic to escape being pulverized once again by the United States.

And hanging over everything in those first postwar months was the question that went to the heart of Williams's writing project: WMD (Weapons of Mass Destruction). The core rationale for the U.S. invasion was Saddam's supposedly huge stash of these weapons, hidden somewhere in Iraq's western deserts but now mysteriously missing in action. So where were all those chemical warheads and biological agents, alluded to by U.S. Secretary of State Colin Powell as he brandished a vial of fake anthrax at the United Nations? Increasingly it was becoming evident they did not exist, a fact that appears to have bothered Williams not at all as he made his case. "That evidence of these [WMD] programs has not been uncovered some nine months after the fall of Iraq to coalition forces is beyond the scope of this paper," he wrote in a throwaway line of breathtaking alacrity. "Similarly, while aspects of the coalition action shall be used for illustrative purposes, it is not the intent of this essay to critique the Anglo-American decision to launch their attack," he wrote, even though the thesis struggled to do exactly that.

Returning to the missing WMD near the end of his essay, almost as if it were a footnote, Williams does acknowledge that "it would appear that there remains a great deal of progress to be made in the area of intelligence collection and analysis, given, for example, that coalition forces have proven unable to locate the WMD stockpiles they were sure existed." Indeed, the phantom WMD had reinforced the general consensus against preventive war, Williams concedes. But he adds: "Imagine if coalition forces had quickly located the weaponry . . . such discoveries would have softened the reactions of many to the invasion of Iraq, leaving the door open for a less polarized discussion of the merits of preventive war."

The other hurdle Williams had to overcome in trying to make his case was the supposed link between Saddam's Iraq and Osama bin Laden, architect-in-chief of the 9/11 terror attacks. A vague but oft-cited prop in the Bush rationale for the attack, the connection was never there, as most experienced Middle East observers well understood.

Williams, in sum, displayed an intense tunnel vision that in hindsight is illuminating. The people he was chiefly writing about—Iraq's 14 million citizens—are invisible. As with the women Williams would later stalk, molest and kill, it was as if their torment was secondary to his own needs, and irrelevant. His ivory-tower conclusion rosily summarized the post-invasion landscape thus: "Although there are likely to be turbulent periods in the near future, this writer believes that the path to international stability and a more pervasive sense of peace and co-operation between states is straighter than it was just a short time ago."

Whatever its failings, Williams's thesis had the desired effect. He was promoted to lieutenant-colonel, and in June 2004 he took charge of the 437 ("Husky") Transport Squadron at CFB Trenton, the base he would command in its entirety five years later. In August of that year, he and Harriman purchased the cottage on Cosy Cove Lane in the nearby community of Tweed.

At the time, 437 possessed five CC-150 Polaris Airbuses: one configured for prime ministerial use, with a stateroom, a bathroom and other conveniences; two used for carrying people, with a capacity of 197 passengers apiece; and two multifunctional planes designed to haul both people and cargo, called combies. Including civilians, 437 Squadron deployed about eighty people, and troop movements were the staple, with a steady flow back and forth between the Middle East, Bosnia and Afghanistan, the main focus. And as usual, the professional and pleasant new squadron leader gave no hint whatever of his dark side.

Retired air force sergeant and loadmaster Lucy Critch, now a Canada Post employee in Newfoundland, spent twenty-three years with the Canadian Forces, more than a year of it under Williams's command at 437. She remembers him fondly, with nothing but affection and respect. "He was funny, he liked to laugh and was beloved by everyone in the squadron, definitely someone often described as a nice guy." As loadmaster—akin to a purser on commercial flights—Critch flew half a dozen times or so with her boss, who called her Lu. On quick trips to, for example, Croatia, he would cheerfully wander through Zagreb at day's end with the rest of the crew looking for a bite to eat or a quick drink. "Call me Russ," he would often say to them, though no one did.

Critch remembers a court-martial in which Williams took a role, and she was struck by the fairness he showed. But the most compelling thing about him, she says, were his many acts of kindness and consideration, large and small. She recalls vividly a silent-auction fundraiser she once organized for a married cousin in Newfoundland who needed major surgery and had to relocate to Toronto with her husband while they waited for the operation, leaving their young daughter behind. Critch asked Williams, her boss, if she could auction off some of the assorted gifts and keepsakes members of 437 Squadron and other squadrons had picked up overseas. "Of course," Critch remembers him saying, "you have my blessing, and what can I do? Would you like some of my hand-tied fishing flies? I tie them myself." The next day Williams brought in half a dozen of the flies, signed and mounted on a piece of paper with the squadron logo. Critch's husband made the winning bid for them.

Another time, a junior officer Critch still knows well developed serious kidney problems and had to abandon her career with the armed forces after less than ten years' service. The military wanted to pay her off with a lump-sum settlement, but she preferred a small pension instead. Williams went to bat for her and secured the pension.

When Critch learned of his arrest, she was so disbelieving that she rushed upstairs to check the name on the fish-flies memento. Then she woke up her husband to tell him that the police had made some dreadful mistake.

In the summer of 2005, Garrett Lawless met Russell Williams for the first time. He'd just been posted to 437 Squadron as a pilot, and as all new arrivals did, he stopped by his new commander's office for a brief chat. "He asked me if I had kids, I said not yet, then he asked if I planned to have kids, and I said maybe, to which he responded that he definitely wasn't. Other than that, the conversation was quite vanilla. He discussed the importance of the mission I would be carrying out, how he would support me in any way possible to become a better pilot and/or officer, and that he also expected me to make every effort to be the best of each that I could be. My initial impression exactly matched his reputation. He was a consummate professional with exacting standards for himself and those that worked for him."

Lawless got to know Williams well during his spell at 437, and was glad to see him come back to CFB Trenton four years later to take command of the whole base. Yet agreeable as he always was, off the job Williams could be stiff and socially inept. "It's not so funny anymore, but I used to make fun of him behind his back. I used to call him the cyborg because we would be at these mess functions, at Christmas dinner or whatever, and you would see him in a group. Someone would make a joke and everybody would start laughing and he would start laughing as well. But he looked like he never saw what the joke was, and it would be like, 'Oh, I must be seen laughing, ha ha ha.' He just seemed awkward. He was more at ease when he was talking about things like Swiss mechanical watches, which he loved, or anything to do with airplanes. It was the one thing outside work that we talked about, because we were passionate about it: Swiss mechanical watches. He had two Breitlings, I had one. We would always ask each other what watch we were wearing. I could feel the internal mechanism spin, and he said, 'Yeah, that's normal, you'll grow to love it.'"

Despite what took place later, when Williams was arrested and armchair experts began referring to him as a "psychopath," Lawless remains as sure as he can be that the warmth he encountered was not a facade. "He wasn't emotionally detached, he always seemed very friendly and very interested, and if you went up to him he'd give you a big firm handshake. This [Williams's downfall] would be easier if you could think of him as some cold person, but he wasn't. He seemed very genuine—very controlled, but in an admirable way. You'd look at him and say, 'That's the guy that's never going to get flustered.'

"I saw him in stressful situations and he always approached them very logically. Scheduling difficulties, for instance. Say we had a mission and the prime minister said he needed the plane on this date, we now had to figure out a way to rearrange it. Not a life-and-death thing, but we are going to have to tell the prime minister he can't have the airplane. And [Williams] would just come in and sit, with his chin in his hands, look at it and say, 'Try this, this and this.' That might not work, so he'd say, 'Try this and this.' And eventually it would work.

"And he was a really, really good pilot. Take the Airbus. Most people take about a year to get comfortable with it. But I was given my training by the guy that gave him his training, and he said to me, 'Russ Williams, he came into the simulator and the first day, as expected, he didn't know anything. The second day he was a little bit better. And by the third day, it was like, What the hell did this guy do? Because he seems to know the airplane as well as I do.'

"Within six months Russ could handle that airplane as good or better than anybody on the squadron, and there were people who had been flying it for seven years. I would look at Russ Williams and it was just, 'That guy's better than me.' He was deeply impressive in his ability as a pilot, just an excellent officer. If you wanted to model yourself on somebody, he was perfect."

After Williams's arrest, questions also arose about how he had found not only the time but the energy to lead his double life for more than two years. Lawless says his stamina was extraordinary.

"I've never seen him tired. We did most of our flights at night, we would land back here in Trenton at three or four in the morning, and he would go almost straight to work and do all his [commanding officer] duties."

His temper, too, was almost always under control. "The only anecdote I've ever heard about him getting angry was when he flew the Challenger one time and somebody farted in the cockpit. And that's a little strange. You're stuck in a small, confined space with people, and the joke is, you say 'Howdy,' to warn the guys. But he got really angry, he thought it was disgusting."

Nor was Williams's authority ever challenged. "Nobody I ever came across would have dared be insubordinate to him. Not because they were afraid of being crucified but because he was such a picture of professionalism. Everybody felt in awe of him. I wouldn't call it charisma, more like professional authority. Everybody just knew this guy was better than them."

In that same year, 2005, came a curiously revealing episode that sheds light on another side of Williams's complex personality: his near-neurotic modesty, which seemed to prevent him from claiming personal credit for anything.

In May, the Queen made her twenty-second visit to Canada, marking the 100th anniversary of Saskatchewan and Alberta joining Confederation. Protocol called for the host country to collect Her Majesty, as well as Prince Philip, the Duke of Edinburgh, from the United Kingdom and then return them after the visit. So Williams took the controls of one of the squadron's CC-150 Polaris Airbuses and together with a military and civilian retinue of seventeen he headed to London. A posed photo of the crew in Trenton's CF newspaper *Contact* shows him proudly standing in the center of the crew on the tarmac before their departure, with the hulking Polaris, dubbed Flight Royal One, in the background.

The weather was lousy, it rained a lot, but the big crowds were enthusiastic and the week-long royal visit to various stops in Saskatchewan and Alberta went off without a hitch. For most pilots, it might have been the trip of a lifetime, certainly a big feather in their cap. And along with all the congratulations, Williams received a framed, signed photograph of the monarch, thanking him personally. He hung it in his upstairs office at the house on Wilkie Drive, together with his other plaques, and a few months later his old university friend Jeff Farquhar stopped by—one of the very few people who ever visited and stayed over. Farquhar noticed the photograph and remarked on it. Williams just shrugged—no big deal. He changed the subject. "I can't [emphasize] enough how ridiculously modest he had become," Farquhar says today. "I am sure much of it had to do with secrecy regarding security [arrangements], but he just never bragged about anything, even after the fact."

And then, for Lieutenant-Colonel Williams, there surfaced a mission that really did call for secrecy. In late 2005, with more than six months still to go in his two-year posting as commander of 437 Transport Squadron, came the unexpected announcement that he would be wearing two hats. He would keep his position with 437 Squadron, but simultaneously he was taking charge of Camp Mirage, the quasi-clandestine air base post near Dubai, in the United Arab Emirates, that served as the Canadian military's air bridge linking Trenton to the Afghanistan war effort.

In the fall of 2010, Camp Mirage became a very public political issue in Canada, over what looked to be an absurd squabble between the Stephen Harper government and the U.A.E. government. At issue were the landing rights in Canada of the U.A.E.'s two national carriers. Air Canada was complaining that the U.A.E.'s airlines were unfairly scooping up its customers on the shorter-haul flights between Canada and Europe. The two airlines' access to Canada was restricted; in retaliation, the U.A.E. informed the Canadian military that its days in Dubai were over.

But back in 2005, Camp Mirage did not officially exist, and was considered a highly sensitive topic. It was Williams himself who offered to take charge of the desert compound while retaining command of 437 Squadron, and the double duty looks to have been a mark of his ambition. "That was a career move, I think. He could have waited, but it's all about getting through those gates as quick as you can," Lawless says. "He sacrificed the last six months of his two-year tenure as CO, which are generally seen as the highlight of a career—the command of a squadron—to take concurrent command of Mirage. He could have handed it over to his deputy, but he wanted joint command."

Formally known as Theatre Support Element, Camp Mirage was attached to the U.A.E.'s Minhad air base, a short drive south of glittering, skyscraper-choked Dubai, and was the worst-kept military secret in the Middle East. Al Minhad served as a transit point for other Afghanistan-bound coalition troops too, and anybody who wanted to could find out exactly where Camp Mirage was; if not, Google Earth could assist. The consensus, at least in Canadian military circles, was that the vagueness about its location stemmed less from security concerns than from a reluctance to embarrass the host state, the U.A.E., which was not anxious to advertise its military ties to Western powers fighting their assorted wars in Muslim lands.

It would be Williams's first and only spell both in the Middle East and in a war zone, and he appears to have thrived at Camp Mirage. He already had a "Secret" security clearance (as opposed to "Top Secret"), which was deemed sufficient for his new duties. He underwent no additional background screening for the posting.

He was taking charge of an air base as busy as some major European airports, a conduit for flights that streamed in day and night. In all, well over 200,000 passengers have passed through Mirage since it was created in 2002, and when Williams was there most of them arrived and left aboard the aging CC-130 Hercules transport planes that were the backbone of the Canadian war mission, whose hub was Kandahar Airfield in southern Afghanistan. A former air force officer under his command at Mirage described the new CO's performance as "fantastic," saying he appeared comfortable under pressure and was adept at juggling several balls at the same time, always with good humor. And the pace was nonstop, frequently requiring Williams to put in an eighty-hour week.

Camp Mirage's primary function was as a transit point for troops starting or ending six- or nine-month tours of duty. But many Canadian VIPs came and went too, as did soldiers and dignitaries from allied countries. There were also the occasional ramp ceremonies for soldiers who died in Afghanistan—one when their bodies arrived at Mirage and a second when they were sent on to Trenton and then Toronto, for a final autopsy.

There was no combat role for the Camp Mirage personnel (hence no possibility that the genesis of Williams's crimes was some type of post-traumatic stress disorder) and from a distance a stint there might have looked like easy street. In fact, it was highly demanding. Air maintenance was the chief task of the rotating 300 to 400 officers deployed to Mirage for six months at a time, drawn from air bases in Winnipeg, Greenwood, Trenton, Cold Lake, Comox and Bagotville. Also on hand were communications experts, an intelligence unit, military police and civilian support staff. Troops had access to a well-run mess hall, shared with other coalition troops, phone cards, an Internet area, a recreation room, a music room and even a scuba club.

Among those who served at Camp Mirage, three years before Williams arrived, was Corporal Marie-France Comeau, whom he would later rape and murder in her Brighton home. She was part of Operation Apollo, the first group of Canadian soldiers to land in Afghanistan, and was deployed as a traffic technician, driving a forklift truck to load and unload cargo and drawing widespread admiration for her hard work and unflagging good spirits.

Up the road for the handful of senior officers able to pay regular visits was safe, West-friendly Dubai. But the working conditions at Mirage were often brutal, encompassing long work weeks and blistering temperatures that could reach 140 degrees Fahrenheit. In the hottest months, the Persian Gulf humidity was so extreme that much of the work had to be done at night.

As base commander, Williams oversaw everything, from day-to-day duties such as the fire detail, medical detail, kitchen duties and the computer system to the constantly shifting arrivals and departures schedules. Everything was to run like clockwork, he insisted, and for the most part it did. In addition, he had to travel regularly within the region—to the Kandahar base, which he visited at least once a month, to Abu Dhabi, the U.A.E. capital, and sometimes to Qatar, for consultations with senior U.S. military officials based there. It was all very much like being a mini wing commander—a continuous, highly visible job.

Nonetheless, after the murder and sex-assault charges were laid against Williams, voices in the blogosphere speculated that perhaps in his off-hours at Mirage—a tour that wrapped up in June 2006, fifteen months before his first acknowledged break-in— he found time to commit crimes in the Dubai region, possibly other murders. One conspiracy theory that briefly gained attention suggested that a military policeman's unexpected suicide at Camp Mirage while Williams was there might have occurred because the officer had discovered something suspicious about his boss—liaisons with prostitutes in Dubai, for example, who for a high price were definitely available.

There's no evidence whatever to support this thesis, and two factors weigh against it. First, Williams's existence at Mirage was highly regulated, and he was rarely out of view. Every six weeks, the Camp Mirage commander had a 48-hour rest and recreation break off the base, but because of the importance of his job, he would never have been alone. And during those short spells, Garrett Lawless says, "everybody would always need to know how to contact you."

Second, the trajectory of Williams's admitted crimes began with dozens of break-ins committed when the homeowners were almost invariably absent, a pattern that continued for two full years (September 2007 to September 2009) before spiking up sharply and accelerating into sexual assault and finally murder. It is conceivable and in fact very likely that long before Williams carried out the first burglary with which he was charged, targeting a family who lived near his cottage in Tweed, his obsession with women's underwear had manifested itself— perhaps as voyeurism, or sneaking into a bedroom during a house party. And he may well have committed earlier burglaries too. But it seems improbable he did anything illegal in Dubai. One of the hallmarks of his later crimes was that they all took place within what could be called a comfort zone—close to his home, involving people whose movements he had carefully tracked. He had no opportunity to do that kind of research in Dubai, even if had wanted to. Rather, Williams told police—and for the most part they believed him—that it was during his next posting, back in Ottawa, that he first started breaking the law.

Williams's six-month spell at Camp Mirage, with regular side trips to Afghanistan, earned him the circular-shaped South-West Asia Service Medal (Canada). He wore it alongside his Canadian

Forces Decoration, an award given to all members of the military who have completed twelve years of good service. Following his criminal convictions in October 2010, he would be stripped of both, together with his rank, and the medals were shredded.

Back in Canada, still a lieutenant-colonel, he commenced a desk job that was physically much less taxing than his eighty-hour weeks in the desert but no less critical to the air force. In July 2006 he was appointed to the dull-sounding Directorate of Air Requirements, the agency that oversees the acquisition of new airplanes and other major assets. As within any other technically oriented organization, the work flow is constant, as new planes displace older ones and decisions are made about what will be needed in the future, what can be dispensed with and what can be afforded. The job requires both nuts-and-bolts expertise with respect to the planes and other equipment and an acute business acumen, since much of the work involves negotiating with airplane builders and other manufacturers, both domestic and foreign. Many up-and-coming air force officers spend time at DAR.

Williams's particular mandate was to oversee and advise regarding the acquisition of two types of new heavy-lift aircraft: four Boeing CC-177 Globemaster transports (a Conservative election pledge) and a much bigger fleet of C-130J Hercules planes. New search-and-rescue planes were also in the pipeline.

There was another key way in which Williams's new posting in Ottawa differed from his job at Camp Mirage. When he left at the end of the day, and headed either to his Orleans home on Wilkie Drive or to the cottage in Tweed that he used on weekends, nobody was watching him.

6

OVER THE THRESHOLD

Williams spent two and a half years with the Directorate of Air Requirements in Ottawa, working under Lieutenant-General Angus Watt, who would later recommend his promotion to full colonel.

Williams was "unusually calm, very logical and rational and able to produce good-quality staff work in a fairly short time, which is a valued commodity in Ottawa," Watt later told the CBC's *Fifth Estate* program. "You have to be good with people and you really have to be a good leader. You have to be good with the administration, you have to be good with the media, and good with the public. It all has to come together in a package that gives us confidence that you will do well as wing commander, and Russ had all of that package . . . Is there something that we did or didn't do that would have given us a clue [as to his dark side]? Everybody's had the same reaction—there was no clue."

At the DAR operation in Ottawa, he left very much the same impression. "Russ was ahead of the curve. He didn't just see the day-by-day stuff landing on his desk—he was anticipating what's going to be coming next, in terms of possible problems," says another air force officer who worked with Williams at the same time. "The Globemasters were pretty much a done deal when he got to DAR—it would have been a big surprise if they hadn't gone through—but the amount of technical know-how that went with them was vast. These are complicated airplanes, and he was totally on top of it. I'm sure he didn't enjoy doing a desk job as much as he liked flying, but you never heard him complain, he was cheerful. I guess he knew that if you wanted to keep going up and make [the rank of] full colonel, DAR was a place where you had to pay some dues."

But one of his neighbors in Orleans, George White, recalls Williams's demeanor changing perceptibly at around this time, which White put down to the new job. "He became more secretive when he had the job downtown with the Directorate of Air Requirements. That was the environment in which I spent eighteen years, on the civilian side, and so I knew a bit of what was going on. At his level he would be reviewing the specs and making sure they would be presented the right way to the minister. But it also involved knowing the business side, making sure that in the contract all the T's were crossed and the I's dotted, to convince the minister that we've got to get these airplanes. He was a member of that team, but we never discussed it. I would say, 'Hard day at work?' and he would say, 'Oh yeah.' He never brought his work home, it was just idle chitchat."

The aircraft projects Williams was overseeing went through almost entirely as planned. In February 2007, the federal government signed a contract with the Chicago-based Boeing Company for four CC-177 Globemasters, and delivery began six months later. The C-17, as it is abbreviated, is a hulking military transport plane designed to haul both people and cargo, and is also used by the armed forces of the United States, Great Britain and Australia. By April 2008, all four Globemasters had arrived at 8 Wing/CFB Trenton, where Williams took command nine months later. Nor did any major problems arise over the deal with Lockheed Martin for the big new Hercules airlifters. In January 2008, Ottawa signed a $1.4-billion contract with the Bethesda, Maryland, manufacturer for seventeen new CC-130Js, to replace the existing CC-130E and H models. The first CC-130J arrived at CFB Trenton in June 2010, four months after Williams's arrest.

In sum, there appear to have been no significant work-related pressures that might have had any bearing on the colonel's seemingly momentous decision to commit his first acknowledged break-in, fourteen months after he arrived at DAR.

On the second weekend of September 2007, Williams drove the 125 miles from Ottawa to his rural retreat on Cosy Cove Lane. Living close by was a family—father, mother, son and daughter—who probably knew Williams and his wife better than most people in Tweed. Few local residents were even aware of the low-profile 8 Wing commander, but this family certainly liked him. The two couples had bought their cottages at around the same time, and Williams and Harriman had visited the family's home on several occasions for dinner. In the summer months they had sat together outside overlooking the lake, playing cards.

After Williams was arrested, many former neighbors would say that the colonel's relationship with Harriman had seemed stiff and formal, a marriage of convenience perhaps. But possibly this particular husband and wife put Williams and Harriman at ease, because the wife later spoke of a couple who seemed genuinely devoted to each other, and sometimes could be seen strolling, holding hands. And if the parents liked Williams, so did their teenage son and younger daughter. Williams sometimes took the children tubing, pulling them around Stoco Lake in his outboard-powered boat. The boy had an interest in guitar, which Williams encouraged, and in the summer of 2009 the daughter would be given a key to Williams and Harriman's cottage so she could look after the couple's new cat, Rosebud.

Now, in September 2007, at the age of twelve, the girl became the first target of the family's trusted friend.

Williams broke into the family's home twice, and possibly three times, that month, always while they were away. And like virtually everyone else in Tweed whose homes he invaded over the next two years, they never noticed anything missing and had no idea they had been robbed. Not until several weeks after Williams was arrested in February 2010 did they learn to their horror what their neighbor had been doing.

That first break-in took place in the late hours of September 8 and early hours of September 9, a Saturday/Sunday. Twenty-five time-stamped photographs Williams took and stored on his computer hard drive in Ottawa show that after entering the family's house through an unlocked door, he was there for more than two and a half hours, all of that time spent in the girl's bedroom. While he was there, he established a pattern that he would often replicate during his scores of subsequent break-ins in Tweed and Ottawa: he rooted through the girl's underwear drawer, stripped naked and posed for his carefully positioned camera, draping her clothing around his erect penis and ejaculating on it. On leaving this, his first victim's house, he took with him six pieces of underwear.

He came back three weeks later, either once or twice, again arriving late at night. The first twenty photos—all similar to the ones he took the first time—were made before and after midnight on September 28. Then, shortly after eight o'clock the next morning, he took twenty-two more, suggesting he either returned or had spent the night in the girl's bedroom. Many more pictures were taken that day, both inside the girl's bedroom and outside in some nearby woodland, where Williams photographed himself naked wearing her underwear.

The template was set, and in several ways these first two (or three) break-ins are illustrative. They took place on weekends under cover of darkness while the homeowners were away, a modus operandi over the next two years that goes some way toward explaining how he was able to lead his double life. In all, Williams ultimately pleaded guilty to 82 burglaries, encompassing many return trips to the same houses, plus two sexual assaults and two murders, these last four also starting as break-ins. (Two counts of forcible confinement raised the total number of charges to 88.) Of those 86 intrusions in Tweed, Ottawa, Belleville and Brighton, more than half took place on a Saturday or a Friday—28 and 18 respectively—and a further 18 occurred on a Thursday. Seven were on a Tuesday, 7 others on a Wednesday, 5 on a Sunday and just 3 on a Monday.

Eight months later, in May 2008, Williams returned and broke into those same neighbors' house yet again.

Williams entered the dozens of homes he robbed by the path of least resistance. Often he walked through unlocked doors, especially in Tweed, where serious crime was almost unknown. Sometimes he forced a window sash or a screen, usually at the back of the house. If he had to, he could usually—not always—pick the lock, a skill that dated back to his university days. And he did his homework ahead of time, too, often scouting out targets while he was jogging. In and around Cosy Cove Lane, which is a long walk from the center of the village, with no bus service, an empty driveway was a giveaway.

And this first clutch of burglaries also sheds light on Williams's obsessive sexual interests, which drove his law-breaking from beginning to end, and which in large part focused on victims who were young. He told police that the preferred age of the women he targeted after doing his reconnaissance was late teens to early thirties. But of the 48 different homes he invaded, in 13 instances females aged under eighteen were either his sole or the joint target. And child pornography would be found on his computer.

Although he many times posed for himself cross-dressing in women's stolen underwear, he seems to have displayed no sexual interest whatever in boys or young men. The wearing of the underwear, often while he masturbated, looks to be an extension of his need to invade his victims' privacy in the most intimate way. His huge collection of photos included not only the pornographic ones, by far the majority, but also a much smaller number of shots—usually photos of photos hanging on bedroom walls— showing the victim in ordinary, everyday poses, as if the intruder wanted to have a trophy of that too, perhaps to enhance his pleasure when he got home.

In the case of this first break-in, he photographed a news clipping showing the twelve-year-old at a Tweed Legion function, together with two classmates, holding what appears to be a certificate or plaque. Capturing innocent images of his unsuspecting victims, especially if they were young, was a hallmark of Williams's perversity. After he later began expanding his raids to target houses near his home in Ottawa, he photographed himself masturbating in the bedroom of a girl aged about eleven, for instance, with her underwear spread out on her bed. But he also snapped four framed photos that he found in the house, showing three different young girls, none of whom appeared to be over the age of twelve. In another break-in, he photographed a young woman's university degree hanging on her bedroom wall.

The fact that Williams returned at least twice to that first house on Cosy Cove Lane also underscores the repetitive nature of his obsession. He hit numerous houses two or three times, and one, also near Cosy Cove Lane, he burgled on nine different occasions. There too, the homeowners knew nothing about it until he was arrested.

His total haul almost defies belief. In all, he admitted to stealing and cataloging around 1,400 pieces of clothing, nearly all of it women's lingerie, and in one raid alone he took 186 items. Some of his loot he destroyed, when the collection became too large to manage, but hundreds more pieces—barely hidden—were found at his Ottawa townhouse and Tweed cottage when they were searched by police. And along with the underwear were many of the thousands of photos he took, artfully concealed inside folders and subfolders within his computer system, together with a near-complete log of all his admitted crimes, recording the dates, the places, the nature of the offense and other details.

After his first repeat trip to his neighbors' home on Cosy Cove Lane, Williams waited a few weeks before striking again. Once more it was on a weekend in Tweed, close to his home, and once more he broke into the same residence twice, stealing thirteen undergarments and a bathing suit. But this pair of early burglaries stands out from the others.

The burglary at the second house is the only known time that Williams came close to being caught in the act, inside someone's house. The home belonged to a couple with twin eleven-year-old daughters, and nobody was home at the time, as the family was attending an evening after-dark barbecue at a neighbor's house. But when the parents briefly returned to pick up a couple of items, they noticed a tall intruder inside, wearing a hoodie, shorts and running shoes. He ran into the woods and they chased him, without result. They noticed nothing missing, and only reported the burglary ten days later when they heard of another break-in, which proved to be unrelated.

That house belonged to the adult daughter of Williams's Cosy Cove Lane neighbor Larry Jones. Two years later, as we have seen, Jones would become a suspect in the two sex assaults Williams went on to commit. This abortive break-in, however, which Williams would later describe to police as "a close call," appears to have had no bearing on Jones's future troubles, and looks to have been no more than coincidence, one in a rash of burglaries Williams carried out in the immediate area.

As with the multiple break-ins he would later commit in Ottawa, the proximity to his own home provided Williams with an excellent fallback card in the event he was spotted on or near someone's property. He would simply have been able to say: "I was passing by and saw something suspicious, so I thought I should check." And who would have doubted him? He was, after all, the colonel in charge of the most important air base in Canada. As Jones put it, with regard to the break-in at his daughter's house: "If I would have seen Russ Williams walking on the trail back there [near the house], I'd have said, 'Russ, did you see a kid running through here?'"

Perhaps the close call gave Williams a fright, because after committing one more break-in on November 1, he abruptly ceased for more than four months before resuming on March 15, 2008, the longest gap in his two and a half years of home invasions. When he did start again, the pattern was the same. All ten of the first Tweed burglaries occurred within a short walk of Williams's cottage, and all showed the same grotesque behavior: intrusions into homes while the owners were out, protracted masturbation sessions where he cavorted and posed for the camera with his underwear trophies, and then the theft of those items, often a dozen or more stuffed into bags he had brought with him, before he slunk off into the night. Almost all the first Tweed burglaries took place around the weekend; during the week, while he continued to work at DAR, he lived at his home on Wilkie Drive in the Orleans area of Ottawa.

Then, in May 2008, eight months after the first break-in in Tweed, his focus abruptly widened. The predator grew bolder, and began targeting houses in Orleans. As with almost all the Tweed burglaries, they were close to his own home, and once again he used his regular jogging routine for reconnaissance missions.

But the Orleans neighborhood of Fallingbrook where Wilkie Drive is located is an urban subdivision of neat, curving streets, in contrast to the houses on and around rural Cosy Cove Lane in Tweed, which typically could be approached from several sides. Most of the 34 thefts and attempted thefts in Orleans, involving 25 different homes, required Williams to make his approach from the front of the house, walking up the side driveway and then usually gaining entry from the back; in only a couple of instances was he able to approach from the rear, through parkland. He was no less stealthy, because he was never caught in the act, although at least once he had to flee when he was spotted trying to force a window at a house on Apollo Way, close to his own home.

Another difference between the two locales where the break-ins were carried out is that the Orleans homeowners were much more rigorous about keeping their houses locked up, meaning that in a number of instances Williams had to force his way inside. As well, his quest for trophies was gathering pace and he started stealing more items, in one case raiding a house that was home to a mother and two daughters and grabbing every piece of underwear they owned. As a result of such wanton theft, almost two-thirds of the Orleans break-ins did get reported to Ottawa police. Of the 25 homes Williams raided in Orleans over the next fourteen months, about 15 of the owners filed a report, although often not right away. In many instances, however, the owners were unable to say whether anything had been stolen.

While the Ottawa police had no idea who might be responsible, it was plain that a prowler was on the loose, and in October 2008 an investigation was launched, deploying undercover cops who watched the street from unmarked cars and posed as residents out for a late night stroll.

Among the homes broken into in Orleans was that of retired couple Patty and Milt Mitchelmore, who live on Caminiti Crescent, a couple of blocks from Williams's home on Wilkie Drive. It was in August 2008, and they had just returned from their cottage when they noticed that a screen was missing from one of the dining room windows, and that there was dirt from the garden on the hardwood floor below the window. As well, a side door was unlocked, marking the burglar's departure.

The Mitchelmores looked through the house and found nothing missing (Williams had left empty-handed) but reported the incident to police anyway. "The police constable did a tour of the house inside, and then he found the screen hidden in some shrubs in the backyard," Patty Mitchelmore says. "We have patio furniture on the deck in the backyard, and apparently one of the patio chairs had been put in the garden so the intruder could use it to get in, because the constable could see the markings of the four feet of the chair, though the chair had been returned to its place."

Two years later, she could joke about the incident. "Maybe he didn't find anything he wanted." She was, nonetheless, extremely unnerved when, a few weeks after Williams was arrested on charges of murder and sexual assault, she was told he had been in her home. "If we'd noticed anything missing, if I'd seen my underwear spread out on the bed, that would have had much more of an impact than seeing some dirt on a hardwood floor. So we were grateful, thinking that maybe we'd arrived home at just the right time."

On the last day of October 2008, Ottawa police issued a warning urging the public to be vigilant, after two break-ins that month that they described as unusual. "It should be noted that the only items taken in the two Break & Enters were women's undergarments," the statement read. "Due to the peculiar nature of these incidents, the Ottawa Police wishes to remind the public to be vigilant and ensure that they secure their home at all times."

As part of their investigation, Ottawa police also revisited some older, possibly related cases, including a January 2005 double break-in at a high-rise building on the west side of Ottawa, where dozens of women's undergarments were stolen by someone described as a tall, clean-cut man in his thirties. No connection to Williams was ever established with that or any other break-ins beyond his tightly circumscribed comfort zone of Fallingbrook.

Meanwhile, some additional expertise was called in, in the shape of Detective Sergeant Jim Van Allen, a seasoned criminal profiler attached to the OPP's Orillia-based Behavioural Sciences and Analyses Services unit who has taken a role in hundreds of murder and sex-assault investigations. Van Allen's task was to assess the disparate information about the break-ins and make a highly educated guess as to the type of person responsible. He didn't like what he saw at all.

The intruder was becoming more aggressive, even as he stealthily evaded detection. In one Orleans home, he left a message on the home computer taunting the occupants by telling them he had been there. In another, he left a trail of leaves leading into the house. In a third, he placed on the floor a photograph of the woman whose underwear he had stolen and he masturbated on it.

"He was messaging the victims and the victims' family by disturbing their living space, and he was getting a kick out of it," says Van Allen, who has since retired after thirty-one years with the OPP and is now a criminal profiling consultant in the private sector. "I look at all behavior on a continuum, and one of the things I'm seeing here is this: He could have just stolen the underwear off of a clothesline or something like that, but he's getting into the homes. He's in the beds, he's trying the underwear on, and I see that as a psychological movement toward the victims' bodies."

In hindsight, Van Allen is unsurprised that Williams went on to rape and kill, although he says the speed at which Williams raced up the sexual deviance ladder is startling. "The guy we were looking for was right in that neighborhood, and the frequency of the break-ins and the repetitiveness showed he had this arrogance. And I thought: 'This is a guy who could escalate.' You can't forecast whether it will be days, weeks, months or ever, but it certainly suggested he was going to continue in that manner. I concluded that he seemed to be very careful about avoiding contact with people, but that anytime that changed, the danger of a hands-on sexual assault would go right up."

The geography of the burglaries, all clustered in the Fallingbrook subdivision, underlined the likelihood of there being a single predator who lived in the neighborhood. But who he might be, the Ottawa police and Van Allen had no idea until Williams was arrested. And there was no predictable time pattern. More than once a cluster of burglaries was followed by a long pause before the next one took place.

For a while, suspicion in Ottawa centered on a local man who had been charged with possessing child pornography. When police spoke to him, he reacted very cagily, and shortly afterward a pile of burned lingerie was found in a nearby field, marking one of two occasions when Williams disposed of some of his loot. "It was very coincidental, and it didn't do much to help eliminate this guy," remarks Van Allen. But when a further

break-in occurred while the suspect was under police surveillance, it became clear he was not responsible.

If Williams was worried about the October 31 police alert, it
didn't show, although he had by now begun monitoring the
Ottawa police website as it tracked and publicized the mounting
number of occurrences. On November 4 he raided another
house in Tweed, and then on the 12th he struck in Orleans again,
with another break-in following on the 20th. Then came three
more in December and three more in January 2009, all while the
area was under police scrutiny.

It was in January 2009 that Williams's career trajectory passed
another milestone, his spell at DAR complete.

Still a lieutenant-colonel, he was posted to the Canadian
Forces Language School at the Asticou Centre in Gatineau,
across the river from downtown Ottawa and fifteen miles from
his home in Orleans. There he spent the next six months
immersed in learning French, an essential step toward reaching
the next rank of full colonel. The CFLS is a big operation, cur-
rently providing more than two-thirds of all the language training for the Canadian Forces. Commanded by a lieutenant-colonel
who oversees about 200 civilian teachers and administrative staff
and a further 30 or so military members, the curriculum blends
classroom instruction with written exercises and tests, conversation and one-on-one tutoring.

It wasn't Williams's first stab at learning French; he had
acquired some basics years earlier while training for the Challenger
jet in St-Jean, Quebec. But this was far more intense, and he
emerged reasonably proficient. "Russ really enjoyed learning
French," recalls Jeff Farquhar, who himself is fluent in both
French and German. "In what I think was our last telephone

conversation, in the fall [of 2009], we conversed primarily in French as practice. He threw in the odd local slang, which he had picked up from someone either in class or from someone in town. He definitely had fun with it, but he was always self-critical about his English accent coming through. He paid careful attention to the grammatical side, as per class, but he knew that he needed more 'immersion' to truly speak and understand it well . . . There would be long pauses at times, broken finally by his laughing and saying, '*Pardon, qu'est-ce que tu as dit?*' [Sorry, what did you say?] Then he would say words to the effect: 'Man, I'll never get this down like you!' He would pick my brain, how I picked it up and what worked for me in helping to memorize grammar rules, et cetera. He took it all very seriously and with great ambition."

Though nobody at the time could have had the least inkling, Williams's diligent efforts to become fluent in French would later have a direct bearing on the sex slaying of Corporal Marie-France Comeau, his first murder victim.

His secret nighttime life, meanwhile, had taken a couple of alarming turns. Photos Williams took at the time of a November 2008 burglary in Ottawa and carefully stored and concealed on his computer show his perversity reaching new levels. The dwelling he broke into was the home of two children, including a fifteen-year-old girl. In all, he stole twenty-two pieces of clothing: panties, bras, a bathing suit and a nightshirt. And as usual, he took scores of photographs. A total of seventy pictures show him with a pair of panties bearing a menstrual bloodstain. In the pictures, Williams is seen wearing, licking, kissing and finally ejaculating on it. When a couple of the photos were shown in court at the sentencing hearing that followed his guilty plea, spectators shuddered, turning their heads away and gasping in shock.

He was also becoming more brazen, even reckless. During a December break-in he committed on his own street in Orleans,

Wilkie Drive, he left footprints in the snow leading up to the back patio door, which he damaged, along with several window locks.

Shortly thereafter, on the first and second days of January 2009—the same month Williams began taking French lessons— he twice hit a house on Cara Crescent, a few minutes' walk from Wilkie Drive. This too was the home of a fifteen-year-old girl, robbed of dozens of pieces of lingerie. But Williams also stole many of the girl's personal photographs, including headshots done for a modeling agency, together with a piece of paper con- taining lip-gloss lip-prints. Other items in her bedroom, such as paintings, had been altered and moved. When the Ottawa police examined the room, they also found dried semen in her under- wear drawer. When the physical evidence came to light, one of the many photos Williams had taken inside her bedroom showed him holding her makeup brush to his penis as he gazes steadily into the camera. He left the makeup brush behind.

The double break-ins left the girl so frightened that she began sleeping in the spare room with her dog. Williams, meanwhile, marked the occasion differently. On the computer records he kept of his intrusions, he labeled this one with the initials HNY: Happy New Year.

And as he grew bolder, he was also becoming more vigilant. A file folder containing scores of photos taken during a burglary in April, also in Orleans, contained a 148-page monthly crime report downloaded from the Ottawa police website, together with a screenshot of the police report on the break-in.

His pace began to pick up. On a weekend return visit to his Cosy Cove Lane cottage in Tweed the same month, he hit nearby homes on three consecutive nights: April 17, 18 and 19, a Friday, Saturday and Sunday. Over the next few weeks he broke in or tried to break in to homes in Tweed and Orleans five times, flee- ing with his customary trophies.

In mid-June, his behavior took a further strange twist, demonstrating new peculiarities. The event was a burglary on Cara Crescent in Orleans, a few doors down from where Williams had struck in January and home to a woman in her twenties and her father, both of whom were out of town at the time. On returning, the woman discovered that her underwear drawer, closet and laundry room had been looted, in what would be Williams's largest-ever single haul: 186 pieces of clothing. She also noticed that some of her ID had been laid out on a dresser in the spare room and her laptop opened. What particularly surprised her, she told the Ottawa police when they arrived, was that there in plain view was some valuable jewelry, untouched. Entry had been made through a basement window.

Williams's record-keeping was in this instance almost unbelievably thorough, even for him. As usual, he had taken scores of photographs, not only of himself but of the numerous pieces of lingerie he had stolen, spread out on the woman's bed and on the floor. The photos were subdivided into categories and labeled, showing where he had found them: bedroom; bedroom laundry; basement laundry; spare room. Once again, his obsessive need to organize his trophies was on display. When police later seized his computer hard drive and searched it, they also found a saved screenshot of the woman's Facebook page, together with five screenshots of the Ottawa police website recording the break-in.

And there was more. Police would later discover a bizarre letter on Williams's computer, addressed to the woman he had just robbed. Dotted with misspellings that were clearly deliberate, the letter read as follows:

Beautiful [followed by the woman's name]. I'm sorry I took these because I am sentamental to. Don't worry because I didn't mess with them. Also I am sure you know your beautiful but trust me your pussy smells fucking awesome! I should know because I been doing this for awhile. But I am going to stop because my moms will fucking kill me if I get caught. She is pretty sure I can be something. Besides your place was kinda like the motherload and I really like that I have a bunch of undies you put on just after you got fucked. I started this with a chick I knew from high school called . . . who lives down the road from you. I thought it would be cool to have some of her undies. It seems right that I finish with a special chick like you. If you decide to call the cops tell them I am sorry for the trouble and they won't here from me again. Now that I know all about you, I think it might be cool to meet you. Maybe younger guys don't turn you on but I think we could be good together. To me teenage chicks are impressed to easy. I guess I would like to be with somebody more experienced. You guys really need to clean out the bath in the basement. It is some gnarly. I hope what I did ain't pissed you off to much.

JT

Ps. Since I sorta feel guilty about wasting the cops time these are the places I hit so they can close there books.

Remarkably, Williams then itemized all the break-ins he had committed in Orleans, from the first one in May 2008 up to and including this one, thirteen months later. The list matches exactly the inventory of offenses to which he later pleaded guilty. (The dozens of fetish break-ins he had by then committed in Tweed went unmentioned.)

There is no evidence that he ever mailed the letter to the woman, or even intended to, and she was unaware of it until after his arrest. Nor, quite plainly, should it in any way be taken at face value. The overall tone, however, seems apparent: Williams is apologizing for stealing her underwear, even as he gloats about what he has been doing with it. The faulty grammar and spelling and self-reference to "younger guys" show him pretending to be someone even younger than she is (she was twenty-four), as does the reference to "my moms." Further, he is also suggesting that this will be the last of his break-ins and that "it seems right that I finish with a special chick like you." Tell the police I won't do it again, he says in the next sentence.

Conceivably, the letter is evidence that Williams was at this point struggling with himself in an effort to cease his break-ins before he was caught. And had he done so then, before he had physically harmed anyone, he might have stayed below the police radar forever. But he didn't or couldn't stop, and perhaps the letter is a sign that he realized that.

Williams waited three weeks before striking again, this time in Tweed. And when he did so, he displayed a terrifying new boldness.

The incident took place just up the road from his cottage on Cosy Cove Lane, at a residence that he was clearly fixated upon, because he broke in there a total of nine times. This was intrusion number six, on July 10, 2009.

Williams had been watching and waiting in the wooded backyard, and at around one-thirty in the morning the woman of the house stepped into the shower. No one else was at home. Williams stripped off his clothes, leaving them outside, broke into the house and walked naked down the hallway, past the bathroom where the woman was showering, and into her bedroom. He stole from her a black thong, took no photographs and quickly departed. But a note that he later wrote to himself, found by the police on his computer, showed what might have happened. It read as follows:

> . . . on naked walk from back forty—after having watched [the woman's name] for 30 minutes or so, and confident that she was home alone. I entered her house naked just after she got into the shower (approx 1:40)—very tempting to take her panties/bra from bathroom—decided it would be entirely obvious that some-one was in the house while she was in the shower—took panties from panty drawer instead.

Williams's willingness to take risks was clearly accelerating, and—coincidentally or not—his new audacity coincided with the successful conclusion of his French-language studies in Gatineau. In July 2009, the same month, he was promoted to full colonel, and together with his new rank came a new and immensely pres-tigious posting: he was to take command of 8 Wing/CFB Trenton, the busiest air base in Canada.

7

WING COMMANDER

Being handed the keys to 8 Wing/CFB Trenton marked the pinnacle of Williams's 23-year career in the military. Canada's chief hub for air operations of any size at home or abroad, 8 Wing has roughly 3,000 regulars and reserves on the base (one-quarter of the air-force-uniform total) and 600-plus civilians. When Williams arrived there in mid-July 2009, the war in Afghanistan remained the main event, and it was a bad month, with four repatriation ceremonies. Rich in symbolism, 8 Wing is where the bodies of slain Canadian Forces personnel arrive home before being driven down a stretch of Highway 401—dubbed the Highway of Heroes—to Toronto, where autopsies are held. Arctic operations are also based at 8 Wing, as are all major search-and-rescue missions in central Canada. As well, 8 Wing is a key jumping-off point in responding to foreign disasters, such as the earthquake that struck Haiti six months later, in January 2010, just two and a half weeks before Williams committed his second murder.

One of thirteen wings (bases) nationwide, from Gander, Newfoundland, to Comox, B.C., 8 Wing is also a big economic contributor to adjoining Trenton and Quinte West, and as in the village of Tweed, ties between the military and local citizens are strong. The base dates back to 1929, when close to a thousand acres of farmland near adjacent Trenton were bought up by the federal government. Royal Canadian Air Force Trenton, as it was then known, was officially opened in August 1931. In the summer of 2009, when Williams took charge, the base was in the throes of a big, five-year, $1-billion construction boom.

He was replacing Colonel Mike Hood, whom he had known for almost twenty years, and the changing of the guard took place on July 15 in front of 8 Wing headquarters, in a parking lot that occasionally doubles as a parade ground. The 230 or so participants included representatives from all sections of the base, an assortment of civilian dignitaries, Williams's wife, Mary Elizabeth Harriman, his brother, Harvey, his father, David, and his mother, Nonie Sovka (seated separately). Also invited were some neighbors from Wilkie Drive in Orleans.

"He was happy that day. He seemed very relaxed and confident, the usual Russ," recalls a retired air force officer who attended the handover. "Maybe it was like he finally felt he'd arrived, but without making a big deal about any of it, which he never did with anything. But obviously it was a real big deal for him. Mary Elizabeth was very proud too."

George White, Williams's friend and neighbor from Orleans, also remembers the day well. "I met his mother. Her voice sounded familiar, so I approached her, a tall, thin lady with grayish hair, and asked her if she was so-and-so and she said, 'No, I'm the mother.' She was sitting in the front row, but she seemed to stay out of the limelight, and I didn't see her at the reception afterward."

Williams was selective, however, about whom he asked along. Nobody in Tweed was invited, although he'd lived intermittently in the staunchly pro-military village for more than five years. Nor was his longtime friend from university Jeff Farquhar, a conspicuous omission. Farquhar and a girlfriend had stopped by Williams's cottage in Tweed just two or three days before he took up his new post. They were driving from Toronto to Ottawa and Williams had suggested they swing by en route to catch up, after a hiatus of several months. So they did, stopping off first at the Tim Hortons down the road (the one that Williams never visited) to pick up coffee and bagels. When the couple pulled up to the cottage, Williams was outside, fixing a roof panel in the interior of his BMW. As usual, he greeted his friend heartily with a bear hug, explaining that he couldn't chat for too long because he had a flight to Winnipeg to catch.

What he didn't tell Farquhar was that he was heading to air force command headquarters to finalize the arrangements for taking charge of 8 Wing a couple of days later. Farquhar only learned of his friend's glittering promotion afterward, and was mildly hurt to learn he had not been invited to the handover. He chiefly perceives the omission as further evidence of Williams's extreme self-effacement and lifelong reluctance to talk about his own achievements. Conceivably, his modesty about success also cloaked deep shame regarding his double life. Whatever the reason, Farquhar only learned Williams was a colonel in charge of his own air base when he read about it online.

The swearing-in ceremony went ahead under sunny skies with band music and all the requisite pomp and ceremony. Chairs were set out for the guests, each of whom was escorted to an assigned seat. The outgoing Colonel Hood addressed the crowd and introduced Williams, and as cameras snapped, the two commanders signed what are termed the handover scrolls, and Williams was given the pennant that went with his new job. He inspected the troops and there was a march past the reviewing stand, to the accompaniment of the 8 Wing Pipes and Drums Band. Colonel Hood presented Harriman with a bouquet of flowers, and Williams did the same for Hood's wife.

"These are exciting times for the air force," Williams told the crowd after formally taking the reins. "I am confident that the team here is up to the task, and I look forward to getting right into that work. We're going to have a number of exciting milestones to witness as we go along."

Presiding over the ceremony was Major-General Yvan Blondin, commander of 1 Canadian Air Division in Winnipeg and Williams's immediate superior. Observing that Williams was "a leader not of machines but of people," Blondin urged the new wing commander not only to lead but to mentor, and to be a role model. And in remarks that today bear a terrible irony, Blondin also told Williams he should be asking himself this question: "What more can you do than what you are doing now to take care of our people? . . . It's a real command so enjoy it, and take care of your family."

Williams responded: "It shall be an honor to represent you, the men and women of 8 Wing for the next few years, and I guarantee we shall give you our very best in terms of both leadership and support. You will have our complete and undivided attention." At the time he was uttering these ostensibly sincere words, Williams had already committed sixty-two of his fetish burglaries. The next would come just six days later, and of course, far worse was soon to follow.

The formalities over, a reception took place in the officers' mess, open to all ranks, and in the early evening Williams held a small party at his lakeside cottage on Cosy Cove Lane. In a subsequent interview with *Contact*, 8 Wing's weekly in-house newspaper, he spoke modestly and gratefully about being awarded the prestigious job. "Certainly, I was keen to get the opportunity, but you never know. There are a number of qualified people who could do the job and that's why I say that I feel very fortunate to have been appointed." He was also pleased to note the continuum between his previous job at the Directorate of Air

Requirements, overseeing the acquisition of the four big C-17 Globemasters and the fleet of Hercules planes, and his new one at 8 Wing, where the aircraft would be based. "I've had the opportunity to keep a close eye on the development necessary to support these fleets and the collateral advantage the rest of the base has enjoyed, and will enjoy, in the coming years."

Many of the uniformed and civilian members of 8 Wing already knew Williams from his earlier spell at the head of the 437 Squadron, and among them was transport pilot Captain (now Major) Garrett Lawless. Williams was clearly glad to see him again, and asked what kind of watch he was wearing these days—a reference to their shared enthusiasm for Swiss timepieces.

At the same time, however, friendships between soldiers of different ranks only go so far, underlining the highly compartmentalized, often isolated life of the man at the top. "I was a familiar face, a bit of history, but I don't think I was any better friends with him than anybody else," Lawless says. "He was two ranks ahead of me, and then three, so I would never have expected to have close, in-depth personal interactions, especially at a base like this, where it's not impossible but very difficult to develop friends. When you're on the road together you hang out and talk, but when we come back we never make plans to get together because our schedules, working within the transport community, are all so erratic. You might not cross paths with someone again for three weeks or three months.

"And it gets progressively lonelier as you climb the ranks. The higher you go, the more you hang out with your rank level plus or minus one. For him, the closest other full colonel was a hundred miles away, in Kingston, with a completely different background. And when he does go down to the mess, he's the wing commander, so the people he's talking to will talk to him as the wing commander. There's not going to be any small talk."

Williams settled into his new life, commuting from his cottage in peaceful Tweed, where he was largely unknown, to 8 Wing, where the pace was almost invariably hectic, a nonstop assembly line of formal duties and informal functions. His first full day on the job, July 16, brought bad tidings from Afghanistan. In a rare firefight with Taliban insurgents in the Panjwayi district south of Kandahar, 26-year-old Private Sébastien Courcy of St-Hyacinthe, Quebec, had been killed when he stepped on a hidden roadside bomb and was thrown off a cliff edge, the 125th Canadian soldier to die in the Afghan conflict.

July 19 saw Williams attend the Ottawa funeral of a young air force squadron corporal. Four days later he was at a Trenton charity event, smiling cheerfully and donating televisions to needy children. Shortly after that, he presented a commendation to a military policeman for his role in helping secure the scene of a crime scene investigation. (A 36-year-old civilian living on the base had been stabbed to death; a second man was charged with second-degree murder.)

Meanwhile, he had resumed his parallel secret life with a quick succession of break-ins. On July 21, he burgled a house on Cosy Cove Lane; on the 24th, he broke into a home on nearby Sulphide Road; and on the 25th and 26th, the last weekend of the month, he committed two back-to-back burglaries at the same address on Mathieu Drive in Orleans. Williams later told detectives that he returned for a third time on the 27th, but he noticed the residents had returned home and walked away. In all, he stole fifty-two items from the house during the course of his two break-ins and took dozens of photographs, all similar to the earlier ones.

It's far from unusual for serial killers and predators to keep careful track of their crimes. Williams, however, took the process to a whole new level. His photo-taking was nothing short of obsessive, and as with most things technical in his life, only the best equipment would do. His preference was a Sony digital single lens reflex camera, a type he had used for many years, which employs a sophisticated mechanical mirror system to direct light from the camera's lens to an optical viewfinder on the back of the camera. He had many different lenses for it, and his knowledge of memory cards and memory sticks was extensive too. It was the same with the home computer into which he would download his stolen images. He had long been an Apple enthusiast, and at the time of his arrest he owned a model of Macintosh computer more common in commercial applications than in home use.

August was another busy month for Williams at 8 Wing, a steady flow of functions, ceremonies and charity events. Midway through, the base welcomed a new commander at its Canadian Forces Land Advanced War Centre, which teaches combat skills in assorted different environments, from the jungle to the desert to the Arctic. Williams also provided 8 Wing with an update on construction of its new Canadian Forces Aerospace Warfare Centre, begun a year earlier. The $20-million project was on track to be completed in the summer of 2010, he confidently told the base in a mass mailer.

In his off-hours, he was working just as hard. He committed five nighttime break-ins that month, all on Cosy Cove Lane in Tweed or on adjacent Charles Court. He broke into one home three nights in a row, the same place that he targeted a total of nine times, stealing underwear in eight of the nine raids. There, once again, he posed for his camera in front of a bathroom mirror, wearing the woman's bra and panties as he masturbated.

In September, his calendar was again full. On the 3rd, he toured 8 Wing's new six-story, state-of-the-art air traffic control tower, six years in the works and now nearing completion. On the 8th, he helped launch Operation Santa Claus, dispatching tractor-trailer loads of donated gifts to Canadian troops in far-flung locations. "Having received one of those boxes, and speaking with others who have, I can say that it means a great deal, it really makes Christmas a lot easier," Williams told an enthusiastic crowd gathered outside a Sobeys supermarket in Brighton. "It's a connection to home, that link to the local community. It's hugely important."

But he was not always to be seen. On September 12, for example, he skipped 8 Wing's annual Scottish-Irish Festival, a big event, dispatching Chief Warrant Officer Kevin West in his place. "I've been MC-ing the Scottish-Irish Festival since its inception, sixteen or eighteen years, and I can't ever recall a wing commander missing that function," says Loyalist College media studies professor Steve Bolton, a lifelong supporter of the military who helps run 8 Wing's remarkable National Air Force Museum and helps out with many other activities. Bolton brushed shoulders with Williams several times, generally finding him stiff and awkward. "He struck me as a get-it-done kind of character. He certainly didn't seem to be breaking any mold. I didn't know him as well as I knew some of the other wing commanders, but there seemed nothing out of the ordinary. He just seemed like another good colonel who'd come in to run this big base, and it's got huge challenges."

Toward the end of September, Williams once more raised eyebrows by being a no-show, this time at the annual dedication of memorial stones at the museum, an event attended by about two thousand people. At the last minute he once again sent someone to speak on his behalf. Over the next few months, there would be several other nonappearances.

Meanwhile, he was quickly getting to know not only the principal players at 8 Wing but also many of the civilians who had dealings with the base, in particular another man named Williams—Quinte West mayor John Williams, first elected in

2006. The 8 Wing base has for decades been integral to Trenton, now part of the City of Quinte West. Its five thousand or so military members and dependents are spread across the city and adjoining Belleville, and issues of mutual interest constantly arise, from fundraisers and celebrations to jobs programs and traffic. The bond is strong, seen everywhere on billboards and ubiquitous "Support Our Troops" bumper stickers, and in recent years the emotive repatriation ceremonies for soldiers slain in Afghanistan have made it stronger still. When a flag-draped casket begins its journey from 8 Wing to Toronto, hundreds of Trentonians routinely gather outside the fence and line the road to watch and pay their respects.

"There's always been a good relationship between 8 Wing and us. It's a big part of the community, and whenever there's a change of command it always includes the mayor's office," John Williams said later. "So I would talk to [Russ Williams] maybe a number of times a week, at an event or over the phone. There were a lot of events that both of us would be at—Christmas at the base, museum events. He was fairly quiet and difficult to get close to, not one to kibitz. It was difficult to carry on a conversation. He was not a warm person, just, 'Here's my job.' I've found other wing commanders to be very outgoing, but he was not. He was very correct and military, very well respected by those who worked with him, and obviously they thought he was going to the top. You don't get to be a colonel and be in charge of a major base without that kind of reputation."

Midway through September, in an episode whose timing would later leave Mayor Williams stunned, the new wing commander issued an invitation. He was heading to the Arctic for a couple of days to have a look at operations up there. Would Mayor Williams like to come along for the ride? The mayor said he would, and packed a small bag.

In one of the soon-to-be-replaced Hercules CC-130s, which usually hauled freight, they flew to Canadian Forces Station Alert, on the tip of Ellesmere Island in the territory of Nunavut—the most northerly permanently inhabited place in the world. Administered by 8 Wing, the small, remote base is what is termed a signals intelligence intercept facility, a combination weather station/science station/listening post, home to a rotating group of about sixty military personnel and civilians attached to the defense and environment departments, chiefly scientists.

The trip required a twelve-hour flight each way, and Mayor Williams recalls it well. The group left on September 14 and returned two days later. Colonel Williams was not at the controls of the aircraft and seemed preoccupied, sitting at the back of the plane by himself, where it was chilly because a heater had malfunctioned. There's not a lot to see at CFS Alert, which dates back to the 1960s and the Cold War era: an airstrip, a handful of equipment-filled buildings and a beautiful, dramatically empty Arctic landscape. But the mayor nonetheless found the experience interesting, and on returning to Trenton at around seven in the evening on the 16th, he thanked his host and went home.

So too did Colonel Williams. He headed up Highway 37 toward his cottage in Tweed. He had a big night ahead.

The young Russ Sovka, as Williams was known then, as a student at Birchmount Park Collegiate in Scarborough.

[above] Yearbook photo from Upper Canada College in 1982. Sovka, as he was still known, was a talented trumpet player in his teenage years.

[left] During his first year at the University of Toronto's Scarborough campus, Williams grew a beard and reverted to the use of his birth name. His interest in the trumpet was soon to disappear, and he rarely mentioned it in later life.

The 8 Wing/CFB Trenton headquarters, where Williams's office was on the top floor. He was base commander from July 2009 until his arrest in February 2010.

The National Air Force Museum of Canada at 8 Wing, home to the largest number of stationary military aircraft in the country. Thousands of memorial stones bearing the names of honored air force members line the walkway, including that of Corporal Marie-France Comeau.

Williams on the day of his swearing-in as the new base commander of 8 Wing/CFB Trenton, in July 2009, attended by both his father and his mother, who sat separately. The photo was taken by an Ottawa neighbor—but no one from Tweed was invited.

Victoria Street, the main street that cuts through the center of the village of Tweed.

The cottage at 62 Cosy Cove Lane, which Williams and his wife Mary Elizabeth Harriman purchased in 2004.

The house on Wilkie Drive in the Ottawa suburb of Orleans, where Williams and Harriman lived for fourteen years, the longest he lived anywhere in his life.

Corporal Marie-France Comeau. "She had found her calling," her former boyfriend said of the slain flight attendant.

Comeau's house on Raglan Road in Brighton, west of the 8 Wing base. Williams broke in twice, each time through a basement window on the east side of the house, on the right.

Jessica Lloyd. "Many people have said it took our angel to bring Russell Williams down," Lloyd's aunt said at the killer's emotional sentencing hearing.

Lloyd's house on Highway 37, which connects Belleville to Tweed. Williams drove past it twice a day as he commuted between his cottage in Tweed and the 8 Wing base.

Looking out onto Stoco Lake from Williams's house on Cosy Cove Lane, where Jessica Lloyd was held captive for about sixteen hours before she was murdered.

Williams being interviewed by Detective Sergeant Jim Smyth at Ottawa police head-quarters on February 7, 2010.

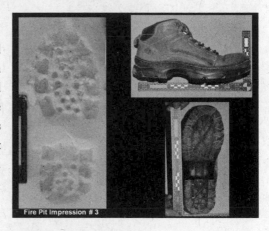

The boot print found at the back of Jessica Lloyd's house, and photos of one of the boots Williams was wearing when he went in for the interview.

Fire Pit Impression # 3

The patch of woods, off Cary Road in Tweed, where Jessica's body was left by Williams amid a cluster of rocks.

A small sample of Russell Williams's meticulously organized collection of stolen lingerie.

Countless photos were found of Williams modeling the underwear of women and girls. These were taken in November 2007, two months after the first break-ins to which he later pleaded guilty.

Andy Lloyd, older brother of Jessica, speaking to reporters outside the court-house during a break in the sentencing hearing of Russell Williams.

Russell Williams leaving court on October 21, 2010, after being sentenced to life imprisonment. He was dispatched directly to Kingston Penitentiary.

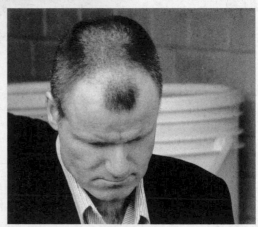

Mary Elizabeth Harriman, Williams's wife, February 2010.

8

UP THE LADDER

I t was shortly after midnight on September 17 when Williams stepped out of his cottage on Cosy Cove Lane and walked through the surrounding woods toward his target, once again a thief in the night. Well inside his comfort zone, he was probably feeling confident, and perhaps just a little nervous. Two years had passed since his first break-in in Tweed, just around the corner from where he was heading now, and aside from the one close call in November 2007, he appears to have entirely eluded scrutiny. Since then, he had carried out more than thirty lingerie thefts in Tweed, and not one had been reported to police. Now he was about to dramatically raise the ante.

In his confession, and in the two highly detailed pages that he wrote and concealed on his home computer, Williams said he decided to attack Jane Doe—the name that he himself gave to his twenty-year-old victim in his records—after glimpsing her one day when out in his boat on Stoco Lake and thinking she was "cute." That could be true. While accurate in its broad brushstrokes, the confession was also replete with self-serving untruths and evasions, all of them evidently designed to "minimize the impact on my wife," as he put it. And particularly suspect is the apparently casual manner in which he claims he selected his victims, most notably Corporal Marie-France

Comeau. "I didn't know any of them," he told Detective Sergeant Jim Smyth, suggesting he had acted on the spur of the moment rather than having stalked the women.

In fact, great planning and preparation preceded Williams's attacks, and the one he was about to commit was very likely no exception. But he may have been speaking truthfully when he said he first spotted Jane Doe from his boat, because she was at home with a newborn daughter, her house was not on any route that he normally traveled, and she had only lived there for about a month. Certainly she had never previously met the colonel, she told police after his arrest.

Alone with her infant child in the lakeside cottage, Jane Doe was sleeping in her bedroom when Williams broke in through a side window by cutting a screen. He was wearing a sweatshirt and dark pants, his face partly concealed with a small dark hat. When the attack began, she thought she was having a bad dream.

She awoke to the realization that someone very strong was holding down her head as she lay in bed, clad in a tank top and pajama pants. A struggle ensued, in which Jane Doe broke a chain around Williams's neck, but he subdued her by pressing the weight of his body down on hers. Over the next thirty minutes or so, her head still firmly in Williams's grasp, a conversation of sorts took place. Jane Doe asked him if he was going to kill her and he said no. He told her it was around one o'clock in the morning and inquired where her spouse was. She refused to say.

He then maneuvered her onto her stomach, sat on her, and after a brief struggle struck her hard on the head three times with his hand, warning her to be quiet and to make no attempt to see his face. A curious exchange followed, a further illustration of Williams's contradictory impulses: Jane Doe told him he did not seem to be the type of person who would do something like this, upon which, she said later, he seemed to get "nicer."

With some difficulty, Williams tied her up. He first tried to use a pillowcase, then a couple of blankets, before finally succeeding in binding her hands with the pillowcase. Another pillowcase was placed over her head and repositioned to turn it into a blindfold, and she heard him take what proved to be his camera out of the bag he'd brought with him. In a desperate bid to make him go away, she told him that giving birth had left her fat and unattractive. Not at all, he said, she was "perfect," and once again he assured her he was not going to hurt her. Nor would her baby be harmed.

In all, Williams was inside Jane Doe's house for about two hours. The photo session began with him pulling down her tank top, fondling her breasts, removing her pajama pants and forcing her to pose with her legs apart, hands still tied behind her back, eyes still blindfolded. She became extremely distressed; Williams reassured her that there was no need to fret because he was soon going to leave. She heard him leave the room, then return and open the drawers of her bedroom dresser. She later discovered he had stolen bras and other undergarments.

After pawing her breasts one last time (and asking her the age of her infant daughter), he told her he was leaving and ordered her to count out loud to three hundred. She stopped at seventy, but he was still there and instructed her to resume counting. At the two-hundred mark she paused once more, yelled out loud and removed the blindfold. He was gone.

Using a flash, Williams had taken just nine photographs. The two pillowcases he used to restrain Jane Doe he left in her daughter's bedroom. Before fleeing into the night, he stripped a sheet and a baby blanket off her bed and took them, along with a shirt she owned, most likely because they were items he had touched; he didn't want to leave any of his DNA behind. (Williams kept the five underwear items he had stolen, but later told police he'd disposed of the sheet, blanket and shirt at the Tweed public dump.)

In acute distress, Jane Doe called her mother-in-law, then 911, and police and friends soon arrived. As it got light, forensic experts and a police canine unit scoured the area in and around her home but found nothing useful. No one in the area reported having seen or heard anything. No cars or boats had been spotted leaving the vicinity.

The OPP officers trying to make sense of these events were perplexed. Nothing remotely similar had ever happened in Tweed before, and they had no physical evidence at all to go on, save for the two pillowcases. All they had was the account of the extremely distraught Jane Doe, who, never having seen her assailant, could offer only the vaguest description of him. She guessed he was between thirty and fifty, with a demeanor she described as fatherly—seemingly thoughtful and concerned, even as he was tormenting her, something that the detectives found particularly puzzling. She said it sounded as if he had tried to make his voice sound deeper than it was—a ruse Williams repeated when he attacked Jane Doe's neighbor, Laurie Massicotte, two weeks later. Jane Doe also said she thought he was wearing hiking boots and a tight sweater, which she ripped during the short struggle at the beginning. He was clean-shaven and wore a ring on one of his hands. He smelled dirty.

As a crime and a crime scene, it was as baffling as anything the police had seen. And once again, they sought guidance from Detective Sergeant Van Allen, the OPP criminal profiler who, among his other tasks, was also assisting Ottawa police in the Orleans lingerie break-ins. He opened a fresh file. No one, least of all Van Allen, had the remotest idea the two sets of circumstances were connected: different types of crimes in jurisdictions more than 120 miles apart. And none of the earlier lingerie thefts in Tweed had been reported.

Van Allen examined the OPP's two-and-a-half-page report on the Jane Doe assault and was unsure whether he was dealing with fact or fiction. Over the years he has encountered many false accusations of sexual assault, and his tentative conclusion was that this might be another one. There was no physical evidence of an intruder, no description of him, and Jane Doe had declined to seek any medical attention because she had not been raped or sexually penetrated. What also puzzled Van Allen was Jane Doe's account of the almost conciliatory way in which the intruder had spoken and behaved. "She said—and this was a direct quote—the guy had told her to roll over on her tummy. I couldn't ever remember a sex offender using that phrase, 'Roll over on your tummy.' So I thought her disclosure was problematic, and it wasn't until the second one happened [the Laurie Massicotte assault] that we knew for sure that what she had said was probably true."

In the detailed, diary-style account of the attack that Williams wrote shortly afterward, he gave a slightly different version of events than would later appear in the agreed statement of facts. Rather than first seizing her by the throat, he said that he stood over the sleeping Jane Doe for several minutes and then finally struck her hard on the side of the head, "trying to knock her out." Instead she awoke, and the struggle began.

In flat, casual prose Williams described the encounter as though it had been the most ordinary of everyday events. He wrote that after snapping her picture a number of times, "she stood up to let me pull her pants back on—very civilized." Yet he was also acutely aware of the risks he was taking. After the assault he walked back through the woods to his cottage; his account noted that "a white police car went down the lane within 8 minutes of my return."

What the police were completely unaware of until after Williams confessed was that his assault on Jane Doe didn't mark the end of his activities in her house. Incredibly, just twenty-four hours later, on the night of September 18, he returned to the scene. Only Jane Doe wasn't there; she and her baby had gone to stay with friends. Williams broke in again, this time through an open window. He stole another fifteen pieces of lingerie, took more photographs and left.

He came back again the following night, September 19, but he noticed that the father of Jane Doe's child had returned home and decided not to venture inside. Earlier that same evening, before heading down the road to Jane Doe's house, he had had dinner at his Cosy Cove Lane cottage with his wife, Mary Elizabeth Harriman, and a friend, Jeffrey Manney, who was staying over. Before retiring for the night, Harriman remarked to Manney that her husband often liked to go for late night walks before he went to bed.

And then Williams showed up a fourth time at Jane Doe's house, on September 22, when the house was once again empty. He stole more undergarments and took more photos, including a couple of himself standing naked, wearing only one of Jane Doe's thongs.

In between these raids, the almost unbelievably brazen Williams resumed his normal life. A few hours after the September 17 attack, he met in Belleville with members of Criminal Intelligence Service Ontario to discuss an upcoming charity event for wounded soldiers. Later the same morning, at CFB Trenton, he watched a strongman (Lutheran pastor Kevin Fast from

Cobourg) break a Guinness world record by pulling one of the newly acquired, 200-ton C-17 Globemasters across the tarmac. Then he visited the 8 Wing engineering shop.

September 18 saw him exhort members of the air base to take a role in the Wing Commander's Challenge, an annual medley of games and races in support of the United Way. "I very strongly encourage members of 8 Wing/CFB Trenton, military and civilian, to achieve a healthy lifestyle, including regular exercise," he said in an address. "General [Rick] Hillier used to say that if he could find time to exercise he was pretty sure that the rest of us could as well . . . That's my challenge to you." Later the same day he attended a Belleville Bulls OHL junior hockey tournament press conference where they dedicated their 2009–10 season to the "heroes" of 8 Wing. His friend Jeffrey Manney attended the game too, then accompanied Williams back to his cottage for dinner and a stay-over.

On September 19, Williams attended a special hockey ceremony where he and his right-hand man, Chief Warrant Officer Kevin West, dropped the pucks for a game between the Bulls and the Peterborough Petes. On the 20th he was on hand at 8 Wing to greet the returning coffin of Private Jonathan Couturier, Afghan casualty number 131. He also attended a Battle of Britain commemoration that day. And still on the 20th, he found time to compose on his home computer an extremely detailed account of his assault on Jane Doe three days earlier.

On September 22, Defence Minister Peter MacKay—someone Williams appears to have liked and respected, judging by complimentary remarks he made to his friend Jeff Farquhar—stopped by 8 Wing to announce another $334 million in funds for the ongoing base expansion. On the 23rd, Williams hit the first ball at the annual wing commander's charity golf tournament, where almost $10,000 was raised.

Two days after that, midway between the September 17 attack on Jane Doe and the subsequent one on Laurie Massicotte on September 30, a most peculiar episode took place at the Forces' flying school in Portage la Prairie, near Winnipeg. The event was the graduation dinner for the newest batch of proud pilots to be getting their wings. Williams had been asked to fly in and attend as reviewing officer and guest of honor, and after the dinner he rose and started to make his congratulatory address to the half-dozen new pilots and the crowd of eighty or so guests.

Someone who was there that evening tells what happened next. "He's there making his speech, and he has everyone's total focus and attention. It was kind of somber comments he was making, talking about very serious things. He was standing there in his mess kit, everyone else sitting there at their tables. And then he suddenly just stopped. People at these things sometimes like to have a pregnant pause—it focuses everybody—and I thought it was just one of those, and we're all just sitting there.

"But the pause went on. He just stood there looking at everybody with this grin on his face. Not a word was said, everybody was just stone quiet, any conversation that was going on while he was talking just totally stopped. People started looking around and looking at him. I remember looking at the people I was with and going, 'That's really odd, that's a long pause.' It was very out of character for him."

The pause lasted for up to a full minute, the witness says. "And he's just standing there looking at everybody. It wasn't like he'd zoned out, he didn't have a lost look on his face—he just stopped. I thought he'd just lost his train of thought and was trying to regroup and refocus. But he didn't, he just stopped. Finally, after the minute or whatever was up, he says something along the lines of, 'Well, that was different,' and everybody just chuckled, and he went on with his little speech and everything was fine. And at the time I just put it down to the pressures of being a wing commander, with so much on his mind. Afterwards I said to him, 'That was a pretty good speech, but not quite sure about that pause.' And he says, 'Yeah, that was a little different.'"

And perhaps it happened with good reason, because by now Williams must have been firing on all cylinders. He made his awkward speech on September 25, a Friday, flying into Portage la Prairie and returning almost immediately to Trenton. One day before that, on September 24, he had broken into the home of Laurie Massicotte, three doors down from his cottage in Tweed, when she wasn't home. He stole just one pair of panties, and the next day—the same day he gave his speech to the graduating pilots—he photographed himself wearing them. Then, on the 26th, after returning from Manitoba, he broke into Massicotte's empty house once again. This time he stole four pieces of lingerie.

The two burglaries were a prelude to Williams's second sexual assault, in which the victim would be Massicotte herself. As to why he targeted Massicotte, after his arrest he would once again offer vague explanations to the effect that he didn't know her name and had only spoken to her once or so but he knew she lived alone. Such statements were almost certainly disingenuous and self-serving, intended to make the assault appear spontaneous rather than premeditated. Certainly that's what Massicotte believes. "Thinking back now, I think he had been in my home many, many times, he'd been stalking me many times," she says.

As with Jane Doe, the most peculiar component of Massicotte's terrifying experience was the attacker's blend of vicious domination and purported concern for her well-being—getting her a couple of aspirin, repeatedly reassuring her that if she cooperated he would be out of her home and on his way. Williams also made clear to her the paramount importance of him getting his photographs. When he stripped her clothes off by slicing them with a sharp blade, she panicked, thinking she was about to be raped. He responded: "No, there'll be no need to rape you if I get these pictures."

In the attack on Jane Doe, Williams took just nine photos, but in this instance he took twenty-nine, and they provide an indication of how his sexual aggression was accelerating. Most are pictures of his captive, in her blindfold and restraints, being forced to present herself in assorted pornographic poses. But in the final three, Williams is seen too, displaying his erect penis and—the final picture—standing fully clothed in front of a mirror, wearing a black tuque, his face wrapped in one of Massicotte's undergarments so only his eyes are visible.

A week or so later, he augmented that photo file by taking additional pictures in his home of his most recently acquired lingerie trophies. And shortly thereafter, he added still more—photos of the October 7 edition of the weekly *Tweed News*, whose front page gave a prominent account of the two attacks on September 17 and 30. Williams had placed the newspaper in the fireplace of his Tweed cottage, set it alight and photographed it seven times while it burned. Also found in the same group of photos were more than a dozen screenshots of news and police websites reporting on the two sexual assaults.

Clearly, Williams had by now crossed a major threshold, and conceivably it made him cautious for a while, because he did not carry out another break-in for more than three weeks. Meanwhile, he lost no time in resuming his regular life. A few hours after the September 30 assault on Massicotte, he was back at 8 Wing for a ribbon-cutting ceremony. The same day he also presented a $700 check to the Heart and Stroke Foundation of Canada—the Ottawa-based charity of which his wife was an executive director.

Williams's schedule at 8 Wing during October reveals nothing remarkable: a workout and photo op for Fire Prevention Week, the colonel clad in a bright yellow firefighter's protective suit; a speech at the Air Force Association of Canada's annual meeting, held that year at the Trenton base; an appearance as a "celebrity chef" at a United Way fundraiser.

His life of crime, too, was relatively low-key that month. The only break-in he committed, on October 24, targeted an all-male household of a father and two sons, who lived in Tweed down the road from Cosy Cove Lane. Williams walked in through an open door, realized there were no women living there, and departed without stealing anything, though he did take four photos.

Then he became bolder. On November 5, he hit a home on Minnie Avenue in Tweed, closer to the downtown core than his usual zone of operations, stealing nine pieces of women's underwear and snapping nine photos. He had raided the same home almost exactly a year earlier, and he marked the anniversary in a post-burglary note he wrote to himself, illustrating not only his customary obsession with detail but a new temerity:

Unlike last year's entry, after which I'll guess they had no idea that I'd been in the house, I made no effort to conceal this entry. In fact, I left plenty of signs that I was there (screen from back door was removed, with window left wide open, and the screen from the lower bathroom, where I actually gained access (like last year) was left removed—again with the window open. As well, I closed the door but didn't lock it.) On the way home the next night (Friday) at 8.00-ish I noticed that they had returned home, and that the outside light above the back room door was on (I'd never seen this light on . . .) Note: The time on these shots is one hour later than actual. "Fall back" was the past weekend and

I hadn't yet reset the camera. Pics in Untitled Folder 2 have the
correct time . . .

Two days later, on November 7, and farther still from his
usual geographic comfort zone, Williams was in the home of a
mother and her teenaged daughter on Tweed's River Street,
where he stole twenty-two items of clothing, including a skirt
and a slip. Mother and daughter were out of town for the weekend, visiting the daughter's older sister in Ottawa, and like
almost everyone else in the village who was robbed, they knew
nothing about it until after Williams was arrested.

When they did find out, they were deeply perturbed, and wondered why he had targeted their house. "I have to walk to my bus
stop to go to school, so we figured he maybe saw me walking or
something, because there's a story he was seen at the nursing
home across the street," says the teenager, Ruth, who requested
that her full name not be printed. "I cried, I was so shocked. To
think of some man coming into your room, and knowing he was
probably in my room and touched my stuff—I don't know what
he touched. After we found out, I searched through my room,
wondering what he could have taken, because we don't know if he
took my underwear or my mom's. When I found out it had happened, every time I walked in my house, or up my driveway, it was
like, 'He took these steps, he went into my house.'"

Discovering that Russell Williams was responsible was a
three-stage process for Ruth and her mother. Shortly after he
was charged with murder and began chronicling for police his
scores of lingerie raids, the family were visited by detectives, who
assured them they were not in danger but were vague as to
what was going on. "They sat down with our mother and asked
who all lived here and how long we'd lived here, if we'd noticed
anything was missing. They asked that question multiple times

and we didn't really know what it was about," recalls Ruth's older sister, Ann. Their mother asked neighbors if they too had been questioned, and learned they had not. "So we knew it was something specific to do with us."

The evening before the break-in charges were announced in April, Ruth and her mother were advised over the phone that an arrest had been made in connection with their case. But not until the next day was Williams named as the perpetrator.

When the family did finally connect the dots, there was a further dimension to their dismay. Tweed is a small place, and Ruth and her mother knew both Jane Doe and Laurie Massicotte, the two women Williams had attacked back in September, and were keenly aware of what they had been through. "When all this was happening, we were sleeping with stuff beside our beds, like a hammer," Ruth recounts. Now they were being told by police that the same intruder who had committed the bizarre twin assaults had been in their home as well. "Looking back at it, we were thinking, 'What if we would have been home,' if that would have made any difference, if we could have been killed," Ruth says.

And they were not wrong to be so fearful, because the predator's appetite was growing.

Nine days elapsed before Williams struck again, and when he did so, he strayed again from his usual territory. On the evening of Monday, November 16, he drove his Pathfinder toward the small town of Brighton, just west of Trenton. He was heading for the home of a 37-year-old flight attendant under his command at 8 Wing, a soldier he knew by sight and by name and probably much better than that: Corporal Marie-France Comeau.

9

A SOLDIER STALKED

The well-kept brick house on Brighton's Raglan Street that belonged to Corporal Comeau was empty that evening when Williams arrived there. She was away on a mission accompanying Prime Minister Stephen Harper to Singapore, Japan and India. As base commander with ready access to her schedule, Williams would have known that. He nonetheless took precautions, parking his vehicle in a wooded area about 650 yards from her house. He broke in by removing the screen of a small basement window at the side of the house and squeezing through. Once inside, he looked around, then headed for the bedroom and the lingerie drawer. He played with and put on some of Comeau's garments, stealing seven pieces when he departed. And, as usual, he took dozens of photos, including images of his erect penis as he modeled the undergarments and shots of Comeau's military uniform, with her name on it. After about ninety minutes of this, he left by one of the doors, carefully replacing the screen on the basement window, and headed toward his cottage in Tweed.

Later, Williams would tell police that he barely knew Comeau, that he had met her just once before, on a flight. All the evidence, however, suggests that is untrue and that they had had several previous encounters. Garrett Lawless describes one at 8 Wing

Trenton: "We had a squadron mess dinner just after I got back from Afghanistan, about four months prior [to her murder]. She was sitting right across from me, and he was sitting about five seats up, at the head table. We later conjectured that would have been the first time that he saw her, because he would have seen her, he would have been aware of her, she definitely would have stood out." Others say the same. Corporal Comeau is remembered not only as generous, with a sunny, outgoing disposition, but also as attractive and very fit.

And she had also helped Williams with his French. In September 2009, a few weeks before Williams killed her, he had a telephone conversation with his old university friend Jeff Farquhar, in which he specifically mentioned Comeau's name and said she was giving him some pointers in learning French. Farquhar recalls the exchange because he asked Williams if "Comeau" was spelled the same way as Baie-Comeau, former prime minister Brian Mulroney's Quebec parliamentary constituency.

Nothing suggests there was any romantic relationship between the two, which for a colonel and a corporal serving on the same base would have been conspicuous and highly unacceptable. But it appears certain that Williams and Comeau knew each other better than he ever admitted and that—as with numerous aspects of his confession—he was striving to make his actions appear spontaneous and unpremeditated, and hence perhaps marginally less heinous than they were.

His lingerie trophies in his burglar's bag, Williams sped away from Comeau's house. But he was not yet done for the night. During his almost two and a half years of known break-ins, encompassing more than eighty different burglaries, there were only four occasions on which Williams raided two different homes on the same night. This was one of them, and he returned to the second home the next night as well, in a pair of back-to-back intrusions that illustrate how swiftly his aggression and risk-taking were picking up pace.

After leaving Comeau's house in the early hours of November 17, he drove east along Highway 401 then headed north on Highway 37, which links Belleville and Tweed. On the rural outskirts of Belleville, close to the city limits, he pulled into the driveway of a darkened 150-year-old farmhouse with outbuildings, on the west side of the highway. The house belongs to transplanted Quebecer Anne Marsan-Cook, an artist and musician in her late forties who moved to Belleville in 1999 with a degree in mining technology but chiefly makes her living through teaching music. A lively, engaging figure with a ready laugh, she has two adult sons who have left home and is married to a mining engineer and consultant who is often out of town on business, as he was that night.

Williams told police after his arrest that he selected Marsan-Cook's home after noticing that a relatively young woman lived there. And that may be true, because the house sits right by Highway 37, the front door and driveway visible from the road. But once again, he was very likely downplaying the planning and preparation he put into his break-ins and attacks, because among other assignments, Marsan-Cook taught piano and organ at two different schools at the 8 Wing base in Trenton. She says she was never aware of Williams until his arrest, but he may have spotted her on the base, and as its commander it would not have been difficult for him to figure out who she was and where she lived.

Sometime after three a.m., he climbed through an unlocked window into her sprawling, deserted farmhouse and followed his usual routine. He grabbed more than forty pieces of Marsan-Cook's underwear, along with three sex toys and a sex movie, and he took an assortment of photos, including six shots of himself wearing some of the lingerie and masturbating.

Then—at some point—he departed. A key question would later be when that was.

November 17 was a Tuesday, and Marsan-Cook had spent the previous night away from home. Late that afternoon, she returned briefly to change her clothes because she was going out again that evening, just down the road to a friend's house, to celebrate her forty-eighth birthday. She tells what happened next: "I came home. I'm a party girl, I love drinking and dancing, and I was in a rush to get out. So I went straight to my bedroom, and the two drawers [in the bedside table] were open, and I thought, 'How unusual.' I had been alone for a few days and I knew nobody had been here. So I looked in and there was nothing missing on my husband's side . . . but on my side I realized there were a couple of sex toys that were gone."

Marsan-Cook didn't immediately notice that any underwear was missing, but the theft of the sex toys was evident, and at first she thought it was a practical joke. After calling friend and neighbor Howard Gray, who rushed over, she realized it was probably not a joke, and they debated calling the police. Confused about what had happened and wary of not being taken seriously, she decided not to do so. So she and Gray checked the downstairs doors and windows and then headed to the small birthday party, where she stayed over for the night.

The next morning, November 18, Marsan-Cook had to work, and Gray drove her home and waited downstairs while she went up to the office on the second floor, where she needed to make some photocopies. That's when he heard her scream.

On the screen of an older, rarely used computer (no log-on code was needed) was a message in place of the screensaver. It was still dark outside, and the text was visible as soon as she walked into the office. In large letters it read: "GO AHEAD. CALL THE POLICE. I WANT TO SHOW THE JUDGE

YOU'RE REALLY BIG DILDOS." Marsan-Cook noticed this time that her lingerie drawer had been ransacked.

In this, his second theft from the Marsan-Cook home in less than twenty-four hours, Williams stole a total of 116 pieces of her underwear. For a while she thought the culprit was perhaps a long-ago, unstable boyfriend who had stalked her and resurfaced a couple of years earlier and sent a threatening email telling her she had wrecked his life. But whoever the intruder was, the terrifying implication of his message was that he had been in the house the previous afternoon, when Marsan-Cook and Gray were debating whether to call the police about the first theft, and had overheard them talking. Certainly that was how things appeared to her at the time. "He was hiding in the linen cupboard up there in the hallway. We know that, because all the things there were upside down and it's big enough for three people in there."

Indeed, Williams may well have rooted through the linen closet during one of his intrusions. But he was probably not there when Marsan-Cook and Gray stopped by her house on the afternoon of the 17th. The telltale date-stamped photos he took in the house were in two batches. The first group was recorded between around 4:30 and 5:30 a.m. on the 17th, while the second was shot shortly after midnight on the 18th. Williams the prowler was very much a nighttime creature, and it seems unlikely that he lingered in Marsan-Cook's home through the day until she and Gray showed up in the afternoon. He told detectives that he broke in two separate times, and that's likely true. On his second visit to the house, empty of occupants once more, he would have realized that Marsan-Cook had returned home in the interim and noticed her sex toys were missing. So he tormented her by leaving the message, which he also photographed before departing. (He even took a picture of one of her cats.) And the incorrect spelling of the word "your" to read "you're" was almost certainly no accident. As with the clumsy, quasi-apologetic message he had written but never sent to the young Ottawa woman, this looks to be another effort to make himself appear less educated than he was.

Beyond dispute is that the close encounter left Marsan-Cook badly shaken. She had heard something about the two unsolved home-invasion sex attacks up the road in Tweed a few weeks earlier, and she immediately drew a connection. The Belleville police who subsequently came to her house, however, appeared to know nothing about those incidents, which were under investigation by the OPP and had garnered little attention outside Tweed. Marsan-Cook says that one of the uniformed Belleville officers asked her, "Why, what's going on in Tweed?"

Marsan-Cook emerged from the experience with a deep sense of gratitude for having survived, which was later heightened when she learned what Williams did next. "Ever since, I've realized I could have been killed. But I realized I was meant to live, that I was being protected at that moment. This wasn't about learning a lesson, this was bigger than that. I was spared, and there was a reason for that."

10

A SOLDIER SLAIN

Quebec-born Corporal Marie-France Comeau joined the reserves in 1995 and had been with the military full-time for twelve years. Her family was originally from New Brunswick and she was raised in Quebec, New Brunswick and Germany. Like her father, Ernest, who spent forty-two years with the Canadian Forces, and like her grandfather before that, she was a career soldier. At thirty-seven, she owned the house on Raglan Street, part of a tidy new Brighton subdivision that was home to many other military households, having moved in a little less than a year earlier.

She was content. "She had found her calling, she had no worries and everything was going well," says Canadian Forces basic-training instructor Alain Plante, who had lived common-law with Comeau for four years. Comeau had become a devoted stepmother figure to Plante's two teenaged sons, one of whom, Etienne, in a later tribute on Facebook called her "the best stepmother that could possibly have set foot in our lives."

In the late 1990s, Comeau was stationed at the big NATO base in Lahr, Germany, as a member of the army, before switching to the air force. Then followed a tour of duty in which she shone. In 2002 she was posted to Afghanistan, part of the first Canadian contingent of troops to be rotated through after the

U.S.-led invasion and the ousting of the Taliban. There and at Camp Mirage, the air base in the United Arab Emirates that served as the chief conduit for the Canadian mission in Afghanistan, Comeau served as a traffic technician, moving cargo. She drove a forklift truck, loading and unloading the big Hercules aircraft that ceaselessly flew in and out, and it was a taxing environment—hot, dusty and demanding long hours.

"She did an incredible job," a former colleague, retired Master Corporal France Breault, told the *Northumberland News* newspaper. "Tough conditions, but I never heard Marie-France complain. She did her job with her usual smile, really making a difference . . . She was just the friendliest person there is. All her supervisors were thrilled to have her working for them."

Comeau had been at 8 Wing for about a year, attached to the base's 437 Squadron, where she initially worked the Trenton–Germany–Camp Mirage run. But in the early summer of 2009, shortly before Williams took charge of the base in July, she was picked to work on the VIP flights that flew the prime minister and other dignitaries, a highly prestigious position in which social skills were considered paramount.

Seven days after breaking into Comeau's home the first time, Williams returned. Late in the evening of Monday, November 23, he switched off his BlackBerry, locked the door of his top-floor office at 8 Wing headquarters in Trenton and made the short trip to Brighton. He arrived there shortly before eleven, and once again he parked his vehicle a few hundred yards away in a patch of woods and walked down Raglan Street to Comeau's house.

Her travels with Prime Minister Harper to Japan, Singapore and India had taken her right around the world—first west across the Pacific Ocean and then back to Canada via Europe and across the Atlantic. It had been a tiring haul and she was still recuperating, so she wasn't expected in at work the next day. With his easy access to her work schedule, Williams was well aware of that fact.

He paused outside her house and listened. She was talking on the phone. When the house went quiet, he once again used the same point of entry to slip inside: the horizontal, two-foot-by-five-foot basement window on the east side of the house. He was wearing a sweatshirt, Dockers pants and running shoes, his features masked by a small black cap and a wide black band that concealed his lower face, so only his eyes were visible. With him was what could be called his rape kit: rope, duct tape, lubricant, a flashlight and of course his camera equipment, all of it carried in a blue duffel bag.

The unfinished basement looked like countless others in newish homes: a concrete floor; pink glass fiber insulation in high wood-frame walls that had not yet all been closed in with drywall; a spare bed; a furnace in one corner. And it was there by the furnace that Williams silently stood for more than half an hour, waiting for his prey one floor up to retire for the night. In his hand was the same weapon he had used to club Laurie Massicotte, his heavy red tubular flashlight.

But Comeau did not go to bed. Instead, dressed only in a shawl, she walked down the wooden basement stairs in search of one of her two cats, calling out to it. Of course, there was a reason the cat was lingering in the basement: it had spotted the intruder hiding by the furnace and was staring fixedly at him, Williams later told police. And as Comeau came downstairs, she caught sight of him too. In the dim light and with his face covered, it is unlikely that she recognized the base commander—Williams later insisted she did not—but her reaction on finding an intruder in her home was swift and vocal. She shouted out, "You bastard," began screaming, and a struggle ensued. It ended when Williams struck her over the head several times with the flashlight, forcefully enough to cause extensive bleeding and bruising.

Comeau made an attempt to escape, but he pushed her to the floor, binding her arms behind her back with the rope, so tightly that it left burn marks on her forearms and wrists. He wrapped her entire face in the silver-colored duct tape he had brought along, leaving an airhole around her nose for her to breathe through. He hauled her to her feet and tied her to a metal post in the center of the basement that served as a ceiling support. Among the numerous injuries sustained by Comeau and recorded by pathologist Dr. Michael Pollanen was a wound to her back, inflicted by a metal pin in the post. Then Williams reached for his camera and took a couple of photographs.

His captive secure and blindfolded, he began taking elaborate precautions to ensure he would not be disturbed. First he went back outside the house and replaced the screen on the basement window through which he had entered; bloodied footmarks were later found in the walkway between the two houses, and also on the basement stairs. He found a key for the front door of the house, inserted it in the lock and snapped it off, so the door could not be opened from the outside. He went into Comeau's bedroom and draped a sheet over its single window. He removed all the small night-lights from the living room and the spare bedroom.

Then he returned to the basement, untied Comeau from the metal post and hustled her to the foot of the basement stairs, where another struggle took place as she once again fought back against her attacker. Large quantities of blood were found spattered about, and a section of the drywall was dented. Comeau was knocked unconscious and she ended up lying on the staircase, naked with her hands still tied behind her back. Williams took four more photographs, carried her upstairs to her bedroom and reapplied the duct tape to her face. She was still bleeding from the head wounds, which stained the bedroom carpet.

He placed her on the bed, the long rope binding her hands lying on the floor and neatly coiled in a figure eight. Around her head he wrapped a burgundy towel, tightly secured with duct tape. Then he turned on his video camera and proceeded to create a macabre record of his deeds, not to mention the most damning physical evidence imaginable.

Over the next two hours, he repeatedly raped Comeau, recording the assault with video and dozens of still, close-up photos, shot with a handheld camera. He seems preoccupied with obtaining as much variety in his footage as possible, in terms of angles and close-ups. And he too is very much part of the nightmarish photos and video clips that police found on one of his computer hard drives. The first glimpse of him on camera shows him naked except for the balaclava-like mask on his head and face. He even shot video of himself taking still photos, the video camera's lens trained on the Sony camera he grasped in one hand, held inches away from what he was photographing. That way he had two sets of images for his collection.

There is no merit in describing in detail Comeau's ordeal over the next two hours. Suffice to say that the colonel tasked with protecting the country and the people serving under him shows not a shred of mercy. At one point Comeau struggles to speak through the duct tape; he leans in and whispers, "No." She can be heard saying, "Get out, get out, I want you to leave." His response is to sit back thoughtfully, then take more pictures of her face.

At one point he kisses her on the cheek, then mugs for the video camera with a half smile, having removed his balaclava. At another time she is heard pleading with him to loosen the rope tightly binding her hands behind her back. He ignores her.

He produces a tube of lubricant jelly and displays it for the video camera, holding it between his knuckles.

And still Comeau fought back. Midway through the two hours Williams paused and went to the living room window to make sure no one was coming. She struggled to her feet and ran to the bathroom, still tied and blindfolded, where he caught up with her, struck her several times more on the head with his flashlight and dragged her back to the bed.

He removed some of her lingerie from a drawer, placed it on her and took more pictures. He began raping her again, and as he did so, Comeau was crying out: "I don't want to die, I don't want to die." Williams placed a pillow over her face, but even though still bound and gagged, she briefly managed to pull it away and fight him off. He forcefully ordered her to "Shut up," saying that if she did, he would allow her to breathe. The autopsy showed that Comeau also sustained injuries to her eyes and neck, thought to have occurred at around this stage when Williams exerted pressure on the jugular veins on the side of her neck.

He reached for his roll of duct tape and there was a further struggle, leaving Comeau on the floor screaming, "No." Again he warned her to be quiet or he would suffocate her. He got dressed, ordered her to get to her feet and led her by the rope still binding her hands to a corner of the bedroom.

"I want to live so badly," Comeau can be heard saying. "Did you expect to?" Williams replies, and the mumbled response is, "Yes . . . Give me a chance. I'll be so good, I don't deserve this . . . Please go, please go away, please."

He told her he was not going to kill her, but as with Jessica Lloyd two months later, it was a lie. As Comeau cowered in the corner, her face still wrapped in the duct tape save for an airhole for her nose, Williams completed the act of murder by placing another piece of tape over the hole. She slumped to the floor, her last words a muffled plea for her killer to "Have a heart, please. I've been really good. I want to live." And Russell Williams watched her die, the video camera still rolling. He then took two more still photos, the last one at 4:23 a.m.

He cleaned up. He took the sheets from the bed and ran them through Comeau's washing machine, dumping in a bottle of bleach, shooting yet more video and still photos as he did so. He went back to the bedroom and removed the duct tape from Comeau's face, placed her body on the bed and covered it with a duvet. Finally he took nine pieces of her underwear, put them in his duffel bag and left her house by the back patio door. He walked up the road to where his Pathfinder was parked and drove away up to Highway 401, headed for Ottawa. He switched on his BlackBerry. It would still be dark for another couple of hours. He had an early morning meeting to attend.

11

BUSINESS AS USUAL

Marie-France Comeau was murdered in the early hours of Tuesday, November 24, and her body lay undiscovered for more than thirty hours. Still on leave after her long-haul overseas trip to Asia, she was not expected at 8 Wing that day, and it wasn't until almost one in the afternoon on the Wednesday that the Northumberland OPP got the 911 call. It was Brighton's first homicide in more than thirty years.

Retired printing-press operator Terry Alexander lived directly opposite Comeau's house, and he had never had a conversation with her. But he knew her well enough to say hello as she came and went, driving back and forth from work or picking up groceries. He was outside on his front porch, awaiting a visit from a plumber, when he realized that something was terribly amiss. "It's sometime after twelve and a guy comes out of the house and he's crying. He said to me, 'Did you see anybody around here who shouldn't have been here? Did you see any strange people or strange cars? She's laying in there dead.' That's what he said to me. Then he sat down in the driveway, leaned against the wheel well of his car. He'd already phoned 911, because about two minutes later all the cars came rushing down—police cars, ambulance, the fire chief, everything."

The man was Paul Bélanger, Comeau's boyfriend, also in the military and stationed in Quebec, and it was he Comeau had been chatting with when Williams was lurking and listening outside her house on Monday night. They had arranged to have dinner the following evening, and when she didn't show and didn't answer the phone he drove over to her house on Wednesday to find her silver-colored Toyota Yaris still parked in the driveway. First Bélanger tried the front door, then he went around to the back, where he found the patio door unlocked. He gave a shout, got no response and went inside.

Crime in Brighton is rare, and still more so in the tranquil subdivision nicknamed Brighton by the Bay. So for the next several weeks residents remained extremely uneasy, despite police reassurances that there was no cause for alarm over what looked to be a domestic-related incident. Williams's intrusion via the basement window had gone undetected, despite the blood traces in the walkway, and police found no other sign of a forced entry, suggesting that Comeau had known her killer and had let him into the house. For that reason, Bélanger was of immediate interest to the detectives pursuing the murder investigation. They also learned from him that after the burglary on November 16, Comeau had noticed her belongings had been disturbed and that she had accused him of being the culprit. Not until Bélanger passed a polygraph test several days later was he cleared.

Then another possible suspect surfaced, a pilot at 8 Wing who was put through two extremely distressing high-pressure interrogations, with a third one scheduled for the day on which the murder charges against Williams were announced.

In the meantime, Comeau's neighbors were wondering if a killer was in their midst. Police wouldn't release the cause of death, viewing it as holdback evidence, but it was obvious the quiet, pleasant air attendant from 8 Wing had been murdered.

Terry Alexander and his wife, Mary, had sold their house in Mississauga and moved to Brighton three years earlier, in part because Mississauga, just west of Toronto, was experiencing too much crime. "I moved away from all that, I came from a place where there's murders, I come here and there's one right across the road. It was mind-boggling for me," Terry Alexander says. "Everybody was very nervous, it was very tense, because we didn't know anything. All that I wanted to know was that he [the murderer] was out of here. We didn't know if anybody had been remanded or if someone down the street might be next, or what. The police didn't mention anything. We kept asking, 'How did she die?' and they said, 'We can't divulge that.' But they asked all kinds of questions and they were around here for weeks. Everybody on the street was interviewed, and on the next street too."

Comeau's house was torn apart in the search for evidence, from the floors to the ductwork to the insulated walls, requiring extensive repairs when the police were done. The best clue they had was the bloodied footwear impressions Williams had left behind in the outside walkway (he subsequently discarded the running shoes he'd been wearing), but of course there was nothing to compare them to. And the same was true of the DNA traces Williams left in Comeau's bathroom sink, where he had washed his hands.

The killer colonel, meanwhile, once again resumed his normal life.

As Williams would later tell police, on the Tuesday morning, a few hours after murdering Comeau, he drove from his cottage in Tweed to Gatineau, across the river from Ottawa, where he participated in an 8:30 a.m. meeting regarding the recently acquired C-17 Globemasters. He remembered the meeting, he said, because the big aircraft—a vital component of the Afghanistan war effort—had been so much a part of his job when he'd been working in

Ottawa at the Directorate of Air Requirements a couple of years earlier. It was very foggy on the morning he made the drive, he also recalled.

The meeting wrapped up mid-afternoon and later he had dinner at a restaurant with his wife, kissing her goodbye and then heading back to Tweed, he said. But in an odd memory lapse, he was unable to tell Detective Sergeant Jim Smyth where the couple had dinner, even when pressed, except to say that it was somewhere in Westboro, the upscale Ottawa neighborhood where their new house was being built, now nearing completion. Nor could he remember who paid for the meal, only that it would have been paid with MasterCard.

On November 25—the same day Comeau's battered and bloodied body was discovered in her home—Williams took part in a charity stunt that in hindsight can only be described as grotesque. As the 8 Wing commander usually did, he lent his weight to Trenton's annual United Way fundraiser. In a corny but effective attention-getter known as Jail 'n' Bail, organized at numerous workplaces across Canada, bosses and celebrities get rounded up and "arrested" on absurd charges, sometimes by good-humored cops. From a mock jail, the prisoners then frantically appeal to friends and colleagues to bail them out, and the money goes to charity. Williams cheerfully pitched in. He was arrested on a charge of being "too young to be a wing commander" (he was forty-six), while Lt. Col. Sean Lewis, 8 Wing's Logistics and Engineering Officer, was accused of "having a full length mirror in his office and looking at it too often." Under the caption "Jail and Bail event locks up the worst Wing offenders," the December 4 edition of 8 Wing's weekly newspaper carried a picture of Williams grinning into the camera, his hands tied behind his back.

It was not long before official word of Comeau's murder reached the base commander. Before he confessed, Williams told police he wasn't sure when and where he found out—an astonishing gap in the memory of such an efficient, detail-oriented commander—but emails obtained under an Access to Information request show that a few minutes after midnight on Thursday, November 26, he was informed there had been "a significant occurrence" and that Corporal Comeau was dead. From his Tweed cottage, Williams acknowledged the news at 6:40 a.m., firing off a rather antiseptic message in reply. "Understood. Thank you," he typed on his BlackBerry. "I'll catch up when I get in, if there is additional information." He then drove to the base in Trenton.

Over the course of the day, numerous emails went back and forth between the senior 8 Wing officers, who were dealing not only with the police who had carriage of the investigation and were trying to reach Comeau's next of kin, but also with a flurry of media calls. Late in the morning, a press release went out from the base, after a couple of minor amendments by Williams. He corrected Comeau's first name to read Marie-France instead of Marie, and the reference to 437 Squadron, to which she belonged, was changed to read "437 (Transport) Squadron." Early in the afternoon, the 8 Wing military police commander emailed him a news update from *The Trentonian* newspaper's website, and Williams replied with an assurance that if he learned anything new, "I'll keep you in the loop."

Williams's breathtaking sangfroid held firm over the next few days. Comeau's funeral, which he did not attend, was held on December 4 at the National Military Cemetery in Ottawa. Hundreds of friends, family and military personnel were there, including both Alain Plante, her former longtime boyfriend, and Paul Bélanger, whom she had been seeing more recently. Padre Paul-Alain Monpas delivered the eulogy, lauding the murdered soldier's accomplishments, her great sense of adventure and her integrity and devotion to duty. "Marie's respect for those around her aided her career in the military," the pastor said. "She always found the words for those having difficulty. She was never scared to get involved, she was full of talent, and whoever knew her can say she made a difference in their lives. Marie, a ray of sunshine to her friends and family, embarked on a lifelong quest to seek truth in her life. She lived her life to the fullest."

Other tributes were paid, and Williams had made a contribution too. Earlier in the week, he had written to Comeau's father on his official letterhead, expressing his condolences on behalf of the 8 Wing base. "Please let me know whether there is anything I can do to help you during this very difficult time," he concluded. "You and your family are in our thoughts and prayers. With our deepest sympathy . . ."

After the funeral, he was given an update by a senior officer who was there. "I'm pleased to hear that the service went as well as could be expected, given the very sad circumstances," Williams replied in an email. "Take care. Russ." He had spent the day in Trenton, attending another charity function, and at a turkey-carving later in the day, smiling broadly, he posed for a shot with the youngest private at the base, who was declared honorary Wing Commander for the Day.

On December 8, a memorial service for Comeau was held at the 8 Wing chapel. Williams did not attend that ceremony either, possibly because he was flying. At around that time, early in December, he helped pilot an Airbus 130 on the Germany–Ottawa–Trenton leg of a return trip from Camp Mirage in the U.A.E. Garrett Lawless had brought the plane from Mirage and the flight home marked the last time he chatted to Williams before the arrest. It would also be Williams's last overseas trip, though he flew at least once to Edmonton over the Christmas holidays, always a busy time at an air base. Designed for medium- and long-haul flights, the wide-bodied Airbus was bringing home twenty or so assorted celebrities who'd been entertaining the Canadian troops in Kandahar with a morale-booster: folk singer Bruce Cockburn; retired hockey great Guy Lafleur; Canadian Football League hall-of-famer Peter Dalla Riva. Williams was introduced to them and was his usual courteous self, but he seemed subdued. "In hindsight, I remember he was very twitchy, though he may just have been tired," Lawless remarks. "He talked about how he was going to miss flying if he was further promoted or transferred, because very rarely does a full colonel have an operational flying position. Flying to Trenton from Ottawa, I remember him saying his favorite time to fly was at night because the air was so smooth."

Right around that same time, on December 6, he and Harriman took possession of their new house in Ottawa. They had already sold the home on Wilkie Drive in Orleans, where they had lived for fourteen years, and now they were relocating to Westboro, an established upscale neighborhood a few minutes' drive from the city center. Former neighbors on Wilkie Drive say the upkeep on the old house had become too time-consuming for the couple and their busy schedules, but the move also shortened the commute for Harriman, whose offices are situated in a downtown high-rise office tower.

Most of the homes on Edison Avenue have been there for many years, but like the property next door, number 473 was brand new, purchased from the Prestwick Building Corporation. For $693,819, Williams and Harriman got a three-story, three-bedroom townhouse comprising 2,200 square feet. As often happens with new houses, completion ran a bit behind schedule, so Harriman had stayed with friends for a few weeks after selling the Orleans property, while Williams had lived in Tweed.

On December 15, Williams welcomed the Olympic torch when it stopped at Trenton en route to the Olympic Games in

Vancouver. In all, fourteen military bases took part in the ritual. "It's very exciting to be a part of this," he said.

In the December 18 issue of *Contact*, his Christmas message to the men and women under his command urged them to "reflect upon our collective accomplishments and to look toward the future." He and Chief Warrant Officer Kevin West listed some of 8 Wing's achievements for the year: "We have maintained the support lifeline to our mission in Afghanistan, saved fellow Canadians through Search and Rescue operations, conducted all aspects of Air Mobility support, whether VIP or materiel transport, and returned to Canada our fallen [soldiers] with honour and dignity." With the approach of Christmas, Williams concluded, "We know that many of you will be thinking of our comrades serving elsewhere, away from their loved ones. We thank you for the support we know you will provide their families here at home."

Christmas came and went, then New Year's Eve, which Williams marked by attending two parties at the 8 Wing officers' mess—a formal, dress-kit function followed by a more relaxed get-together with some of the civilians attached to the base. He stayed for a drink and then departed.

January 3 saw one of the largest-ever repatriation ceremonies to stem from the Afghan conflict. In a biting wind, Williams watched as the coffins of Sergeant George Miok, Sergeant Kirk Taylor, Private Garrett Chidley, all from the Princess Patricia's Canadian Light Infantry, and Corporal Zachary McCormack, a reservist with the Loyal Edmonton Regiment, were unloaded. And there was a fifth coffin, that of award-winning journalist Michelle Lang, seconded to the Canadian Press from the *Calgary Herald* and reporting from the Kandahar area for less than three weeks before she was killed. Lang had been traveling with the others when their armored vehicle was ripped apart by a roadside bomb.

The New Year brought fresh demands for 8 Wing. Along with its ongoing, multi-million-dollar infrastructure expansion and the ceaseless back-and-forth supply mission to Afghanistan, it was gearing up to provide air support for security operations at the Vancouver Olympics. As well, the seventeen-strong fleet of new CC-130J Hercules transport planes was soon to start arriving. Williams told the Belleville *Intelligencer* that his first half year as wing commander had been "a lot of fun, but very, very busy, some major pieces are getting under way." One of the big challenges, he said—probably the biggest—was juggling day-to-day operational needs with the big infrastructure changes afoot at 8 Wing in the shape of new roads and buildings. He also offered thanks to the people of Trenton and Belleville: "What has really impressed me in the last few months is how outstanding the support from the local community continues to be. I can think of very few events that have been less than positive."

On January 5, 2010, he attended the swearing-in ceremony of Belleville's new deputy chief of police, Paul Vandegraaf, where he mingled and spoke with the police officers and other dignitaries.

Then, on January 12, a huge earthquake devastated Haiti, killing more than 230,000 people and posing a major, obviously unforeseen challenge for CFB Trenton, which overnight became ground zero for relief operations and Canada's Disaster Assistance Response Team. Operation Hestia, as the Canadian Forces humanitarian response to the earthquake was dubbed, was a very big deal for Canada in general and for 8 Wing in particular, which was the main point of departure for a 2,500-mile "air bridge" linking Canada and Haiti via Jamaica. As the base funneled the first of two thousand troops and hundreds of tons of food, water and medical supplies to the stricken country, on January 17 it was toured and praised by Defence Minister Peter MacKay and General Walter Natynczyk, Chief of the Defence

Staff, Canada's top soldier. Other visitors included Chief of the Air Staff Lieutenant-General André Deschamps along with Honorary Colonel Pamela Wallin, who spoke of being struck by "the incredible amount of energy here."

Other, less urgent matters helped fill up the colonel's calendar. On Wednesday, January 27, he attended a meeting for the 8 Wing museum's board of directors, where it was proposed that a memorial wall be erected to honor the Canadian soldiers killed in Afghanistan. Williams suggested that some sort of finance committee be set up to examine costs.

And amid the hectic schedule, there was special recognition for the base commander. At a black-tie dinner on January 15, Deschamps presented Williams with the Canadian Forces Decoration First Clasp, marking his twenty-two years of "faithful service." The award was a kind of upgrade for a medal he had already received, fastened to his chest alongside the South-West Asia Service Medal he'd been awarded for his work in Camp Mirage and Afghanistan. Presented after a town hall meeting at an 8 Wing gymnasium, the recognition apparently came as a surprise to the colonel, but he was unfazed. The career soldier and pilot who a few weeks earlier had raped and murdered a corporal under his command, and who two weeks later would rape and kill another woman, smirked into the camera.

12

ROADBLOCK

S now lay on the ground and a raw February wind whipped across the surrounding farmland as the police cruisers maneuvered into position, blocking the two-lane highway in each direction. A checkpoint was being set up, with cars from two police forces, the Belleville Police Service and the Ontario Provincial Police. Behind the wheel of one of the OPP cars that pulled up was Constable Russell Alexander, a career officer from the small Madoc detachment who was nearing retirement. He stepped out onto the asphalt.

It was this same constable who in late October had suspected Larry Jones, Williams's next-door neighbor, of being responsible for the twin home-invasion sexual assaults on and near Cosy Cove Lane, and his presence at the roadblock may have been a coincidence. But what was rapidly becoming clear in the fast-widening investigation was that those two attacks were almost certainly linked to the recent mysterious disappearance of a popular young Belleville woman, and that the unsolved murder of Corporal Marie-France Comeau two months earlier in Brighton was probably part of the picture too.

This was an early Thursday evening, February 4, 2010, around seven o'clock, and the checkpoint on Belleville's northern outskirts, where Highway 37 stretches toward the sleepy village of

Tweed, was what's termed a rolling roadblock. Mobile and set up without warning, rolling roadblocks are routinely deployed in rural Ontario to nab drinking drivers and—increasingly, under toughened provincial legislation—speeders. And at first glance that would have seemed to be the purpose of this one, which in part it was. As a trickle of motorists slowed down and obligingly rolled down their windows, the first question was friendly, unremarkable: "Good evening, sir. Good evening, madam. Any alcohol tonight?" On this evening, however, something more than drunken drivers was on the minds of the cops, whose roadblock remained in place through the night until almost six the next morning, long after Belleville's bars had closed for the night.

One week earlier, almost to the hour, a vivacious, independent-minded woman of twenty-seven had inexplicably vanished overnight from the brick-and-siding bungalow where she lived alone, right where the police checkpoint now straddled Highway 37. So as the passing motorists pulled up and the police discreetly sniffed for a whiff of booze, drivers were asked to cast their minds back a few days. Had they been traveling this way the previous Thursday evening, January 28, or early on Friday? Did they recall seeing anything unusual? Did they know of anyone else who did?

Belleville is a mostly blue-collar city of fifty thousand inhabitants, a two-hour drive east of Toronto along Highway 401. And like authorities anywhere else, its police are well accustomed to fielding missing-person reports. Unless they involve youngsters or the elderly, such disappearances rarely stir much concern at the outset. Sooner or later, and usually sooner, most people turn up unscathed and perhaps apologetic for having caused such a fuss.

But from the first hours of Jessica Lloyd's vanishing, alarm bells rang. She'd texted a friend shortly after ten-thirty at night to say she'd arrived home safely after spending the evening with him at a mutual friend's house and was turning in for the night.

But she'd failed to show up for work the next morning at the bus company where she'd worked for the past two years, Tri-Board Student Transportation Services Inc. in nearby Napanee. And because she was always punctual, colleagues at work swiftly realized something was very wrong.

January 29 was a Friday, and at around nine o'clock Lloyd's mother, Roxanne McGarvey, got a call from the school bus company in Napanee telling her that her daughter had not shown up for work that morning. McGarvey headed for Jessica's house, stopping off en route at the office of Jessica's doctor in Belleville to see if by any chance she was there. On arriving at her daughter's house, she found the car still in the driveway, the doors locked and no signs of a break and enter. Inside was everything Jessica would normally have had with her: her purse and identification, her BlackBerry, her eyeglasses, her keys. McGarvey began phoning family members and friends, and Jessica's older brother Andy, to whom she was close, was among the first to get the call. A confident, burly figure who had a warehouse job with the Beer Store, working the midnight shift, Andy Lloyd would become the public face of his sister's family and many friends in the weeks and months ahead, answering the barrage of reporters' questions with unfailing patience.

"It drew a red flag so quick," he said of Jessica's disappearance. After Williams was arrested, Andy Lloyd recounted to CBC television how he had learned something was amiss. He had just come home from work. "I'd only been laying down for half an hour and my mom phoned and told me she was missing and it didn't really register . . . So I rushed right over to my sister's house, where my mom was, and it all just kind of converged from there. Within an hour a lot of friends and family were over. And the police were there obviously. We called them right away and they were there very quickly and it just kind of exploded from there."

The police arrived shortly after noon, and quickly spotted two sets of footprints in the snow, leading from the house to a set of tire tracks about 150 yards away, on the edge of the corn-field at the north end of the property. Scores of volunteers began fanning out and scouring the woods and surrounding fields, and they were joined by personnel from CFB Trenton together with police from Belleville and from the small, neigh-boring Stirling-Rawdon police department. The OPP brought in a helicopter, as did the military at 8 Wing, a big yellow search-and-rescue Cormorant, the deployment of which was approved by the base commander, Colonel Russell Williams. Hundreds of posters were quickly printed and distributed, plastered on cars and hydro poles, seeking a young woman who was five foot five, weighing 125 pounds, with bright green eyes, brown shoulder-length hair and an intricate, L-shaped tattoo across her lower back. There was widespread concern about the disappearance, as Lloyd had lived most of her life in Belleville and was extremely well liked. An ad hoc Facebook group, "Find Jessica Elizabeth Lloyd," sprang to life, as more than 48,000 people—including family and friends, but mostly strangers—pitched in with sympathy, thoughts and advice. Deputy Belleville Police Chief Paul Vandegraaf called the col-lective response "amazing."

Despite the blitz, however, a week after Lloyd had disappeared without a trace, there had been no breakthrough, nor any sign of one. And the sense of foreboding that built with the passing days soared on Wednesday, February 3, when Belleville police issued a stark warning to the city's women, especially those living alone: keep your doors locked; vary your daily routine; try to be with friends; report anything or anyone suspicious.

———

There was good reason for the police alert because, sinister as Lloyd's disappearance was, the larger picture police were by now looking at was becoming more threatening as they joined up dots from the past four and a half months: the two bizarre sex attacks in Tweed, the murder in Brighton of Corporal Marie-France Comeau, and now what looked to be the abduction of Lloyd in Belleville—different types of crimes, in different places, under scrutiny by different police. Still absent from the mix was any connection to the dozens of lingerie break-ins in either Tweed (all but one of which had gone unreported) or Ottawa, more than 125 miles away. Nonetheless, the ingredients were in place for what could have been a reprise of the cross-jurisdictional chaos that hampered the big Paul Bernardo murder investigation in the early 1990s, which was badly marred by interdepartmental police rivalry in Toronto and Niagara Region.

But this time, it didn't turn out like that. Jessica Lloyd was a Belleville resident and her disappearance was a Belleville case. Because it was so entirely out of character, however, the city's new police chief, Cory McMullan, had approached the OPP shortly after Lloyd vanished to see if there might be a connection to any other unsolved crimes.

Indeed there might, she was soon told. One of the most useful tools in the OPP's inventory at its headquarters in Orillia is what is termed the VICLAS computer system, acronym for Violent Crime Linkage System, part of a national network that's mostly run by the RCMP. VICLAS grew out of a still-earlier investigation, in the 1980s, involving British Columbia serial killer Clifford Olson, and its broad function is to track and analyze common threads in seemingly disparate investigations. Scrutiny of these four recent incidents showed several possible links: all took place within an hour's drive of each other, all involved home invasions and all took place late at night. As well, the Comeau murder and the Tweed sex attacks a few weeks earlier showed similarities in the way the predator had tied up his victims. Could that same assailant now be responsible for the disappearance of Jessica Lloyd? Quite possibly, the police had concluded—hence the warning to Belleville's women.

But where Lloyd might be, no one had a clue.

Jessica Elizabeth Lloyd was born in Ottawa, where her father, Warren Lloyd, spent more than twenty-five years at CFB Ottawa in the Canadian navy's communications section. On retiring in 1990, when Jessica was eight, Warren Lloyd and his small family relocated to Belleville. Home was the red-brick bungalow on Highway 37, which was built for her parents and which later became Jessica's property after her father died of cancer and her mother moved into a smaller place in Belleville. At the time of her death, Jessica had owned the house for less than nine months.

After graduating from Quinte Secondary School in 2000, she attended Belleville's Loyalist College, graduating after three years with a diploma in business administration and human resources. After a couple of interim jobs, she was hired by Tri-Board Student Transportation Services in Napanee, where she worked as a transit planner. She was famously reliable, which was the reason the alarm was sounded so early when she didn't show up for work that Friday morning.

The search for Lloyd went full tilt. "It felt like the world rallied," one friend said. Some of the Missing posters went beyond listing the facts of her disappearance, and included details about a possible suspect (these posters were soon taken down). And there was so much activity and speculation on Facebook that while lauding the collective effort, Paul Vandegraaf, Belleville's deputy police chief, urged caution in sifting fact from fiction.

"It's wonderful how quickly this information got out, the picture and the description," he said. "It's amazing how fast that got around the province. The other angle, though, is that it's gotten so big that nobody is validating the information . . . so we're cautioning people about what they read, what they believe and what they post."

Investigators, too, were pulling out all the stops. Close to three hundred homes up and down Highway 37 and within a half mile of Lloyd's home were canvassed. So too were four convicted sex offenders who lived in the area. In addition, a highly specific vehicle canvass was undertaken. Along with the tire tracks discovered on the far northern edge of Lloyd's property, there had been two separate sightings of what looked like an SUV parked there on the night she vanished. Its make was unknown, but using the tire tracks, identification specialists were able to measure the width between its wheels. Those two bits of information were fed through a provincial government database, and roughly 450 vehicles that might be the suspect one showed up. They included but were not limited to: Toyota 4Runners, 1996–2002; Jeep Cherokees 1999–2004; and Nissan Pathfinders, 1998–1999.

Of those 450 SUVs, police had traced 178 and were still in the process of interviewing the owners when the roadblock was set up on Highway 37 on that chilly February 4 evening. So Constable Alexander and his partners were carrying a tape measure and photos of the tire-tread marks. OPP forensic specialists had photographed the tread, magnified the image and pasted it onto a sheet of cardboard, along with an estimate of the wheel width.

And now came what proved to be the moment of truth. The roadblock was set up shortly before seven o'clock, and one of the very first vehicles to pull up, within a minute or two, was a 2001 silver-colored Nissan Pathfinder piloted by the air force colonel who commanded the 8 Wing military base in Trenton. Still in his crisp blue uniform, he was heading toward his home in Tweed and was in a hurry, he explained.

Much later, Williams suggested that the way he handled the situation was his undoing. After he'd pleaded guilty but before he was shipped to Kingston Penitentiary, he confided to a jail guard at the Quinte Detention Centre that he reckoned he'd made a big mistake at the roadblock by being too assertive and trying to bluster his way through by pulling rank. In particular, Williams blundered by telling Constable Alexander that he was in a big hurry because he was rushing home to take care of a sick child. Certainly when he was summoned for police questioning in Ottawa three days later, that lie by the childless colonel would have stirred deep suspicion, even though it was never raised during the interrogation.

In the end, however, whatever Williams said at the roadblock would have made no difference. The timing of his arrival was undoubtedly fortuitous, because had he left 8 Wing even ten minutes earlier, he would have escaped scrutiny that night. But once he had been stopped, there was nothing he could do, because the cops' instructions were twofold: If any vehicle matched the description of the suspect SUV, the owner was to be questioned in detail, and the particulars of the vehicle recorded. Then—and this was a direct order from OPP Detective Inspector Chris Nicholas, who was in charge of the mushrooming investigation—the driver was immediately to be placed under surveillance.

When Williams pulled up at the roadblock, he was politely quizzed by Constable Russ Alexander, who had with him the detailed questionnaire. When Williams was interrogated in Ottawa soon afterward, he remarked approvingly on how extensive the questioning had been, noting casually that the constable had the same first name as him.

Alexander looked at Williams's Pathfinder, measured the width between its wheels and concluded that there wasn't an exact match with the mysterious SUV. But the Pathfinder's Toyo Open Country H/T tires were a different story. Particularly notable was the front left tire, which appeared to closely resemble one of the telltale tracks. Alexander said nothing, filled out his questionnaire, and with a nod and a wave the colonel was soon on his way up Highway 37, heading toward his lakeside hideaway on Cosy Cove Lane.

But back at the roadblock, an animated discussion was taking place about whether to pull the alarm cord and place surveillance on the colonel. Alexander knew who Williams was—he was a distinguished guy, the boss of 8 Wing—and he made the case that even though his tires seemed to match the tracks, it was probably a coincidence. If anyone would be above suspicion, it surely must be Colonel Williams. One of the Belleville officers vigorously disagreed, and after an argument Alexander relented. So as Williams drove up the highway, Alexander was speaking into his cell phone, his tone urgent and insistent.

"Surveillance," he was saying. "Now. Right now."

13

THE HOUSE ON HIGHWAY 37

It must have been a bad moment for Russ Williams when the phone rang at his new Westboro house in the early afternoon of Sunday, February 7. On the line was Detective Sergeant Jim Smyth of the OPP, asking politely whether Williams would mind stopping in at the main Ottawa Police Service building on downtown Elgin Street. Further to the questions he'd been asked at the roadblock three days earlier, there were some loose ends to be tied up, he was told. No problem, Williams replied, he'd be happy to drop by in an hour or so.

He'd been under surveillance since Thursday night, and his house on Edison Avenue was being watched now, by under-cover police parked up the street. That morning he'd been tailed by the OPP surveillance unit to an Ottawa car wash, where he'd vacuumed and cleaned his Pathfinder. After he departed, police seized the contents of the vacuum canister. Search warrants were meanwhile being sought and granted for his two homes in Ottawa and Tweed and for his Pathfinder. Later, the scope of the warrants would be widened to encompass his office at 8 Wing Trenton and his medical records there, a Bank of Montreal safety deposit box Williams shared with his wife, along with his bank records, his cell phone/BlackBerry records and a DNA sample.

No one expected Williams to make a run for it. Where could he go? Of greater concern was the possibility that he might try to hide or destroy evidence—which is exactly what he did. After getting off the phone with Detective Sergeant Smyth, he grabbed two 500 gigabyte Lacie hard drives from the computer in his upstairs office and went to the basement, where he concealed them in the ceiling above the electrical panel. The contents of those two hard drives were identical: video clips and close to 3,000 photographs, many of them depicting the tortures inflicted on Comeau and Lloyd, along with screen grabs from police and news websites. In addition, the hard drives contained a complete and detailed inventory of all the scores of burglaries he'd committed over the past two years, buried so skillfully in computer file folders that he later had to help police locate them.

Also in Williams and Harriman's house was a wealth of incriminating evidence he had planned to take to Tweed that same evening and destroy. By the bed in the master bedroom was Williams's blue duffel bag containing the black skull cap that formed part of his disguise. In the basement spare room was an Epson printer box containing more than fifty lingerie items, lubricant and photos of Lloyd, including her student ID card. A second box had more underwear, vibrators and commercial sex videos. In a corner of the garage was a pillowcase that held more vibrators and more underwear, including children's panties. And when police later searched the house on Edison Avenue they also found a book entitled *LSI Guide to Lock Picking*.

It was too late to do anything about that now; he would have been acutely aware that he was very likely under surveillance already. After hiding the hard drives in the basement ceiling, he had about an hour to compose his thoughts. Yet he doesn't seem to have been reaching for the panic button, because on his feet were the same incriminating leather boots he had been wearing when he kidnapped Lloyd nine days earlier. Williams had made a career out of wearing his confidence on his sleeve, and of putting people at ease with his low-key, self-effacing worldliness. Maybe it would work this time. Either way, there was no dodging what was ahead. Shortly before three that afternoon, he drove to Elgin Street for his rendezvous with Detective Sergeant Smyth.

When he'd been questioned by Constable Alexander at the road-block three days earlier, Williams had said he had never seen or spoken to Lloyd, adding that, of course, like everyone else in the area, he'd been aware of her disappearance. How could you not be? The Missing posters were everywhere and the story was all over the airwaves. And he stuck to this fiction during the first phase of his interview with Smyth. Then, in his confession several hours later, he told Smyth he had targeted Lloyd after driving past her home on Highway 37 on January 27, the evening before he invaded her home and kidnapped her. He'd glimpsed her through a window, he said, working out on a treadmill, and decided then and there that she would be his next target.

As with his account of having met Corporal Marie-France Comeau just once, there is no reason to believe there's much truth to this astonishingly casual cause-and-effect explanation. And certainly the post-arrest rumor mill offered numerous alternatives: the two had been dating; they'd met at Belleville's Trillium Wood Golf Club; there was even a scenario that had Williams lurking at another property just up the road, wearing a wig and dressed as a woman while watching Lloyd's house.

There's no evidence any of that speculation is true. But equally improbable is Williams's claim that he just noticed Lloyd and attacked her on an impulse. Lloyd's house is set back from the road by at least fifty yards, and the aboveground basement window through which he said he'd spotted her exercising is small. Much more likely is that he had seen her several times and had stalked her. He drove past her home twice a day on most days, as he went back and forth between Trenton and Tweed, and the hours of her daytime schedule as she commuted between Belleville and Napanee roughly matched his.

As for the timing of this attack, two factors may be relevant. Over the previous two years, the bulk of Williams's crimes had taken place near the end of the week or on weekends, as this one would. And perhaps much more telling, on the same day he targeted Lloyd, a news story had appeared regarding the unsolved sex slaying of Comeau in November. Under the headline POLICE ANTICIPATE A LENGTHY INVESTIGATION IN MARIE-FRANCE COMEAU MURDER, the Brighton-based *Northumberland News* reported on its website that afternoon that progress was slow, and that detectives were renewing their appeal for public assistance. "We're looking for any information at all," lead investigator Detective Inspector Paul McCrickard said. "If she visited someone, got gas, or went into a Tim Hortons, we want to know. She could have been on foot or in her car, we believe she was in her car. We just want to confirm her whereabouts and who she might have been with. At this point in the investigation, we really have no idea." McCrickard added that he anticipated the investigation would be lengthy, which conceivably reassured Williams that for now, at least, the heat was off. And he'd been keeping his head down. In the two months since he had raped and murdered Comeau, he had not committed a single break-in anywhere.

January 28 was a Thursday, and Lloyd spent most of the evening, from roughly seven till ten, with a friend, Dorian O'Brian. And it was while she was out for those three hours that Williams first showed up at her house. He had stayed late at the air base that day, leaving at around nine o'clock, Lieutenant-Colonel Ross Fetterly, the base's chief administration officer, later told police, and he seemed cheerful when he departed. It had been taco night in the officers' mess, a Thursday evening ritual of a post-work bite to eat with a beer or two. Someone asked Williams if he would be back at the mess the next day for a luncheon at eleven, and he replied that he would.

From 8 Wing, Williams headed directly for Lloyd's house, near the south end of Highway 37, on a reconnaissance trip. He broke in through an unlocked kitchen window, looked around to make sure she lived alone, and quickly exited. He had parked his Pathfinder in the cornfield, about 150 yards away, and had made his way to the house indirectly, walking around the perimeter of the field.

As he lurked in the cold darkness preparing to leave, what can only be seen as a piece of extraordinarily bad luck took place. At around nine-thirty, a uniformed Belleville policewoman who knew Lloyd personally was on patrol alone when she drove past Lloyd's house, spied Williams's truck out in the field, thought it looked odd and decided to make a check. Hidden at the back, Williams saw the lights and heard the cruiser pull up. He couldn't see it, didn't know it was a police car, and initially thought it was Lloyd returning home. The policewoman knocked at the door of the darkened house, but there was no reply. Since everything seemed to be in order, she drove away.

Given what she knew, there was no reason for her to have done anything else. The house seemed secure, no one was home, there was no sign of anything wrong. Much later, when it emerged that Williams had been there all along, waiting for Lloyd to come home so he could kidnap her, it was suggested the Belleville cop had been negligent for not driving across the cornfield to the truck 150 yards away and running its license plate through the provincial data bank, which would have determined the ownership. If that had happened, so the reasoning went in a series of newspaper stories and columns excoriating the police, Jessica Lloyd's life might have been saved.

In theory, that may be true. Certainly if Williams had seen the policewoman drive over to his Pathfinder and examine it, he would likely have been scared away, at least for that night. But in the real world rather than the hindsight world, the cop was not negligent at all. Lloyd had not yet gone missing, no crime had been committed, and there had been no calls for help. Above all, at this stage there was no sense in and around Belleville that a predator was on the loose. None of Williams's lingerie raids in Tweed had been reported, and the murder of Comeau down the highway in Brighton two months earlier looked to be a self-contained episode. The only local sex crimes that had stirred any public alarm thus far had been the two strange home invasions and photo sessions in Tweed, back in September, and most Belleville residents were entirely unaware of these.

The Belleville cop's judgment call would look different had the Pathfinder been sitting by the road or in some other public place, appearing abandoned. But it was parked on private property in a field, and there were any number of reasons why it might be there, even if it did look out of place. Up and down rural Highway 37, plenty of other trucks and vehicles were not parked neatly outside their owners' houses either. In this instance, the remarkable thing is that when driving by at night the officer had noticed anything at all, and had taken the trouble to stop to knock at the door.

Williams waited a little longer in the darkness, then drove back up Highway 37 to his cottage, where he changed his clothes and collected what he needed for what he was planning.

Then he headed back down the highway toward Belleville and Lloyd's house, leaving his BlackBerry behind.

This time Lloyd was home, her white Dodge Neon in the driveway. Once again Williams parked his Pathfinder on the far northeast end of the property by the fence line and walked around the edge of the field, pausing at the back to watch the house. Then he moved in. Lloyd had returned sometime after 10:15 p.m., and at 10:36 had sent a text message to her friend Dorian O'Brian telling him she was safely home. It was the last time anyone ever heard from Jessica Lloyd. She was in bed asleep when Williams re-entered her house, this time through the patio door.

The precise timing of this second entry is unclear, but the first photos Williams took were time-stamped at 1:19 a.m. on January 29, suggesting he came back at around 1:00 a.m. As with Jane Doe and Laurie Massicotte, he had intended to strike or seize Lloyd while she slept, he later told police, but she awoke as he stood over her. He ordered her to lie on her stomach, then he tied her hands behind her back with a rope he had brought along and blindfolded her with duct tape.

For the next three hours, he orchestrated another horrific photo session, taking scores of still photos and recording long segments of videotape, all of it illuminated with elaborate arrangements of table lamps. Throughout the long sexual assaults he constantly gave his victim orders, with which, plainly terrified, she complied. "You want to survive this, don't you?" he says calmly at one point. Lloyd nods and says yes. "Okay, good, you are doing good," Williams responds.

As with the murder of Comeau, he videoed himself taking still shots with a handheld camera, close-ups recording the multiple attacks in nightmarish detail. But that was not the worst of it. He also forced Lloyd to perform oral sex on him, placing a zip tie around her neck and telling her: "I feel something I don't like,

I pull on that and you die, got it?" As well, he compelled her to pose in various pieces of underwear, still blindfolded, her arms still tied behind her back with rope.

Like Comeau, Lloyd displayed extraordinary courage. Comeau, who was physically strong for her size and had some knowledge of self-defense, fought back physically. Lloyd struggled for her life by doing something that in such a terrifying situation was surely harder still: she made every effort to placate her attacker by cooperating with him—behavior that must have been truly unbearable for such a strong-spirited, independent woman, but which was her only hope.

As the attack was under way, there was another sighting of Williams's Pathfinder parked in the cornfield. At around 3:20 a.m., a local handyman named Lyle Barker and a relative were driving along Highway 37 when they spotted it. It looked odd, as it had to the Belleville policewoman, and after Lloyd's mysterious disappearance began to reach the local airwaves later the same day, they informed police of what they had seen, though they could not say what kind of a truck it was.

Sometime around four-thirty, Williams marched Lloyd across the field to his truck, still tied and blindfolded with duct tape, and with his captive in the passenger seat he drove up the highway to his deserted cottage in Tweed. An hour or so after arriving, he forced her to take a shower with him, and he photographed and videoed the spectacle, Lloyd still bound and blindfolded, the zip tie still around her neck. He then allowed her to sleep for a few hours, he told police. Meanwhile, he dispatched an early morning message to 8 Wing, saying he had stomach flu and would not be able to make the luncheon in the officers' mess at eleven.

Lloyd awoke, and at some point soon after, she experienced what appears in the video to be a seizure. Later, when the admitted facts of the case were entered as evidence, it was suggested by a relative of Lloyd's who attended the court hearing that she had no history of seizures, and that this one may have been a desperate ruse designed to induce Williams to take her to a hospital, as she repeatedly implored him to do. Something she said, captured on video, suggests it was indeed a trick. "We have to go [to the hospital] because I only have twenty minutes from the time it starts," Lloyd tells Williams, as if seizures were something she was familiar with. What is clear is that she is in enormous torment, and Williams again displays the same macabre quasi-compassion he had shown during the two sex attacks in Tweed, alternating between merciless cruelty and what in another context could be construed as concern. "What can I do to help you?" he says at one point. "Relax, Jessica, don't bite your tongue . . ." All the while, he kept taking more photographs and video, and as he did so she was crying, begging him to dress her and take her to the hospital.

Near the end of that segment of the video footage, as he is pulling a sweater over her head, she is still weeping. She says, "If I die, will you make sure my mom knows that I love her?" She continues to cry and Williams says nothing. And then he turns off the camera.

He pulled some clothes on her and allowed her to sleep some more, on the floor, shooting video of that too. She woke up at around one o'clock in the afternoon, and Williams told her he was going to set her free but that he first wanted to take some more pictures of her modeling her underwear, which he had brought with them from her house in Belleville. He used the zip tie again, for the same purpose as before, and he once again raped her, gazing calmly into the video camera as he did so.

After several more hours of degrading sexual assault, Williams dressed Lloyd in her blue jeans and a hooded Roots sweatshirt, gave her some fruit to eat and told her once again that she was going to survive. And perhaps she believed him, because in one of the most chilling moments of the video she appears sitting up on the bed, still blindfolded with duct tape and with her hands still roped together behind her back, but with a broad smile on her face.

At around eight-fifteen that evening, still tied up and now with duct tape over her mouth as well as her eyes, so she had to breathe through her nose, Lloyd was led toward the door of the cottage. As she walked through the living room, Williams clubbed her from behind with the same heavy red flashlight he had used in his earlier attacks on the other women, cracking her skull and knocking her unconscious. He then strangled her with a piece of rope. He told police it was the only time he hit Lloyd during her almost-24-hour ordeal, and that before he did so he had spent some hours pondering how to murder his prisoner. But it was not the blow that killed her; the cause of death was strangulation, the autopsy found. As she lay on the floor of his cottage, blood pooling around her head, Williams took three more photographs.

He carried Lloyd's body out to the garage and cleaned up some of the blood in the living room. Then, somewhere between nine and ten that evening, he got into his Pathfinder and drove back down Highway 37 to the 8 Wing base in Trenton, where he said he spent the night.

Once again, Williams was able to resume his normal life with astonishing ease. Early the next morning, Saturday, January 30, he flew with some troops to southern California, where they were to do some training, and he returned to Trenton early the same evening. He worked in his office for a while, then drove to Ottawa, rejoined his wife at their new home in Westboro and spent the rest of the weekend there.

On the Tuesday night, Williams drove back to Tweed and retrieved Lloyd's clothed, frozen body from the garage, and late that evening or early Wednesday morning he took her out to the thick woodland that surrounds Cary Road, a little-traveled gravel road fifteen minutes' drive east of his cottage—the same patch of woods where Larry Jones's hunting camp was. He left Lloyd's body in a clump of rocks, not concealed as such but hard to find unless a person knew the precise place, particularly at night with snow on the ground. After he confessed, Williams had to take police there, in handcuffs, because they were unable to locate it. It's a lonely and distinctly spooky spot, about forty feet in from the road, surrounded in winter by bare deciduous trees, and unmarked by any memento or shrine.

It took Williams no more than a minute or two to dump Lloyd's body there. Then he returned to his cottage on Cosy Cove Lane and did some more cleaning up, vacuuming and wiping the floors as best he could and doing the same with his Pathfinder.

That Wednesday evening he traveled to Toronto to attend a top-secret conference addressing security plans for the upcoming G8 and G20 summit meetings in June. His task was to help coordinate the arrivals and departures of the hundreds of dignitaries, and to assist in arrangements for protecting the airspace. The meeting was held at the Denison Armoury, headquarters for Joint Task Force Central, which coordinates army, air force and navy operations in Ontario. Brigadier-General John Collin sat at the head of the table, surrounded by his support staff and the various commanders, all of them gazing at a PowerPoint presentation projected onto a big screen. Williams didn't say much, according to a person who was there.

The meeting ended sometime after midnight and he drove back to Tweed right away, arriving home in the early hours of Thursday, February 4. In the morning, he went to work at 8 Wing.

14

"CALL ME RUSS, PLEASE"

When he walked into Interrogation Room 206 at the Elgin Street police building on Sunday, four days after dumping Jessica Lloyd's body in the woods and then attending the meeting in Toronto, Russ Williams was familiar enough with rudimentary criminal law procedures to know that he didn't have to say anything at all. The rules in Canada and the United States in these situations are not quite the same, in that an American suspect's so-called Miranda Rights provide slightly more leeway to abort a police interrogation than do their Canadian equivalent. Nonetheless, Williams was free at any point during the ten-plus hours of interrogation that lay ahead to exercise his constitutional rights and reach for the lawyer of his choice, who would assuredly have instructed him to clam up immediately. Doing so would have made him look even more suspicious than he already did, but it might have bought him some time.

And no one was more keenly aware of that fact than OPP Detective Sergeant Jim Smyth, as he prepared for what would be a duel of wits between two extremely intelligent men. By three in the afternoon, when the interrogation began, Smyth and his police colleagues were fairly sure Williams was responsible for the disappearance of Jessica Lloyd, among other crimes—the lie he'd told Constable Alexander at the roadblock about the sick child looked particularly suspicious—and as the afternoon wore on and the off-site investigation progressed, they became completely sure. The trick would be to keep Williams talking until he admitted his guilt.

But there is a catch-22 with extracting a confession. If a suspect has not been advised very clearly of his right to remain silent and of his right to counsel, any subsequent admission of guilt is not admissible as evidence in court, although it can be useful to police in other ways. On the other hand, once those rights have been read, more often than not the interview abruptly ends, especially in something as serious as a murder investigation. So for the detective stickhandling such a conversation, a key question is always one of timing: when will I advise the suspect of his rights? There is no obligation to do so at the outset, especially if the interrogation begins as an informal chat, but until that caution has been issued, any confession that spills forth is at best only half usable.

So it is instructive to see that Williams's rights were not only explained to him by Smyth at the very beginning, right after the pleasantries and the offer of coffee, but also repeatedly emphasized. Three separate times Williams is also told that audio and video recorders are monitoring everything taking place inside the small room. Such cautions are routine in police interrogations, but the thoroughness in this instance suggests two things. First, it was of paramount importance to the police that down the line no defense lawyer would be able to argue that Williams's rights had been infringed upon. But it also seems apparent that the detectives and the forensic psychiatrist who crafted what would later be hailed as a brilliant, even textbook interrogation believed Williams was confident he could steer his way through the shoals up ahead and would not be scared off.

Certainly he looked brash enough as he strode in, removed his yellow rain jacket, sat down, grinned into the closed-circuit video camera overhead and agreed that, yes, this was the first time in his life he'd been seriously questioned by police. He exuded cooperation, even as he prepared to give an account of events that was almost entirely a lie.

Yet even early into the interview he was clearly struggling, as shown for example in his insistence that he had met Comeau—"one of my people," as he called her—just one time, which as has been seen was by every indication a lie. They had flown together once, soon after he took command of 8 Wing in July 2009, he told Detective Sergeant Smyth, but he couldn't recall the precise circumstances. Here is what he said:

> Uh, I can't even remember I think it was a one day trip uh I did a number of trips uh in Canada transporting um our um you know troops for the first leg out of Edmonton uh and we tend to hop-scotch them across uh until they get into [unintelligible] so anyway I, I can't remember which trip it was but uh I did a number of them out to Edmonton just to pick up the troops bring them to Trenton and then uh put a fresh crew on and uh cause we fly out and back in the same day so pushing the edge of that uh fresh crew on and continue on after a couple hour delay.

His mind in overdrive, Williams was sputtering nonsense, as he did a moment later when asked when and where he learned about Comeau's death. Given the gravity of the news, most people would have a vivid recollection, especially a person as sharp-minded as the base commander. This was his tortured reply:

> Well, I can't remember what again what day that uh the message came in just a second um no I can't remember what day the day of the week but I um let me just think there was all a bunch of activity uh spun up as a result obviously [sighs] no I, I can't

remember the day of the week um I'm just trying to think through
the news reports I read no I, I'm sorry I can't remember what day
from act was that the um the MPs [military police] had learnt uh
of her death I think quite a bit after her body had been discovered . . . I had been in Ottawa earlier in the week uh for some
meetings over in uh in Gatineau for one of the um [unintelligible]
C17 [Globemaster aircraft] acquisitions, I was a project director
when I was here in Ottawa for that so just some follow up stuff on
that . . . so I had been here um at some point in that week again I
can't remember how the days all fell together but um I seem to
remember that I got this word shortly after having come back
from Ottawa I, seems to me it was the same week.

In detective jargon this is "dissonance"—a stress-induced
babble, as the brain races and tries to synchronize itself with the
torrent of words pouring out. The interrogator keeps the process going by smoothly but abruptly jumping from topic to topic,
as Smyth—a polygraph specialist—did throughout much of the
long interview.

When Smyth pursued the topic of a possible relationship
between Williams and Comeau, the suspect's response was
equally telling, but in a different way. "Is there any reason at all
that you can think of why Marie-France Comeau would have
specifically referenced you in some of her, uh, some of her writ-
ings?" he asked Williams.

It was an extraordinarily serious allegation: a woman found
raped and murdered was writing about you in her diary—what
do you have to say about that? An innocent person would almost
certainly respond along the lines of, "What? Are you kidding
me? Writing what?"

Williams replied, with a small chuckle: "No, not at all . . . absolutely not."

Smyth may have been bluffing about the diary. In a police interrogation, trickery is par for the course. A detective is allowed to lie and deceive, it's regarded as tradecraft, and in this instance the idea was to see which way Williams would jump. And he didn't jump at all; Smyth's hugely accusatory question seemed of little interest to him.

Smyth continued: ". . . Anything that she ever said to you that led you to believe that there may be something here more than a passing interest with her toward you?"

"No, not at all. We spent, you know, one flight together talking, I'd go back occasionally and talk, no I uh, if that's the case uh that's very surprising."

For Smyth, the game throughout consisted of maintaining the rapport he was steadily building. When he politely asks Williams for his fingerprints, a blood sample and an imprint of his boots, for example, an hour or so into the interview, he explains that the purpose is to "help me move past you in this investigation." No problem, Williams responds—but by now he must have been getting worried.

At the outset Smyth had made clear to Williams why he had been asked to come in. There was a clear geographical connection between him and the four occurrences the OPP were now examining as a group: the two sex attacks in Tweed in September, the murder of Comeau in Brighton two months later and now the disappearance of Lloyd. So when he was asked for the samples, Williams could have had no doubt that he might be in major trouble. But if he did not provide them, or if he walked out of the unlocked interview room—as Smyth had emphasized he could do anytime he pleased—he would look very suspicious indeed, and he knew those suspicions would not fade away, quite the reverse. It was at this point that his world began to crumble.

Smyth and his colleagues did not invent the interrogative technique that was about to unravel Williams's web of deceit. Rather, it is largely based on a type of counseling known as motivational interviewing, developed by two American clinical psychologists, Professors William Miller and Stephen Rollnick, who have done much critically acclaimed work with drug addicts. In contrast to many other forms of therapy, motivational interviewing does not confront the client and dwell on his/her failings. Instead, it is nonjudgmental and confidence-building, empathizing with the person's plight, gently pointing out the contrast between who they are and who they want to be, while offering possible solutions. Adapted to a police interrogation room, that translates into a dialogue built upon courtesy and expressions of friendliness and understanding, even warmth. All through the long interview, Smyth remains the quintessential nice guy trying to help Williams out of the jam he's in, displaying not a hint of frustration or aggression.

"I'll treat you with respect and I'll ask you to do the same for me," he says at the beginning. He stresses repeatedly that Williams doesn't have to talk to him. He explains that he is what's termed a person in authority, "probably similar to what you may be considered on your [air] base." He calls him "Bud," and "Russ." He tells him he has sat across the table from many other suspects in a similar predicament. His body language imitates that of Williams— leaning in, leaning out, sitting back, sometimes thoughtfully cupping his chin in one of his hands. In sum, Smyth behaves as though he is Williams's only friend on the planet. And that approach, which yielded such spectacular results, was not dreamed up on the fly. It reflected the fact that the detectives circling Williams knew that there were key buttons that could be pushed to great effect. But the empathy act was only part of what was going on in the interrogation room. Even as he seemed to drip with goodwill, Smyth kept piling on the pressure, peeling back layer after layer of damning facts, some of which were literally being uncovered as the interview progressed. Throughout the afternoon and early evening, as the search warrants were producing fresh evidence, Smyth was kept apprised of developments, periodically going out of the room to confer with colleagues while Williams was left alone with his thoughts. And he made sure that Williams understood what was going on.

But it had to be done piecemeal—the tire tracks, the boot prints, the anticipated DNA findings, the computer searches—because if Williams were to be confronted with everything at once, there was a risk he would be overwhelmed and simply shut down. So, even as he relentlessly turned the screws, Smyth also constantly emphasized that bad as things were, and rapidly getting worse, Williams could make them marginally less so by summoning up the fortitude to tell the truth. Otherwise, Smyth gently explained, he would be buried in the avalanche of evidence that was about to land. And where would his credibility be then? What if, for instance, Lloyd's body were to be found? "That might even happen tonight for all I know, once that happens then I don't know what other cards you would have to play . . . What are we going to do?" With or without you, it was made plain to the colonel, the facts were going to come out. "Your opportunity to take some control here and have some explanation that anyone's going to believe is quickly expiring," Smyth told him, tapping into Williams's innate, lifelong preference for order and control over chaos.

Long silences were another tool, as they often are in a police interrogation. For a suspect flailing to conceal the truth, it's unnerving to sit face to face with a detective who is talkative one moment and completely uncommunicative the next, staring hard all the while. The suspect's instinct is to try to fill the vacuum by saying something—anything, even if it doesn't make a lot of sense, as happened with Williams several times.

And there was an additional key element to the confession, masterfully deployed: Williams's extreme distress, articulated many times, over what his wife, Mary Elizabeth Harriman, was going through as her cherished, brand new house was being ripped apart by the police.

What follows is the exchange that immediately preceded Williams's admission of guilt. Smyth has just explained that, whatever efforts Williams might have made to clean up the contents of his computer, it was a futile exercise because the police tech guys could readily identify anything that had ever been there. Nor will any expense be spared, Smyth says; millions of dollars are available, whatever the police want for this investigation they will get, they don't even need to ask, that's how big a deal it all is. Even on a Sunday afternoon, sixty or seventy people are working on the file, he tells his quarry. By now Williams knows he is trapped, yet even as disaster looms, his instinct is to reach out to the friendly interrogator. "Call me Russ, please," he says, and Smyth is happy to oblige.

"So what am I doing, Russ?" Smyth concludes. "I put my best foot forward for you, bud, I really have, I don't know what else to do to make you understand the impact of what's happening here . . . Do we talk?"

Williams pauses, his body language saying everything as he slumps forward, gazing downward, defeated. "I want to, um, minimize the impact on my wife," he says finally.

"So do I," Smyth instantly replies.

"So how do we do that?" Williams asks.

"Well," Smyth responds. "You start by telling the truth."

Another long pause.

"Okay," Williams finally says, and Smyth repeats that word. Then Smyth asks: "All right, so where is she [Jessica Lloyd's body]?"

Williams pauses, then speaks the now-famous words that signaled the end. "You got a map?"

There was nothing accidental about Smyth's triumph. The OPP's Behavioural Sciences and Analysis Services unit to which he belongs has grown since it was created in 1995 and now comprises more than a hundred uniformed and civilian members. Based at OPP headquarters in Orillia, a hundred miles north of Toronto, the BSAS's broad mandate is behind-the-scenes sleuthing that not only probes the complexities of criminal behavior but also bridges the information gaps that often keep turf-conscious police at odds. The BSAS houses an array of skills and resources, from criminal profiling and polygraphy to threat assessment and the upkeep of the provincial sex offenders registry. The computerized backbone of the network is VICLAS, the national Violent Crime Linkage System, which constantly seeks links between seemingly disparate crimes. BSAS's expertise has a formidable reputation and is in constant demand by outside police departments. Only two other Canadian police agencies have their own behavioral science units: the RCMP and, more recently and on a smaller scale, the Sûreté du Québec.

A criminal profiler with BSAS before switching to its polygraph (lie detector) unit in 2007, and trained at the FBI's Behavioral Sciences Unit in Quantico, Virginia, Smyth was thus very much part of a team when he went into the interview room with Williams that Sunday afternoon, and several of the other players, unseen, were watching the on-camera proceedings with fascination. Also key to the outcome were the insights of foren-sic psychiatrist Dr. Peter Collins, attached to Toronto's Centre for Addiction and Mental Health and the OPP's longtime in-house expert in difficult cases, particularly sex-oriented ones. Dr. Collins declined to be interviewed about the case, but over the years he has taken a role in hundreds of investigations.

The approach taken by the interrogator varies as much as the suspect does, and in this instance it was clear that the top prior-ity had to be winning Williams's confidence, even as he lied, and retaining it. Smyth had ample experience to fall back on, his courteous demeanor honed in numerous homicide investiga-tions during his twenty-three years as a police officer. He began his career with York Regional Police, north of Toronto, trans-ferred to the OPP in 1997, and has taken a role in two of Ontario's most high-profile homicide investigations, both involving children. One was the 2003 kidnap/sex murder in Toronto of ten-year-old Holly Jones, in which software devel-oper Michael Briere was convicted. After Briere was interviewed by police without result, Smyth and others spent hours scruti-nizing the videotape and shaping a second interview that then produced an exhaustive confession. More recently, he was part of the team investigating the disappearance in April 2009 of eight-year-old Victoria (Tori) Stafford from Woodstock, Ontario, for which two people were later charged with murder. For more than three months Tori's body was unaccounted for, until Smyth pursued what he said was just a hunch and located it in a thickly wooded area near Mount Forest.

Polygraphy and its accoutrements, his specialty, have changed significantly since the early days. Gone is the scratchy pen that leaps upward on the graph paper when the suspect experiences a surge of stress, replaced by sophisticated computer software. What hasn't altered is the underlying physiology of the person under scrutiny, as the interviewer watches for fluctuations in blood pressure, pulse rate and electrodermal (skin) activity. And because that expertise is rooted in the art of separating truth from fiction, and detecting minute but significant shifts in tone, the polygrapher is one of the most sought-after experts when a challenging criminal interrogation arises. Many of the detectives who in 2006 interviewed suspects in the so-called Toronto 18 terror investigation, for example, were polygraph specialists. Which was one of the main reasons Smyth was sitting across from Colonel Russell Williams that day in the windowless interrogation room.

As the pre-confession portion of the interrogation unfolded and Williams's mind raced to keep track of what he was being told, not all of which was true, one of the tricks Smyth used to keep him off balance was to keep changing the topic. Look, for example, at this series of exchanges:

First Smyth asks him once again if he had ever seen or spoken to Jessica Lloyd. Williams reiterates that he never had.

"Okay, all right, and you mentioned doing some renovations at your property in Tweed there, I think you said something earlier about tearing up carpet, correct me if I'm wrong but . . ."

"Oh yeah."

"Okay, when did all that happen?"

"In two thousand and four or five."

"Okay, any recent uh renovations?"

"No."

"Okay alright, just want to make sure I'm covering all the bases here, okay what kind of tires do you have on your Pathfinder?"

"I think, um, I think they're Toyo."

"Okay but do you have a brand name or sorry . . . the make?"

"Um I don't, sorry the, the make is Toyo . . . I don't know the model."

Smyth then turns the conversation to the security system at CFB Trenton, and the swipe cards used to get in and out, noting that Williams didn't use his on the day Comeau was found murdered. Why would that be?

Williams explains that he was in Ottawa that day, attending a meeting and then having dinner with his wife.

So Smyth then wants to know where they had dinner, asking twice, but Williams can't remember. Nor can he recall the moment when he learned Comeau had been murdered, which may have been his most conspicuous memory lapse of all. When her death was first raised by Smyth, near the beginning of the interrogation, Williams had responded much more plausibly. "I mean, obviously [when] one of your people gets killed it gets your attention," he said.

But by now the lies were pouring forth. Never once, however, did Smyth interrupt Williams, correct him or point out the inconsistencies. To do so would have invited exactly what was not wanted: a yes-I-did, no-you-didn't confrontation that could spell an end to the interview.

So Smyth let him ramble on. Williams had dug himself into the deepest hole possible, and in his helpful way Smyth allowed him to keep on digging.

15

BETRAYAL IN UNIFORM

P eople often remember where they were when they learned of something that really stunned them, and so it was with the February 2010 arrest of Colonel Russell Williams. Outside military circles, very few Canadians had even heard of him, but because the allegations were so disturbing and because he'd been running the nation's top air base, with all the political weight that position carried, a wave of bewilderment swept the country. In Trenton, Tweed, Belleville and Brighton, the shock was still more severe, as consternation blended with an acute sense of personal betrayal. After the initial disbelief, few doubted the accusations were true. Mistakes get made in homicide investigations, everybody knew that. But rarely on this scale, and rarely when the killer has admitted his guilt, as became widely reported within a day or two of the murder and sexual-assault charges being laid. The fact that Williams had also confessed to dozens of bizarre lingerie thefts quickly leaked out too—another layer of disgrace. And for those who knew him personally, especially those who had known him well, or believed they had, the impact was devastating.

Major Garrett Lawless, an air force captain with 8 Wing's 437 Transport Squadron at the time, was in a French-language class when he got word. "My legs just gave, they buckled, though I didn't actually hit the floor. Some people in the room were

crying, others were angry, they were all out of their minds."
Many at the base sought counseling and even medical help. Jeff
Farquhar vomited on his living room floor when the news came
on the television that night. The distress that the news caused
the killer's wife, parents and other relatives can only be imagined. His brother, Harvey, faxed to news organizations a statement distancing himself from Russ's recent life, saying he and
his mother had largely lost touch with him. Then, like the rest
of the family and almost everyone else who'd ever been close to
Williams, he retreated behind a wall of silence.

News of the arrest quickly traveled abroad. Britons followed it
with particular interest, not just because Williams was born in the
Midlands, but because the accused rapist-murderer had once been
the personal pilot to the Queen. U.S. television networks, the
Associated Press and the *New York Times* picked up the story too.

And for a handful of women in the Trenton–Belleville area,
the bombshell was especially alarming, because it stirred memories of disparate encounters that at the time had seemed ordinary
enough but which now took on an ominous cast.

Among those who had had an unusual experience is great-
grandmother Buelah Beatty, who lives alone on the outskirts of
Tweed, close to the cutoff leading up to Cosy Cove Lane. In mid-
January, a couple of weeks before Jessica Lloyd was kidnapped
and murdered, Beatty had twice spotted a tall man lurking outside her home in the predawn darkness, clad in a khaki coat. The
second time, she called out to him. He shouted back that he was
looking for a dog, jumped into his vehicle and sped away. Beatty
couldn't see his face, but later found footprints in the snow outside a side window. And it was around the same time that Beatty's
twenty-year-old granddaughter Cattia Beatty, who was staying
with her at the time, said she had been approached and proposi-
tioned by a man whom she was later certain was Williams; she

recognized his Pathfinder too. The incident in a small park overlooking Stoco Lake left the granddaughter shaken and Beatty wondering if the two sets of circumstances were connected, and if her granddaughter was being stalked. "It was very scary after we learned what was going on," she says. "Why Tweed? It was always so quiet. I've never locked my doors before, never. Well, we sure do now. I'm still a little leery of going out at night."

There had been other strange encounters. In the city of Trenton, home to the 8 Wing base, at least two other women who recognized Williams's post-arrest photo told of him appearing unexpectedly on their doorsteps in recent months. In one instance he claimed he was seeking directions, saying he was looking for Wooler Road (a major thoroughfare, not a side street). In the other he had inquired about properties for sale in the area, and asked if he could step in for a moment to see what a house of that design looked like from the inside. (His request was refused.)

Williams appears to have been doing some clandestine research as well. A female civilian employee at the 8 Wing base recounted a conversation with him in which he'd remarked on some house renovations she was doing. He mentioned other details about her home life and told her casually that he'd been chatting with her husband, a pilot at the base. Only later did she discover that her husband had never spoken to Williams at all. Two young women in Belleville who share a home also recalled peculiar conversations with the base commander, in which he seemed to know all kinds of details about their lives. He told each of them he'd been given the information by the other housemate, which was false.

In all those instances there was not much for police to pursue, since apparently no laws had been broken, except perhaps trespassing, and compared to the offenses Williams had already admitted committing, it was relatively minor stuff. But there was at least one other encounter that could have turned out very badly indeed. In response to a magazine article about Williams, a woman wrote in alleging that she was sitting in a park in Trenton on a Sunday afternoon in August 2009 when a very tall man approached her. He left his car idling while he offered to take her for a ride, but she refused. And when she later saw Williams's picture in the newspaper after his arrest, she was sure he was the mysterious stranger. Her account could not be verified, however.

After confessing to Smyth on the Sunday evening, Williams did not remain in Ottawa for long. In the early hours of Monday morning he was driven to the woods outside Tweed where he had left Jessica Lloyd's body, and he showed Smyth and another detective the spot, which police had been unable to locate despite fairly precise directions.

Later that day, he appeared briefly in court in Belleville, where the charges of murder, sexual assault and forcible confinement were read out. From there he was taken to the Quinte Detention Centre in Napanee, halfway between Belleville and Kingston, where he would remain for the next eight months. He made no effort to secure bail, and like most accused murderers had little prospect of getting it.

Williams's new home must have been a rude shock to him. Detention centers for accused criminals awaiting trial or a bail hearing tend to be more confined and generally less welcoming than federal penitentiaries, where there are programs for the inmates and where the rhythm of daily life lends a certain stability. The 228-bed Napanee lockup, visible from Highway 401, is a bleak little compound of concrete and rusting chain-link fence, with a remote-controlled wire-mesh gate that creaks open each time a car drives in or out. Visitors must park on an adjacent mud lot, walk to the gate and speak through the intercom before they're allowed through.

For anyone locked up there, the crashing boredom and the nail-biting uncertainty of not knowing what the future holds are bad enough. But for Williams, daily life was even more restrictive, because on arrival he immediately had to be segregated from other prisoners. There were several reasons for this: he was an accused sex offender, always the lowest and most despised rung in the prison hierarchy; until his arrest he'd been a person of considerable authority, which to many jail inmates is not much different from having been a cop; and added to that was his overnight notoriety. Placed among other prisoners, he'd have been an instant target, so he was lodged in one of the cramped protective-custody cells. That meant being locked up twenty-three hours a day on most days, with one hour to shower, use the phone and walk around the small exercise yard, usually alone. It's an environment that's a recipe for despair, similar to the circumstances in which Williams will almost certainly spend the rest of his life.

What he did not do was stop speaking to the police—quite the contrary. He kept talking and talking, even after he was persuaded (possibly by his wife) to engage the services of Ottawa defense lawyer Michael Edelson. Court records show that while incarcerated at the detention center in Napanee, Williams was interviewed by Smyth six more times—three times in February, twice in March and once in May.

It's unusual in Canada for someone accused of first-degree murder to keep cooperating with the police, unless there's some chance the charge might get knocked down to second-degree murder, a near impossibility in this instance. Unlike manslaughter, which commonly involves an unintended homicide, second-degree murder typically implies that the killing was deliberate but not planned ahead of time. First-degree murder, by contrast, means the homicide was either 1) planned, 2) committed during a sexual assault or 3) committed while the victim was being forcibly confined. The killings with which Williams was charged seemed to qualify on all three grounds. His willingness to continue talking to Smyth thus speaks volumes, not only about his resigned state of mind but about the rapport Smyth had built with him.

In the outside world, meanwhile, Canadians in general and the military in particular were struggling to make sense of an accused sex killer who'd given no clue whatever about his double life. Nor was there any insight from the police, who over the entire eight months of the investigation held just one press conference, at the very outset, when the murder charges were announced. When Williams finally pleaded guilty, the facts of the case were laid out in considerable detail, but until then the police probe remained one of the most secretive ever seen in Ontario, and those involved received no-nonsense warnings from OPP commissioner Julian Fantino (now a Conservative member of Parliament) that they would be wise to keep things that way. Similarly stern instructions came from the provincial attorney general's office in Toronto.

All through the months of brief videolink court appearances and pretrial discussions, the perennial concern among police and prosecutors was that leaks might undermine their case, by providing ammunition for the defense to contend that Williams's right to a fair trial had been compromised. There was also speculation the saturation media coverage in and around Belleville would prompt Edelson to seek a change of venue, a move that would probably have foundered, given that the story was being aired from coast to coast.

But because the events were so extraordinary and the competition for scoops was so intense, the leaks kept coming, the principal ones being that Williams had confessed to murder and sexual assault, that he had also admitted to dozens of fetish-driven burglaries, and that he seemed to have no interest in pretending otherwise. As early as April, six months before he was convicted, the *Globe and Mail* reported that Edelson and the prosecution team headed by Hastings County Crown attorney Lee Burgess had reached an agreement in principal that would see Williams plead guilty to everything.

And because of his acknowledged guilt, the big issue that hovered over the proceedings was whether this was just the tip of some frightful iceberg. It seemed nearly impossible that at age forty-four, a respected military man with an apparently flawless track record would suddenly plunge into a netherworld of sexual deviancy, rape and murder. Surely he must have started before, the thinking went. Williams, however, assured Smyth and the other detectives that he had not, even though his unusual sexual preoccupations stretched back many years. And to some extent they believed him, insofar as there seemed to be no evidence anywhere of prior crimes.

But no one else knew what to think. In the months ahead, when Williams appeared several times in court via videolink from the detention center, frequently on hand was his air force colleague Lieutenant-Colonel Tony O'Keeffe, who had known Williams for nine years and was now acting as a kind of liaison officer between the military and the colonel. O'Keeffe paid several visits to Williams in jail, and he had the courage to talk briefly to reporters about what he had found, summing up the feelings of so many others. "The guy in front of the courts is not the guy I know, this is beyond anything I can imagine," he said after an appearance by Williams in March. "I'm really uncomfortable, I don't even know what I'm looking at."

Without exception, everyone who'd had any relationship with the killer over the years and was willing to talk about it (few though they were) seemed to be saying the same thing, often using identical language: the Russ Williams they'd known was an entirely decent human being, albeit sometimes a slightly awkward one, smart, thoughtful, generous and 100 percent reliable. Now it seemed as though they had been completely deceived. "I worked every day with this man," said Captain Anne Morin, 8 Wing's chief public affairs officer. "He has been nothing but a good leader and to hear of the alleged acts the man has done comes as a complete surprise and shock."

The dismay was widespread. In Tweed, which finally had an explanation for the two sex attacks in September that had so traumatized the village, most people hadn't even been aware of Williams. Then they were learning that a sex killer had been quietly living among them. "And if we were shocked, think of what it was like for the City of Quinte West and the people around Trenton," says Tweed reeve Jo-Anne Albert. "This was someone who was the father to everybody on that base and all of a sudden he's accused of these horrendous crimes."

Kathleen Rankine, morning news anchor at Belleville's Cool 100 country radio station and a staunch, longtime supporter of the military, spoke for many when she described being not just deeply perturbed at the revelations but also angry. "'How dare you? How dare you do this?' That's what everybody was thinking about [Williams]. To take that trust and just throw it all away. For me, sitting in a newsroom writing the story every half hour, trying to find different ways to write it, I found myself saying repeatedly, 'You bastard.' Every time I looked at his name on the page, that was my reaction. Then, when the eighty-two break-in charges were laid, it was like, 'Oh my God, now what?'"

It was the same on Raglan Street in Brighton, where Comeau had lived and died, and which was home to many other former and current members of the armed forces. "It was just unbelievable," recalls neighbor Terry Alexander, who had seen Comeau's boyfriend, Paul Bélanger, stumble out of her house after finding her body. "A top-notch colonel in the forces? Who would ever, ever have suspected?"

And in Belleville, the horror blended with a sea of grief over the dreaded confirmation that Jessica Lloyd was dead. On a frigid Saturday, five days after her body was located near Cary Road in Tweed, close to a thousand mourners converged on the city's John. R. Bush Funeral Home to pay their respects and articulate their affection for one of the small city's best-liked young women. Air force personnel wore black armbands, the strains of "Amazing Grace" were piped out to the overflow crowd in the parking lot, and along with praise for the police, the many tributes included one from her cousin, John Lloyd, who lauded her as "a positive person who could find the light in darkness."

For a while, the bad news in and around Belleville just kept coming. Year-to-year statistics show that, as in most Canadian communities, crime in what has long been called "the Friendly City" was actually falling. A clutch of unrelated homicides, however, suggested otherwise, and one of the worst took place in March: the exceptionally brutal double shooting deaths of a mother and her fourteen-year-old daughter in their Mountain View home, six miles south of Belleville. The alleged killer was an eighteen-year-old, Dean Brown, also accused of badly wounding his former girlfriend in what prosecutors contended had been a fit of jealous rage. Brown had also once lived in Tweed; and in May that village became the site of yet another homicide, when a 27-year-old Mississauga man was beaten to death in the campground area of Trudeau Park. Four visitors were subsequently charged with murder. There was no discernible pattern to the half dozen or so killings that bracketed Williams's arrest, but as short-term crime trends go, through the eyes of some they made the Quinte region look like Murder Central.

As spring turned to summer, the Canadian military, too, had to struggle with other unwelcome baggage. In May, the commander of the 2,800 Canadian troops in Afghanistan, Brigadier-General Daniel Ménard, was ousted from his post and brought back to Canada for allegedly having a sexual relationship with a female soldier under his command. In July, the same thing happened to Colonel Bernard Ouellette, chief of staff at the United Nations mission in Haiti, over allegations he had an improper relationship with a civilian employee working at UN headquarters in Port-au-Prince. Then, in October, during the same week Williams was convicted, infantry captain Robert Semrau was demoted and dismissed from the armed forces for shooting a wounded Taliban insurgent in Afghanistan, in what Semrau—the first Canadian soldier ever prosecuted for a battlefield death—said was a mercy killing.

But those black marks paled against the stain left by the Williams arrest, and along with the collective shock, the blame game swiftly commenced. There were isolated anecdotal reports of soldiers in Trenton being heckled or even spat at by passersby, but nobody suggested that was a strong public sentiment. The consensus among the citizens of the area was, and remains, that the crimes Williams was charged with were an aberration never seen before, and that they had no bearing on the Canadian military as an organization. Instead, the prevailing instinct was to rally round the troops and reassure them that they were still held in great esteem and affection.

But at the more rarefied high-command level, the questions were pouring in fast and furious. How could a sex killer and pervert have been put in charge of Canada's most important air base? Were no checks and balances in place? How had Williams been able to rise through the ranks undetected? Why had the safety nets failed? Three days after the charges were laid, General

Walter Natynczyk, Chief of the Defence Staff of the Canadian Armed Forces, held a press conference at the Trenton air base that Williams had commanded, in the cavernous passenger terminal used by troops on their way to and from Afghanistan. Flanked by Lieutenant-General André Deschamps, who headed the air force, and navy chief Vice-Admiral David Rouleau, along with other senior officers, Natynczyk described how the criminal charges felt like "a body blow, and I was winded," but said that his message to the troops on the base earlier that day had been clear. "I told them to stand proud . . . Let's move forward." Canada's top soldier also spoke of how the "sacred trust" invested in the military had been violated, and of how an administrative review was already under way. "We need to know, did we miss something?' he admitted, on what must have been one of the most difficult days of his 35-year career. Then a reporter thrust a microphone in Natynczyk's face and asked him in an accusing tone if he felt "personally responsible" for having a killer on the payroll.

It was the wrong question. As the complexities of Williams's mental disorder emerged, it became more and more clear that the killer/rapist-in-waiting had stayed off the radar not just because his crimes seemed so wholly out of character and apparently started so late in life, but because they were all committed during the off-work hours of his highly compartmentalized existence. On the job, the near-universal consensus over the previous twenty years had been that his performance was exemplary.

Williams's military medical records contain no mention of mental disorders of any kind. Like everyone else in the armed forces, he'd been subject to an annual performance review, and like everyone else, his in-house career file included a psychology component. In the run-up to each of his half dozen promotions, he'd been examined for any sign of problems in his professional and personal life, and from what's known there were no red flags at all. The military panels that interview candidates for promotion, however, don't normally include psychologists.

There are some members of the armed forces who undergo regular psychological screening. They include members of the special forces (unorthodox combat specialists), instructors who teach captivity survival, military police and soldiers who work in the intelligence field. The screening comprises aptitude tests, clinical psychological tests and the MMPI, short for Minnesota Multiphasic Personality Inventory, commonly used by mental health experts seeking to identify personality structure and detect signs of any underlying psychopathology. The results get analyzed, and the person is asked to address any troublesome issues that may have surfaced.

But most officers rising through the ranks of the Canadian Armed Forces don't get screened, and neither do pilots—although they do in some other countries, including Australia. John Proctor, vice president of Ottawa-based Risk Operations, specializing in security and risk management, is familiar with the military's screening process and suggests its scope could be broader. "If you were extremely bright, you could probably dodge a lot of it. So could [Williams] have bluffed his way through it? Absolutely, because he doesn't fit any profile whatsoever. But if you're not given [the screening] in the first place, there's no chance. He would have done nothing that would have required psychological screening, ever, including getting his security clearance. This is one of the things Canadian Forces is struggling with, and over the years there's been many different ways of looking at it."

Jack Vance, the retired lieutenant-general who lived just down the road from Williams in Tweed but was unaware of it, also knows a thing or two about the promotions process. For five years he oversaw the forces' personnel operations, and he believes that no screening system could have detected Williams's latent criminal instincts. "None of [the major public-oriented] professions use psychological assessment of people. There's no careful decision-making like that," he says, his sense of betrayal by Williams still raw. "Promotions and performance reviews have a completely different focus. You're looking as carefully as possible at core principles: integrity and truthfulness, loyalty, selflessness, self-discipline. The rest is devoted to how well you do your job, and how well you get along with people."

Yet another puzzle, particularly after word leaked out that Williams's house in Ottawa had contained a trove of incriminating evidence, involved his wife, Mary Elizabeth Harriman. How was it possible for her not to have known, or at least suspected, what her husband had been up to for the past two years and more? Along with Williams's parents and many of his closest friends and acquaintances, Harriman uttered not a single word in public, nor did she attend any of the court proceedings, though she did visit her husband regularly at the Quinte Detention Centre. All the police would say was that she was in no way suspected of having been an accomplice or of having broken the law in any other way.

After it transpired that Williams had confessed, many were wondering what he planned to do next. He told Detective Sergeant Smyth that he had no interest in retaining counsel, and that one of his priorities, along with trying to keep Harriman's distress to a minimum, was to keep his legal costs down. The widespread public assumption was therefore that matters would be dealt with quickly, probably within weeks, and that a quick confession would translate into a quick guilty plea. But it didn't work out that way. A few days after Williams was charged, he hired Michael Edelson, well known in Ottawa despite his low profile and with a long-standing reputation as one of the city's most combative legal advocates.

Edelson has had numerous prominent clients over the years, many of them in serious trouble with the law. He defended Margaret Trudeau, the former prime minister's estranged wife, on a charge of impaired driving, and secured an acquittal by successfully arguing that her right to counsel had been breached. More recent clients have included Ottawa mayor Larry O'Brien, found not guilty of influence peddling, and Roman Catholic bishop Raymond Lahey, accused of possessing and importing child pornography.

At age sixty, Edelson was famous for his forceful style. At a conference of the Ottawa Defence Counsel Association more than twenty years earlier, he had advised lawyers defending clients accused of sexual assault to "whack the complainant hard" at the preliminary hearing, the pretrial forum where it's decided if there's sufficient evidence to proceed. "My own experience is, the preliminary inquiry is the ideal place in a sexual assault trial to try and win it all," Edelson told his audience, in remarks first reported by the *Lawyers Weekly* publication in 1988.

> You can do things . . . with a complainant at a preliminary inquiry in front of a judge which you would never try to do for tactical, strategic reasons—sympathy of the witness, etcetera—in front of a jury . . . You have to go in there as a defence counsel and whack the complainant hard at the preliminary. You have to do your research, do your preparation, put together your contradictions, get all the medical evidence, get all the Children's Aid Society reports, and you've got to attack the complainant with all you've got, so that he or she will say "I'm not coming back in front of 12 good citizens to repeat this bullshit story that I've just told the judge."

Other useful tactics, Edelson told the conference, include hiring a private investigator to tape-record conversations with key Crown witnesses, exploring a witness's history of drug use, unearthing criminal records and researching documents from other court proceedings.

His no-holds-barred approach probably made Edelson the most effective advocate Williams could have had. And there could be no issue regarding his discretion. Unlike many other lawyers who defend famous or infamous people, Edelson was not a darling of the media; he would have nothing whatever to say in front of the microphones in the months ahead, despite the huge interest in Williams. Nor did he attend most of his client's brief court appearances in Belleville, dispatching a local lawyer in his place, and entering the court through a side door when he did show up, to avoid the press.

Edelson's problem, however, was that he was playing with an empty deck. Williams had given the police all they needed for a successful prosecution, including the location of his second murder victim's body and the two computer hard drives containing highly detailed accounts of his many crimes, all carefully itemized and stored. As well, he just kept talking to the police, so much so that toward the end, Smyth advised him that—thanks very much, Russ—the police had pretty well everything they needed.

As Edelson and his colleagues began sifting through the thousands of pages of evidence disclosed by the Crown, the police were looking hard at Williams's past. To them too, it seemed highly improbable that he had launched his career as a fetish-driven sex killer so late in life. So they cast their net as widely as they could, examining every phase of his adult life.

In the world of unsolved homicides, DNA technology has become by far the most valued tool, a constantly refined science that grows more precise almost every year. One of the newest frontiers is what's termed "familial search," which tracks connections between the similar but not identical DNA markers shared by close relatives. And it might be thought that when a suspect has confessed to murder and has provided a DNA sample, it would be a straightforward task to run it through the national, RCMP-administered DNA bank on a sort of fishing expedition, to see if it ties in with any other crimes. But until the person has actually been convicted, Canadian law doesn't allow that. Case-by-case analysis can be done; if DNA has been obtained in one investigation, it can be compared with the sample found in another. But for the same reason a search warrant must, for example, specify an apartment number rather than blanket the whole building, preconviction DNA comparisons have to be specific.

There were, nonetheless, plenty of other unsolved murder cases for the Williams investigation team to look at, all involving women. As seen, evidence ruled out any involvement in the 1987 Margaret McWilliam rape-strangulation in Scarborough, where Williams had graduated from university a year earlier. Another case police looked into was the June 2001 slaying of nineteen-year-old Nova Scotia native Kathleen MacVicar, found raped and stabbed to death at the 8 Wing base in Trenton. Williams, who had been living and working in Ottawa at the time, was swiftly excluded in that murder too.

Police in Halifax contacted the OPP in connection with three unsolved murders that took place while Williams was at the Shearwater, Nova Scotia, base from 1992 to 1994: the killings of Andrea King, 18; Shelley Connors, 17; and Kimber Leanne Lucas, 23. In all three, no connection could be drawn. The same was true with an old Winnipeg murder that had occurred in 1991, that of Glenda Morrisseau, 19, while Williams was at the nearby Portage la Prairie flight school. And there was interest in

U.S. law-enforcement circles too. Detectives in North Carolina, where Williams's father, David, had a home, inquired whether there might be a link to the double murder in 2008 of Allison Jackson Foy and Angela Nobles Rothen, both stabbed to death and dumped in a patch of woods near Wilmington. The OPP detectives handling the Williams investigation found no link in that case nor in any of the dozens of other cold cases whose details piled up on their desks.

"They went over everything," says a police source familiar with the Williams case, "his timeline, his travels, his credit card receipts, and they went looking in all those areas for different occurrences that would match anything he is now known to have done, and they've come up with nothing. They've also responded to over a hundred requests from [other police] agencies looking at the possibility of him being involved in some of their unsolved cases. There's zip."

What did emerge a few weeks after Williams was charged with the two murders and the two sex attacks was confirmation that they had been preceded by two years of fetish burglaries. Word of the break-ins had already leaked out, but the sheer number of charges laid in April—eighty-two in all—brought astonishment. Apart from anything else, how had the commander of such a busy air base found the *time* to commit so many break-ins? And that was before it became widely known that Williams's obsession with photographing, uploading and cataloging his stolen lingerie collection, including countless pictures of him wearing his trophies, had generated an inventory of homemade pornography that ran into thousands of images. Managing that, too, would have been time-consuming, even if he didn't often look at the pictures, which presumably he did. Add to that his writing of highly detailed accounts of each burglary—who, where, when, how—and his energy seems almost inhuman.

So how *did* he find the time? One answer is that in the virtual world of email and texting, a decision maker in a high position can do a great deal of his work from afar, which meant, in Williams's case, by means of his well-thumbed BlackBerry. But in addition, an intriguing partial explanation comes from veteran and greatly respected psychologist Bill Marshall, attached to Rockwood Psychological Services in Kingston, Ontario, who has examined and treated thousands of sex offenders over the past forty years. What most people underestimate, he suggests, is how much time they spend on small tasks and small diversions that are of little consequence: ten minutes here, twenty minutes there. Over the course of a day it adds up to more time than you might think. If all those bits of time are devoted single-mindedly to what really interests—or obsesses—you, Marshall suggests, a big window opens. "I had a client back in the seventies who admitted to having molested 426 boys over a 26-year period," he recounts. "And you'd think to yourself, 'What the hell else was he doing?' Because he had to hustle the boys—it was not just the time he spent molesting them. He was obsessive-compulsive, and he kept detailed diaries."

So while the man was incarcerated in Kingston Penitentiary (where Williams is now) Marshall and his colleagues examined his diaries, which itemized everything he'd done. The remarkable conclusion: his crimes took up only 8 percent of his waking hours. The rest of his time was devoted to being a law-abiding citizen with an ordinary life. "He had a job, he was an accountant, he went to an old folks' home, and he read them stories on a Sunday. I was quite amazed, really. You and I do so many humdrum things every day that are pro-social but boring, but this gave me a different way of looking at sexual offenders. Most of them are pro-social most of the time, not anti-social in the everyday sense, but very few of them go this far."

———

In his isolation cell at the Quinte Detention Centre, Williams spent a lot of time reading during his first weeks of confinement. To the jail staff he appeared reasonably good-spirited and compliant, sufficiently so that he was removed from the round-the-clock suicide watch that had monitored him when he first arrived. That meant he was allowed to wear regular prison clothes, instead of a suicide-proof type of smock that couldn't be ripped, to eat regular meals, rather than food that had to be eaten by hand (no utensils permitted), and to enjoy the occasional cup of hot tea.

But his apparent satisfaction with his conditions may have been a trick designed to lull his jailors into a false sense of security, because over the April 2010 Easter weekend, Williams tried to kill himself—and almost succeeded. He had collected some scraps of tinfoil and cardboard, compressed them into a cardboard toilet-roll cylinder and forced the tube down his throat, jamming the lock in his cell door with more tinfoil before he did so. But first, he'd written a message on the wall of his cell, using packets of mustard he'd squirreled away from his meals, telling the world that he'd put his affairs in order as best he could, and that he found his plight unbearable. Through the cell-door window, jail guards spied him choking and managed to force the door open and save his life.

After that, there was a guard watching Williams twenty-four hours a day. But Colonel Mustard, as he was mockingly nicknamed, still appears to have been plotting, because among other things, he began writing letters in code. The sentences alternated between everyday descriptions of his dull life behind bars and gibberish that no one could comprehend, a source inside the center said. There was a short-lived hunger strike too, whose purpose was never clear. The speculation was that

Williams and his lawyers were planning to argue that he wasn't mentally capable of standing trial, meaning he didn't understand what was going on. Shortly before his guilty plea, he was sent to Ottawa for a psychiatric examination, but whatever the outcome of that assessment, the issue of mental fitness never arose in the court proceedings.

In between his short videolinked court appearances, Williams was able to socialize a little, because he was not the only prisoner in the segregation wing. Southeastern Ontario experienced a rash of unrelated homicides in 2009–10, and among the dozen-plus accused killers awaiting trial in the Quinte Detention Centre at the time were Mohammed Shafia, 56, his wife Tooba Yahya Mohammed, 40, and their son Hamed Shafia, 19. Of Afghan origin, the trio had lived in Dubai for many years before immigrating to Canada, and were now accused of murdering the three teenaged Shafia sisters, together with an older woman who was Mohammed Shafia's first wife. The four victims' bodies had been discovered in a submerged car in a Kingston canal in June 2009.

Father and son were in the Quinte segregation wing, standard procedure for inmates accused of murdering women. And Williams, who had once spent six months in Dubai as commander of Camp Mirage, was occasionally allowed to step outside his cell to talk to them. He would spend hours talking to Hamed Shafia about the Middle East, a prison guard said, and perhaps he appreciated the diversion. Certainly it was better than thinking about what lay ahead.

The suicide bid, the message in mustard, the letters in code, the hunger strike: to many of those watching the Williams case and hearing bits of news and gossip that trickled out of the Napanee detention center, it all looked as if he was scheming. And when it transpired that in March, six weeks after Williams was arrested and charged, he and his wife, Mary Elizabeth

Harriman, had expedited a kind of property swap, the suspicions grew. Property records at the Ontario land registry office show that on March 26, Harriman acquired full ownership of the couple's new home in Ottawa by paying her husband $244,500— $62,000 in cash and $182,500 worth of assumed mortgage debt. Simultaneously Williams gained exclusive title to the much less valuable cottage on Cosy Cove Lane where he had killed Jessica Lloyd, for which he paid nothing.

On May 6, the young woman he had blindfolded, stripped and photographed in the first of his two home-invasion sex assaults back in September 2009 cried foul. That day, Jane Doe filed a civil lawsuit in Belleville demanding nearly $2.5 million in damages from Williams for what she described as his "harsh, vindictive, malicious, horrific and reprehensible" conduct. Her statement of claim contended she'd been so traumatized by what he did to her that she'd been compelled to develop "certain psychological mechanisms in order to survive the horrors of the assault," including "denial, repression, disassociation and guilt." Jane Doe said she'd lost the ability to trust other people, and that for practical purposes she'd become unemployable. Her claim broke down as follows: $500,000 in general damages for pain and suffering; $500,000 for loss of future income; $500,000 for aggravated damages; and a further $500,000 in punitive damages. She also sought $250,000 in special damages for lost income; a further $100,000 for unspecified special damages; and $100,000 for the therapy and medical attention she anticipated she would need.

Along with Williams, the lawsuit also targeted Harriman, claiming that the "secret" property exchange—"unadvertised" might be the better word—was a ruse to forestall any civil claims against Williams for monetary compensation: if he had no assets, he would be hard put to pay anybody for anything. The transaction had occurred "in unusual haste" and under "suspicious circumstances," the lawsuit claimed, expressing concern that Williams and Harriman would "remove assets from the jurisdiction or otherwise dispose of or dissipate them in an effort to defeat the plaintiff in any attempt to recover upon the judgment, if the plaintiff is ultimately successful." The Belleville judge's response, on May 13, was to order Williams and Harriman not to sell or otherwise dispose of either piece of property until the lawsuit was resolved.

Williams issued no immediate statement of defense, and had still not filed one when he was convicted and sentenced. But Harriman did. In a sworn affidavit signed on June 2, she denied any wrongdoing and said the sole purpose of the property swap had been to provide her with a measure of stability in the years ahead, now that "my previously anticipated future and financial security have become jeopardized" as a result of the criminal charges against her husband. "The timing of the transfer was not unusual given the crisis facing the marriage," her Ottawa lawyer, Mary Jane Binks, wrote.

As well, Harriman sought a publication ban on the evidence she planned to present if Jane Doe's claim went to trial, including personal financial statements and details about her work at the Heart and Stroke Foundation. "The revelation of the criminal charges against the Defendant Williams and my identity as his wife has been devastating to me," she wrote. "The publication of further particular details of my professional life, personal financial situation, and legal affairs could have a significant negative impact upon me personally and professionally."

The dueling claims and counterclaims stirred fierce debate and much bad feeling in Tweed, still reeling from the criminal charges. Villagers wondered if the property transfer was what Williams had been referring to when he wrote in his April prison-cell message that he had put his personal affairs in order.

"This just flies in the face of what appears to be natural justice. It has a scheming, conniving kind of feel to it," said longtime resident Wayne Kay, a retired accountant and former sales director of Price Waterhouse Cooper. "Frankly, it's outrageous. This has created a lot of suspicion, and anywhere you go, it's the talk in town. The colonel's wife has become a huge discussion point."

Nor was there much applause in Tweed when it transpired that the OPP had agreed to reimburse Harriman $3,000 for damage to the hardwood floors in the Ottawa home, incurred during the police search. In Orleans, where the couple had lived for fourteen years, there was more residual sympathy for Harriman's situation, but those former neighbors could only guess at what she was going through. George White and the other members of the Wilkie Gang had sent her a letter of support shortly after Williams was arrested, but months later they had still heard nothing back. The small group who made up Harriman's inner circle of close friends also stayed silent, as did the Heart and Stroke Foundation, rebuffing all inquiries about her.

Nothing was immediately resolved. As usually happens when civil lawsuits run parallel to criminal cases, the suit took second place and was put on hold. The hearing to address Harriman's bid for a publication ban was pushed back until January, by which point it was expected that the multitude of criminal charges facing Williams would have been resolved.

And now, in October, it was time to do just that.

16

"CANADA'S BRIGHT, SHINING LIE"

Everyone involved in the Williams guilty plea and sentencing in October knew ahead of time that the repulsive facts of the case were going to be tough to deal with. A little of the collective shock had by then eased. Williams had swiftly been replaced as 8 Wing commander by the able Colonel Dave Cochrane, whose competent affability had done much to help cauterize the Trenton air base's wounds. Tweed, too, greatly settled down once it became evident the danger had passed and that the killer the village had barely known would never be coming back.

The close relationship between Tweed and 8 Wing/CFB Trenton, too, was reaffirmed and burnished. All through the investigation the military police at Trenton, part of the National Investigation Service, had been working closely with the OPP to ascertain Williams's comings and goings over the previous year. But the military also made efforts to reach out to the village of Tweed. In June, Cochrane made a special trip there to address councillors and help locals launch a light-hearted Elvis-themed community fundraiser. Cochrane didn't mention his predecessor by name but made clear the village's staunch loyalty was not taken for granted. "People in uniform are amazed at the strong support shown in small communities such as Tweed," he said. "You'll find that all the military members feel a sense of pride being part of this community, and want to work with everybody as we move forward."

But in the midst of that healing process, the day had come to face Williams's crimes head-on. Now, as proceedings got under-way in Belleville, the full horror of what Russell Williams had done was about to go under a microscope. For many of the reporters packed into the courtroom, there was a special chal-lenge: a few days before the hearing got under way, Superior Court judge Robert Scott had agreed to a media request that live blogging be permitted, enabling information to be transmitted to the world in real time via laptop computers and BlackBerrys.

It was not the first time bloggers had been allowed to report from inside a Canadian courtroom, but with the attention the Russ Williams case was getting, this would be by far the biggest venue. The other usual rules remained in place: no photos, no video, no live audio. It was to be a four-day hearing, and perhaps because it was not a trial but rather a largely scripted event, the experiment for the most part worked well, instantly generating heavy traffic on news websites.

The blogging wasn't as easy as it might have looked, and the hardest thing, made doubly difficult in such a fiercely competitive environment, was deciding what could be reported and what could not, because much of the evidence was too frightful to describe. And the horrific material was only part of the pressure felt by reporters, all struggling with ever-demanding editors who seemed to want everything, right now. In the pre-Internet era, reporters could think in terms of the next edition, or the next newscast. Now everything was live, with fresh developments and new angles surfacing all the time—sometimes accurate, some-times not. It was like trying to chase a boulder rolling down a hill.

One of the first to line up in the cold outside the Belleville courthouse early each morning was seasoned CBC Radio reporter Dave Seglins, who like most crime reporters has seen more than his share of murder and mayhem. Here is part of what he wrote shortly afterward for J-Source, a Canadian Journalism Foundation website:

> On the Friday, once home after things wrapped up, I took the day off to decompress. To my own surprise, and terror, I melted down, incapacitated by several bouts of anxiety, panic and uncontrollable dread that I've never felt before—and hope never to again . . . We journalists pride ourselves on steely nerves, detachment, pushing ourselves to the brink, being able to look into the deep, dark abyss of human potential and report back. What the public—and I fear many in our respective newsrooms—didn't fully appreciate was that we reporters were enduring this horror show with only a few hours sleep each night. The competition for good seats in the Belleville courthouse was so intense that the keen among us were lining up just before 5 a.m. each and every day to secure our spots. So we began each day exhausted, our defences down. We sat through four gruelling days of unrelenting evil. I didn't finish work each night until 10 or 11 p.m. Then, I'd slam down some food, a few drinks, and hopefully, my overwrought mind would shut down by just after midnight.

Seglins's frayed nerves were a common phenomenon among the press at the Williams hearing, and the only thing that kept most of us on an even keel was each other. Crime reporters tend to be a collegial bunch—far more than in other areas of news, such as, say, political coverage—because the work is often so difficult, and if you don't need a friend today, you surely will tomorrow.

It was no accident that the agreed statement of facts covering Williams's crimes was so complete and so graphic. Crown attorney Lee Burgess and the rest of the prosecution team had made a strategic decision that almost nothing pertinent would be withheld or glossed over. The decision drew a lot of criticism, because the events were so appalling, but it was the right thing to do. The trauma inflicted on Tweed, Belleville, Trenton, Brighton and the Ottawa suburb of Orleans had been so enormous, and the back-story so complex, that only a full rendition of what Williams had done would suffice. All along, the police investigation had been extremely secretive. Now that it was near its end, a truncated account of events assuredly would have stirred suspicions of a cover-up. Instead, the facts came out, and helpful court officials expedited an efficient system that made the court exhibits readily available.

The hearing began with Williams entering a guilty plea on all eighty-eight charges. One by one, as he stood ramrod-straight in the prisoner's box, the long list of offenses was read out by the court clerk, beginning with the two counts of first-degree murder and then on through the long series of sexual attacks and house break-ins, beginning in September 2007, in which he either stole lingerie or hunted for it. At the end, he was asked how he pleaded to all eighty-eight. "Guilty, your Honour," he replied in a clear voice, and sat down—one of the few people in Canadian judicial history to plead guilty to more than one charge of first-degree murder.

Williams already looked alone, bereft of support, viewed with disgust by almost everyone in the courtroom and by the military, which lost no time in further distancing itself from him. Later the same day, General Walter Natynczyk, Chief of the Defence Staff, issued the following statement on behalf of the Canadian Forces:

The tragic events surrounding Colonel Russell Williams stunned all Canadians and none more so than the members of the Canadian Forces. Today's guilty plea is the first step in a healing

process that will no doubt take many years. Upon formal conviction we will be in a position to officially begin the administrative
process that will lead to Colonel Williams' release from the
Canadian Forces. This will be completed as quickly as possible.
While we are confident that justice is prevailing, we recognize
that this will not diminish the pain and anguish suffered by the
families, friends, and communities so directly affected by these
tragic events. We extend our deepest sympathies to those affected,
and I reaffirm my commitment to promoting the well-being of
the men and women and families of the Canadian Forces.

After entering his eighty-eight guilty pleas, Williams sat down
as Burgess and co-prosecutor Robert Morrison began to read
out the lengthy agreed statement of facts, which Burgess advised
the court would be "extremely disturbing, the evidence will
cause emotional pain for the loved ones of victims." In the body
of the court were close to forty spectators who were either victims or friends and relatives of victims. Jessica Lloyd's mother
and older brother sat side by side, the former clutching a framed
portrait of her slain daughter. Looking on from the jury box
were OPP lead investigator Detective Inspector Chris Nicholas
and Belleville police chief Cory McMullan.

The events were laid out chronologically, beginning with the
first two burglaries in Tweed in 2007 and then methodically detail-
ing how Williams broke into each home, the photographs he took
and the items he stole. Many of the photos were shown on the twin
TV screens at the front of the courtroom, and the killer would
occasionally glance up at them for a moment—never longer.

As the evidence was presented, it became grimmer and grimmer, as Morrison outlined what he called Williams's "dangerous
escalation." Some spectators wept, many just shook their heads
in disbelief, almost everyone was aghast. After court adjourned

at the end of that first day, Andy Lloyd told reporters that as well as being shocked, he was angry. "I have lots of friends with teenage daughters, and it's terrible. Nobody likes to hear something like that. Sitting in there today and just hearing the stuff he did that doesn't even involve my sister makes me just as a Canadian angry . . . as a regular human being it makes me angry."

Day two was immeasurably worse, as the prosecution outlined the circumstances of the two sex attacks in Tweed, and then the two ghastly murders. No photos or video clips were shown. Instead, a detailed written synopsis was read out. It was a chronicle of violence and depravation so awful that neither Lloyd's brother nor her mother were present in court to hear how she died. As Burgess reached the point in his narrative, near the end of Lloyd's ordeal, when she said to Williams, "If I die, will you tell my mom I love her," the sound of weeping filled the courtroom.

Burgess spoke for everybody. "We are a community transformed by his crimes. And no doubt the feelings are the same in the Ottawa suburb of Orleans . . . And what makes this more despicable is that this was a man considered above reproach. He betrayed this community and he betrayed the military . . . No doubt he laughed at us as he [pursued his double life]." Recounting the murder of Comeau, and how she fought for her life, the prosecutor asked rhetorically: "Can there be any greater contrast of courage and cowardice? Can there be any greater contrast of evil and good?"

The agreed statement of facts complete, Williams rose once again and was formally convicted on all charges.

On day three, the court watched and heard segments of his ten-hour interview with Detective Sergeant Smyth on February 7, in which he had confessed, calmly describing the two murders and how he had carried them out. There is a moment near the beginning of the interrogation, before he realizes he's trapped, where he looks up and grins confidently at the police video camera recording the encounter. As he did so, cries of disgust rippled through the courtroom.

The court also released photo exhibits of letters Williams had written to his wife and to his victims during a break in that interrogation, after he confessed. Smyth had asked him if he wanted to do so and he had said yes.

To his wife, Mary Elizabeth Harriman, he wrote:

Dearest Mary Elizabeth, I love you, Sweet [illegible]. I am so very sorry for having hurt you like this. I know you'll take good care of sweet Rosie [their cat]. I love you, Russ.

To Lloyd's mother, he wrote:

Mrs. Lloyd, You won't believe me, I know, but I am sorry for having taken your daughter from you. Jessica was a beautiful, gentle young woman, as you know. I know she loved you very much—she told me so again and again. I can tell you that she did not suspect that the end was coming—Jessica was happy because she believed she was going home. I know you have already had a lot of pain in your life. I am sorry to have caused you more.

The note to Ernest Comeau, the father of Corporal Marie-France Comeau, reads:

I am sorry for having taken your daughter, Marie-France, from you . . . I know you won't be able to believe me, but it is true. Marie-France has been deeply missed by all that knew her.

It was the second time Williams had written to him. As mentioned earlier, a few days after Comeau's death a letter written on the 8 Wing commander's letterhead had dispatched his condolences.

To Jane Doe, his first sex assault victim, Williams wrote:

> I apologise for having traumatized you the way I did. No doubt you're left a bit safer now that I've been caught.

And to Laurie Massicotte, the second woman he tied up, blindfolded and photographed, he also apologized.

> Laurie, I am sorry for having hurt you the way I did. I really hope that the discussion we had has helped you turn your life around a bit. You seem like a bright woman, who could do much better for herself. I do hope you find a way to succeed.

The next order of business was to hear from some of the many people whose lives had been so badly scarred. In Canada, victim impact statements are often read into the court record before a convicted person is sentenced. In this instance, they could have no effect on the actual sentence, since Williams was automatically facing life imprisonment. But victim impact statements are taken seriously and examined closely if and when there is an application for parole.

And rarely are they as compelling as these ones, which chiefly addressed the death and suffering of Jessica Lloyd. Corporal Marie-France Comeau's former longtime boyfriend, Alain Plante, was in court that afternoon, as was Paul Bélanger, who had discovered her body. But there were no victim impact statements made on Comeau's behalf by relatives and friends, who were said (unofficially) to be too heartbroken to stand in front of her killer and try to tell him what he'd done. Their loss was addressed the next day by Crown attorney Burgess in his closing remarks.

Lloyd's mother, Roxanne, dignified and gracious in her sorrow, read out loud the dates of her daughter's birth and death, and told the court she now takes antidepressants and sleeping pills. And she articulated what most were feeling: there could be no forgiveness. "I feel like my heart has been ripped out of my chest, and I wouldn't wish this on anyone. But I can't help wondering why? Jessica never did anything to anyone . . . I have heard that people should be forgiven for their sins . . . but I can honestly say I hate Russell Williams . . . I am a broken woman . . . There's no punishment that can make this better."

Andy Lloyd told the court that he knew from the moment his sister went missing that something was very wrong, but that he could never have guessed what lay ahead. In tears, he said the case had drawn so much publicity that the grieving process had never been completed. He spoke of his happy, ebullient younger sister, saying Christmas had always been an especially joyous occasion for the family. Now, "looking ahead, I can't even imagine what Christmas will be like." Staring hard at Williams, he said: "The only good thing about all of this is that these crimes were stopped . . . I have so many questions that will haunt me for the rest of my life and only Russell Williams has the answers . . . I don't understand how fate or God or any higher power could allow these things to happen."

Applause erupted in the courtroom when he finished.

An aunt of Lloyd's named Deborah said her six-year-old grandson now wanted to be a police officer, so he could catch bad guys like the one who killed Jessica. And she made an allusion to the only fact that gave any shred of comfort to the Lloyd clan—that it was Jessica's rape and murder that had led to Williams's arrest. "I don't know how to close my eyes at night without seeing her scared little face and his piercing eyes. Many people have said it took our angel to bring Russell Williams down."

As she spoke those words, Detective Inspector Nicholas, the tough cop who had overseen the investigation, wiped his eyes.

Andy Lloyd had said the same: "No other woman will be traumatized or murdered ever again by Russell Williams and it is because of my sister," he told the court. "She's a hero for stopping this from happening to another family."

Williams appeared to be listening to everything attentively. When a friend of Lloyd's scornfully accused him of not having the guts even to look her in the eye, he lifted his miserable gaze and did just that.

Another of Lloyd's aunts, named Sharon (Judge Scott asked that their full names not be printed), said that every time she sees a picture of Williams's face, "it's like being kicked in the stomach . . . Jessica was home where she thought she was safe . . . She was powerless to defend herself against such an experienced predator . . . He ended her life and he dumped Jessica on the side of the road like a bag of trash . . . He has ruined so many lives."

Sarah, Lloyd's first cousin, told the court that she is now scared to be alone in her home. "I can't trust anyone, I worry all the time. I have lost my best friend . . . I have lost myself."

And an Ottawa student named Hayley, whose home was robbed by the murderer, told the court the break-in had left her frightened, even after she moved house. She said she had panic attacks and trouble sleeping, and that her life had changed because "I realized how violated I felt."

———

Then finally, on day four, it was time to hear from the killer him-self. A small microphone was placed at the front of the prisoner's box. Williams rose to his feet, blew his nose and began speaking. He proceeded slowly, tearing up and taking long pauses between sentences, as if struggling to summon up the energy to speak.

"Your Honour. I stand before you indescribably ashamed. I know the crimes I have committed have traumatized many people. The family and friends of Marie-France Comeau and Jessica Lloyd in particular have suffered and continue to suffer profound, desperate pain and sorrow as a result of what I've done. My assaults of [Jane Doe] and Ms. Massicotte have caused them to suffer terribly as well. Numerous victims of the break and enters I have committed have been very seriously distressed as a result of my having so invaded their most intimate privacy. My family, your Honour, has been irreparably damaged. The understandable hatred that was expressed yesterday and that has been palpable throughout the week has me recognize that most will find it impossible to accept, but the fact is, I deeply regret what I have done and the harm I know I have caused to many. I committed despicable crimes, your Honour, and in the process betrayed my family, my friends and colleagues and the Canadian Forces."

His chief lawyer, Michael Edelson, then told the court he and his client were in acceptance of everything that was taking place. "There is nothing that can be said to change the legal outcome and consequences here today. It is not the role of the defense to specifically address the victim impact resulting from the crimes. But we wish to acknowledge their suffering and we take no issue with what Crown counsel [is] proposing."

Edelson cited mitigating factors he said Judge Scott should take into consideration in passing sentence, even though the out-come was already certain. He said a long, expensive trial had been avoided because Williams had admitted all his crimes. Edelson also noted how thorough Williams's confession had been, how he had assisted police in locating Lloyd's body and how he had willingly told them where to find all the evidence they needed.

"It is important to note that only 17 of 48 homeowners had reported homes were broken into. Until he confessed, they were unable to identify a suspect," Edelson said. "He cannot stand before this court and expect forgiveness. Indeed, from a fundamental and moral perspective, one could debate whether he's even entitled to ask for forgiveness. We can, however, hope that the act of his pleading guilty might in some way at some time aid in the healing process. We wish to acknowledge their suffering and also to publicly declare that we empathize with these victims and what they've had to endure . . . Their pain is incalculable."

Edelson was not pleased with the way the case had played out, as he made clear in remarks later published in *Canadian Lawyer* magazine, particularly with regard to the many leaks that had taken place. "I think there should be a roundtable of leading defence, prosecution, [and] judges to discuss the implications of new media and management of files that are very high profile and the development of rules of practice and rules of professional responsibility to deal with these issues so that lawyers don't get offside," he was quoted as saying.

He also voiced concern about the ramifications for the witness system of allowing live blogging from a courtroom. "If you have instantaneous communication of the evidence, this means that all subsequent witnesses have access to the evidence in court as it's unfolding. I would like to see our rules of practice amended . . . in order to address these issues and give judges and lawyers clear guidance. I think the law societies across Canada, the federation of law societies, should strike a committee to address the new media issues and how they will impact on trials and court proceedings."

In his closing remarks, Crown attorney Burgess began by saying he would not seek to have Williams declared a dangerous offender—meaning he would be detained indefinitely—because it would prolong the hearing and would be "superfluous" to the proceedings since he did not believe any parole board would ever allow this killer to go free. Along with the two automatic life sentences for the two homicides, Burgess asked the judge to sentence Williams to ten-year concurrent sentences on each of the two sexual assaults, and to one-year concurrent sentences on each of the eighty-two break-ins.

Then he addressed the circumstances in which the two women had died. "They were violated, sir, not only by this man's hands, but by his lens, two young women terrorized in their last hours, just for the sexual gratification of this man," he told Scott. He spoke of Comeau, blindfolded and bloodied yet still fighting for her life, and of how Lloyd had cooperated with her captor, and of how Williams knew he'd kill her but told her she would survive if she did not resist. "David Russell Williams is simply one of the worst offenders in Canadian history," Burgess concluded, to applause. "We are a community that's been shocked and saddened by all that's transpired." But he also emphasized that Williams's brutal crimes were not representative of anything but himself. What really defined Belleville, Tweed and the other traumatized communities was the manner in which they had rallied together, Burgess told the court. "You could hardly open your eyes in the days after Lloyd's disappearance without seeing posters or something about her. We're a community that has also been transformed by his crimes. The impact of his crimes extends far beyond his crimes, what makes it more despicable is this is a man considered above reproach . . . He betrayed this community and he betrayed the military . . . And, as Andy Lloyd put it so eloquently yesterday, it was Jessica and the community that loved her that brought Mr. Williams down."

Burgess then spoke again of Corporal Marie-France Comeau. "The Comeau family has asked me to speak, briefly, on their behalf. They want the court to know how difficult it is to convey to this court the impact that this man's actions have caused on what is left of their family. There was a special bond between Marie-France and her father, Ernie. Marie-France was his only daughter. As he has described it, she was his ray of sunshine, pretty and very much in love with life. He rejoiced in what she had achieved and was comforted by her career choice . . . she had followed in his own footsteps in choosing a career in the Canadian Forces, an honourable vocation dedicated to the service of this country.

"First, they learned that she had died; then that she had been murdered; and finally that she had been murdered by a man of authority, a commander at the Trenton air force base. It is difficult for them to accept that a superior officer in the Canadian Forces would do as he did. They consider it a monstrous betrayal of trust. He has broken their lives. They—that is Ernie's wife, Lise, his son, Marc-André, and Ernie himself—cannot sleep. What were to have been family celebrations have turned into times of mourning for them. The notoriety of this case has only aggravated the impact of their loss. At this most difficult time, they simply want to be left alone, to confront their sorrow and to cry together, in private."

And then came the final act, the passing of double life sentences. But before imposing the automatic penalty, Judge Scott paused and said something that had not been anticipated. Even as he called Williams "a sado-sexual serial killer," he also said he believed he was genuinely remorseful and that his apology was sincere.

"There's been a saying that we've all used over time, and that is, 'Nothing surprises me any more,'" the judge said. "That adage has no meaning here. Fortunately for all, the nature of these crimes are very rare in our society. They do happen and they do occur when least expected. The depths of the depravity demonstrated by Russell Williams have no equal. One suspects that he has contained for most of his adult life sexual desires and fetishes. However, in 2007, these inner thoughts began to control his private actions, pushing him deeper and deeper into criminal behaviour, which culminated in the brutal and senseless murders of two innocents.

"Although not insane, it appears that Mr. Williams was and remains a very sick individual, but a very dangerous man nonetheless. Russell Williams will forever be remembered as a sado-sexual serial killer. Russell Williams lived a charmed life—the best of education, a leader of men and women, a respected rising star in our beloved armed forces. His double life fooled most people. He may be best described in the biographical sense as Canada's bright shining lie, my apologies to Mr. Sheehan [an American reporter named Neil Sheehan, who wrote a 1988 book with that title about the crimes of a U.S. lieutenant-colonel during the Vietnam War]."

As Judge Scott continued, Williams seemed to be listening closely. "Russell Williams's fall from grace has been swift and sure. His crimes have adversely affected this country and our community and the many families and individuals, all victims alike. The residents of Tweed say they've lost their innocence and their sense of safety. Members of the military speak of their sense of betrayal and seek a better explanation from their superiors [as] to what actually happened and why it happened. The victims of the attempted break and enters and break and enters and theft from the many private residences share the common theme that their lives and their homes have been violated. My wish to you is that in the fullness of time, your lives will return to normal.

"But we all understand why we are here today. Not to take away from the seriousness of the other crimes, but it is the serious acts of violence towards four women, two of whom were murdered, that must be the centred focus of our attention. Our thoughts and prayers are with all the victims, but these special victims and their families are the most damaged by the criminal behaviour of Russell Williams.

"Marie-France did not have to die. Jessica did not have to die. May all of you find the peace that you desperately deserve."

Then Judge Scott did something else that had not been anticipated.

Along with the prison time for the sex assaults and the break-ins, he handed Williams twin life sentences for the two murders, which translates into a minimum of 25 years behind bars. A conviction for first-degree murder always means at least 25 years' incarceration, but at the 15-year mark the killer can seek permission for a parole hearing, though few get it. When there is more than one victim, however, that so-called "faint hope clause" does not apply. As well, the judge imposed a lifetime ban on the possession of weapons, and ordered that Williams be registered as a sex offender, provide DNA samples to the police data bank, and pay a $100 victim surcharge for each charge, for a total of $8,800. He also acceded to Burgess's earlier request that Williams's Nissan Pathfinder be crushed, and that his camera be destroyed too, together with the hoard of stolen lingerie and the ropes he used.

What was highly unusual was that he also specified where Williams was to be locked up: Kingston Penitentiary. Normally, in Ontario, men who have just been sentenced to two years or more are shipped to Millhaven Penitentiary, which doubles as a classification center, where they are assessed for a few weeks and then placed somewhere in the federal prison system. But Williams was to go straight to Kingston, which would mean a cell in the facility's high-security segregation block.

And with that, still in handcuffs and shackles, Williams was for the last time led away. He shuffled out of the courtroom without a backward glance, was taken downstairs to the waiting prisoners' van and sped east along Highway 401 toward the ancient penitentiary. He had spent much of his adult life traveling Canada and the world. Now he was heading for a tomb.

Almost as soon as he was gone, the Belleville courthouse began resuming its normal appearance. The black canvas screen erected outside the back door was taken down, the walk-through metal detectors were removed, the parking barriers that had reserved space for the television trucks were dismantled. In nearby Trenton, military leaders gathered at 8 Wing/CFB Trenton for a media conference, where Lieutenant-General André Deschamps, Chief of the Air Staff, said the former base commander would be discharged, stripped of his rank and medals, and forced to repay the roughly $12,000 monthly salary he had accumulated since his arrest. The killer would be able to keep his pension, Deschamps said, because there was no legal basis for removing it.

Back in Belleville, Andy Lloyd and his mother, Roxanne McGarvey, stood on the courthouse steps, thanked everyone who had worked on the case and expressed a measure of satisfaction with the outcome. Ms. McGarvey said she was surprised at Williams's apparent remorse but that she had been glad to see it. "We're just all thankful that it is over and we can maybe now start to get on with our lives," she said, still holding the framed portrait of Jessica.

Her son echoed that. "It's over with, it's done with," Andy Lloyd said. "This is the best thing that's happened to our family since this stuff has happened. We just want to be normal again."

The police, too, had a few words to say outside court. Detective Inspector Nicholas stood with Crown attorney Burgess, Belleville police chief Cory McMullan and OPP Sergeant Kristine Rae, who had handled most of the media inquiries over the previous eight months. Together they praised the justice system for delivering the right verdict, reiterated their sympathy for the many people who had been so grievously harmed by Williams, and voiced hope that now it would be possible to move on.

As for what happens to the convicted killer, it was Andy Lloyd, whose broad shoulders had carried so much of the family's burden over the past eight months, who had the last word.

"As long as he dies in jail, I'm happy," he said.

17

A NEW KIND OF MONSTER

I n the media, Russ Williams was routinely referred to as a
psychopath, as though the term was a synonym for "deranged
criminal." He was nothing of the kind—he was far more
unusual than that. But there were plenty of the genuine article
to be found where he was headed next.

It took less than an hour for him to be whisked east along
Highway 401 to Kingston Penitentiary, where a group of police
briefly gathered outside the front gate to form a derisory welcoming committee. Built in 1835 and extensively renovated in recent
years, the fortresslike maximum-security prison sits on Lake
Ontario's north shore not far from downtown Kingston and has
long been synonymous with doing hard time. Its population is
usually around four hundred, with an additional hundred or so
housed at the Regional Treatment Centre, inside the penitentiary
walls, which treats sex offenders. Each inmate has his own cell,
but most have a measure of contact with other prisoners, at meal-
times and during the various programs made available.

Not Williams. For the same reasons he had been kept segregated from other prisoners at Quinte, he was immediately placed
in the penitentiary's dissociation wing, a cheerless, two-level cell
block whose twenty to twenty-five protective-custody residents
live in almost complete isolation, aside from the inhospitable jail

guards who control their every move. There are no windows in the whitish-colored cells, only a spyhole in the solid door. His next stop, which could also be his last, was most likely the penitentiary's H Block, home to Paul Bernardo, Michael Briere, the killer of Toronto child Holly Jones, and other inmates who would be instantly vulnerable to attack if placed in Kingston Penitentiary's general population. Bernardo has for many years been lodged in the cell at the far end of the lower level of H Block, so other prisoners don't pass him on their way to and from the small exercise yard. Even so, Plexiglas was installed to cover the front of his barred cell, which measures eight feet by ten, and is fitted with a cot bolted to the floor, a desk, a sink and a toilet, because he has more than once been attacked by other H Block residents, and feces were once hurled into his cell. Williams is likely to be no more popular.

It is not a pleasant environment. Meals in H Block are served on trays slid through a horizontal slot in the cell door, which is barred rather than solid to allow better closed-circuit camera surveillance. Prisoners can watch television, if they buy one, and can have writing materials and approved books. But there's no access to email or the Internet. The H Block inmates have no physical contact with each other, although they can sometimes manage shouted conversations with fellow prisoners they rarely see. For one hour each day, alone and in rotation, they are allowed to pace around the high-walled, 65-by-100-foot exercise yard. They can't receive incoming telephone calls, but they can phone people on an authorized call list (provided they pay for the calls) and are allowed occasional visits from relatives and friends, who must also be preapproved. When they gaze through the bars of their cell doors, the view is a concrete wall, illuminated by diffused light that filters through thick, reinforced windows high above.

This would be Williams's new life, an open-ended regimen of crashing monotony likely to be harder for a one-time pilot and military commander than for less worldly prisoners. Not that there was a speck of sympathy for him anywhere. Instead, debate swirled about how and why he was able to retain his military pension, worth close to $60,000 a year and only severable by means of a special, ad hoc regulation that would have to be approved by the Prime Minister's Office. A few weeks after he was imprisoned, public interest was rekindled when it emerged that his wife planned to file for divorce and in the meantime was pursuing a sealing order that—as with similar efforts over the lawsuit filed by Jane Doe months earlier—would shield her financial records and other documents from scrutiny. Every new detail in the Russ Williams saga seemed newsworthy.

Even after the court hearing and the voluminous revelations contained in the agreed statement of facts, many fundamental and haunting questions remain. Who was the real Russell Williams? And why did he begin his criminal activity when he did, at a relatively advanced age and when he was nearing the pinnacle of a glittering career?

It was fairly easy to see what Williams was not. He was clearly not insane, which in a criminal context broadly means not knowing that what you are doing is wrong. Neither was he mentally unfit to stand trial, which means you don't understand what's going on. Technically he could not be classed as a pedophile, despite the child porn found on his computer, because his sexual interests were much wider than that. He didn't fit the usual profile of a panty thief either.

Most important, and in marked contrast to Bernardo, Clifford Olson, Charles Manson and other notorious killers, Williams cannot be described as a psychopath; in fact, he is not even close to being one. Through overuse, the terms *psychopath* and *sociopath* have largely come to mean the same thing, and the definition is not complicated: a detached, indifferent person with no empathy or sympathy for the rest of the human race and its needs, very often a cold, narcissistic manipulator who has learned to hide behind a facade of pretending to care because that's what society expects. Plenty of selfish people in different walks of life show signs of psychopathy, and while most may not be particularly nice individuals, only a fraction break the law. Among those who do, what often accompanies that selfishness is a history of disregarding society's rules, and the criminal courts, of course, encounter many psychopaths.

But Williams was not that kind of murderer at all. The police and assorted justice system officials who dealt with his case quickly realized that he had feelings, emotions and attachments of all kinds: he cared about his wife, he cared about the military, he was devoted to his cats, and he also appears to have a moral compass—a conscience. That's why, in passing sentence, Judge Scott said he believed Williams's remorse was sincere—even as he described him as a sadistic sex killer who had committed some of the most disturbing crimes in Canadian judicial history. In other words, Williams knew that what he had done was wickedly wrong, and he knew so when he was doing it. And it was the fact that he chose to act anyway that made him so immensely dangerous.

Look, for example, at what Detective Sergeant Smyth said to him at one point during the interrogation. The interview had been going on for a little under three hours at this point, Williams was struggling, knew he was sinking fast, and he had just asked Smyth what his options were. Smyth replied: "Well, I don't think you want the cold-blooded psychopath option, I might be wrong eh, cause don't get me wrong I've met guys who actually kind of enjoyed the notoriety, got off on it, got off on having that label, [Paul] Bernardo being one of them . . . I don't see that in you, if I saw that in you I wouldn't even be back in here talking to you quite frankly. But maybe I'm wrong, maybe you got me fooled, I don't know."

Police interrogations can be full of trickery, but this was not a trick. As he did numerous times, Smyth was appealing to Williams's good side, because he knew there *was* a good side—the same positive side that so many other people had recognized and appreciated over the course of his life, and one that was entirely at odds with the heinous crimes he acknowledged committing. Another button pushed repeatedly by Smyth as Williams neared the cracking point was the acute distress of Jessica Lloyd's family as the hunt for her went on. And even as Williams viciously tormented and abused his captive victims, he had displayed peculiar flashes of empathy for them: getting the aspirin for Laurie Massicotte, telling Jane Doe that her baby would not be harmed, reassuring Lloyd that she would be all right when she had her apparent seizure.

The enormous gulf that separates the two faces of Russ Williams was the hardest thing for former friends and colleagues to deal with, because it seemed in hindsight as though they'd been fooled, and that the man they had known for all those years had been a total impostor. This helps explain why so few people had the courage to do what Jeff Farquhar, Garrett Lawless and a small handful of others were willing to do: stand up in public and say that the Russ Williams they'd known had been a thoroughly decent guy. Because as far as can be ascertained, that's true. All those qualities he had displayed—kindness, thoughtfulness, generosity, a certain sense of humor—had been real, but they had in the end been subsumed by a dark internal force that, once unleashed, proved far stronger.

Williams never had many friends, but there were a few people he cared deeply about. Over the years, he'd grown fond of Farquhar's parents and family, for example, and stopped by their

Burlington home many times for dinner and other visits. Then, in February 2009, Farquhar's mother died after a protracted illness, and Farquhar passed along the word to Williams by email. But the message went to an outdated address and Williams didn't learn what had happened until later. Farquhar says today it was the only time in their 27-year friendship that Williams blew up at him. "He said to me, 'What? You could have called.' He was very upset because he was very fond of my mom and my dad, and it was all too bad because my mom was very taken with Russ." Although this incident occurred well after Williams had launched his crime career, he had not physically harmed anyone at this stage. It none-theless seems highly improbable that a psychopath would become upset over not being apprised that a friend's mother had died.

"I am glad my parents aren't around to see any of this, because he was like a second son to them, and my grandmother, same thing," Farquhar says. "Russ was accepted into this family from age nineteen on. And I think that's what he always cherished about my family: he saw us do everything together. He saw us go out for dinners, twelve of us. He saw Sunday dinners at that dining room table, and I know he thought, 'Gee that's nice.' And he was always welcome. Some of the happiest times I've seen Russ was around my family, either at the cottage or around here. He'd spend hours talking to my dad about mechanical things."

The Farquhars weren't the only family to which Williams was strongly attached. Still living in Toronto, near the famous Casa Loma castle, is a retired couple with a son roughly Williams's age who became even closer to him than the Farquhars. They had a cottage in Georgian Bay that he would often visit. Like so many other former friends—including the two women he dated before he got married—they are most anxious not to be in any way identified with Williams. But there is no doubt that he was very fond of them.

The best single piece of evidence that Williams knew right from wrong is the fact that he was not willing to acknowledge possessing the child pornography found on his computer hard drives. Not because it would have made any difference to the sentence of life imprisonment he was already facing, but because it would be too disgraceful. The material had been downloaded from the Internet, and as child porn goes, it was not absolutely the worst of its kind, in that it chiefly depicted adolescent girls in sexual situations—but it was loathsome stuff all the same, and very clearly illegal.

"This was not just one or two images, and it was the one thing he could not summon himself up to admit to," says a source who took a direct role in the proceedings. "He would plead guilty to everything else, but not to that. That's an important clue as to who he is, and so you can see why he did not want a trial. This is a guy who structured his life around how he saw others act, and that's how his morality base came about. In the military you can kill people, it's accepted, that's one of the things that you do, it's within the realm of human behavior. And in war, rape is within that realm as well. The one thing that isn't, and stands outside that, is [sexual abuse of] children. There's no one else within his group that engages in that, so that would make him truly alone."

But it would be a mistake to believe that in providing such an exhaustive confession Williams had undergone some profound character transformation and was telling the whole truth, because very clearly he was not. There are said to be three useful rules to bear in mind when dealing with sex killers: they lie, they lie and they lie. Williams admitted to the eighty-eight criminal charges because he had no choice; he had carefully recorded all the details of his crimes, and he knew the police would find those records. Yet at the same time, it can be seen that his account of events was riddled with self-serving lies and evasions, all designed to minimize his bad intentions and the considerable planning he had put into his crimes.

His disingenuous explanation of how he had come to know Comeau, for example, occurred early in the interrogation, well before he admitted his guilt. But even after he did confess to killing her, he stuck to the story that he had met her just once, and the logic is evident: a sex killer who suddenly spins out of control and perhaps can't help himself—"if I could have stopped, I would have," might be the subtext—could be viewed as fractionally less evil than the methodical predator who stalks his victims and makes elaborate preparations. The outcome is the same, when caught, but the optics are marginally less bad, and possibly the distinction could have some bearing on whether parole is granted, many years down the line.

Williams's attachments and his conscience may set him apart from many other killers, certainly most serial killers, but his conscience is not why he confessed. He did so because the evidence against him was overwhelming, and when forced into a corner, confronted by facts, he reverted to type: he became the realist, too smart to fight a losing battle even in this, the worst moment of his life. So the issue became one of damage control. Trapped, he was willing to admit to rape and murder because he had no choice, but even as he did, he struggled to gloss over his crimes and salvage whatever he could. So he didn't really stalk Marie-France Comeau and he didn't really stalk Jessica Lloyd, he would prefer people to believe; he just sort of noticed them.

Asked by Smyth if he had liked or disliked the four women he attacked, he replied casually, "I didn't know any of them." Williams was a crude and clumsy killer, and an astonishingly skillful burglar who could come and go almost without a trace. But he didn't want to be thought of as a stalker, for the same reason he was not willing to plead guilty to child pornography charges: it would make him look even more hideous than he already did.

So if there was a good component to the character of Russ Williams, akin to Dr. Jekyll in the famous story, how to account for his demons? Some key elements of his twisted personality leap out. The most compelling by far is that by any yardstick he must be classed as a paraphiliac, or sexual deviant, with sexual obsessions rooted so deeply that once he gave them rein, they took over his life.

The American Journal of Psychiatry, the journal of the American Psychiatric Association, lists four criteria used to identify paraphilia, and Williams fits all of them: a preoccupation with non-human objects; suffering or humiliation inflicted on another person or on oneself (hence, perhaps, the grotesque posturing in stolen lingerie, even though he showed no homosexual inclinations); a sexual interest in children; and coercive sex involving nonconsenting partners.

As well, it is evident that he harbored enormous pent-up rage against women. Particularly telling was the violence he used against Comeau, who fought back and paid for it by being beaten very badly before she was suffocated. Where that anger has its origins is moot—Williams told police he didn't know—but in the vast majority of cases, the urges that drive sex killers are traced back to childhood. It is also conceivable, though unlikely, that his long-ago rejection by Misa, his girlfriend at university, had some relevance, and certainly the police were interested in that episode.

As for his fetishes, it is far from unusual for a sex murderer to start out by committing lingerie thefts and then go on to kill, which was Williams's apparent trajectory. Writing in 1999 in

The Journal of the American Academy of Psychiatry and the Law, authors Louis Schlesinger and Eugene Revitch reviewed the histories of 52 American killers aged 17 to 46 who had committed at least one sexual homicide. Of those 52 men, 22 (42 percent) had also committed sexually driven burglaries, a figure consistent with other research. The groundbreaking article cited three similar but smaller surveys that put the figure in the range of 32 to 46 percent. Indeed, some of the most infamous serial sex killers of the twentieth century also committed sex burglaries. They include Ted Bundy, executed in Florida in 1989 after he killed at least thirty women; Jerry Brudos (1939–2006), nicknamed the Shoe Fetish Slayer, who killed four women in Oregon in 1968–69; Albert DeSalvo (1931–1973), better known as the Boston Strangler, who murdered thirteen Massachusetts women; and Richard Ramírez, the Satan worshipper dubbed the Night Stalker who terrorized Los Angeles County in the mid-1980s and is still on death row at San Quentin prison for murdering thirteen women and men. There are numerous other examples.

But that link to sex burglaries among sexual killers is not strong the other way around. Within the much larger pool of sexually motivated burglars—a bigger group than some might suspect—very few do what Williams did, over a relatively short period of time (slightly more than two years): accelerate from theft to sexual assault to murder. A composite picture of the lingerie thief shows a furtive, lonely misfit, frequently a voyeur, who plucks up his courage and commits a hasty, often impulsive snatch-and-run. Williams's meticulous planning, his willingness to linger at the scene, often for hours, the vast amounts of underwear he stole and hoarded, and later his extreme aggression—all those factors set him well apart from most fetish burglars.

What also separates him from most of the pack is an underlying psychiatric disorder that many who knew Williams well had long recognized, and which in part explains why he was such a good military commander. He was obsessive and fixated on detail, and he had been all his life. But by the time of his arrest, what had once been no more than a mild and even amusing neurosis—the Drill Sergeant and Mother Goose were two of his nicknames at university—seems to have evolved into a full-blown case of obsessive-compulsive personality disorder (OCPD). Proof is found in his extraordinarily detailed accounts of his many crimes. It is not unusual for serial killers to keep track of what they do. Convicted in 1982 for the sex slayings of eleven young people in British Columbia, Clifford Olson wrote long, rambling accounts of each homicide, complete with sketched maps. But Williams took the process to a whole new level.

The chief hallmark of OCPD, which may be genetic in origin, is an extreme and constant fixation on tidiness, orderliness, rules and regulations, and a need for everything to be perfectly in place. With Williams, it seems this trait became more and more pronounced as the years passed. Farquhar recalls an event that occurred when he visited him one time at his home in Orleans in the fall of 2004. "I remember joking with Mary Eliz in Ottawa about Russ and his o/c, because he'd gotten so much worse than I remembered. Over the past two or three years he'd become much more fastidious with details. When I first came into Wilkie Drive that day, I wanted to hang up the coats, opened the closet door and I thought I was in Eaton's or something. Everything was lined up an inch and a half apart."

Then Farquhar made the mistake of touching Williams's new stainless steel refrigerator, leaving a mark. "Mary Eliz had poured us a couple of drinks and we were standing there at the center island and I put my hand on the fridge while I'm talking to Russ. And he's there staring at my hand. And I said, 'Oh, for Chrissakes Martha [Stewart], would you get over it.' I thought it was ridiculous." Williams reached for a special cloth to remove the mark. "And he says to Mary Eliz, 'I told you we shouldn't have bought stainless steel.' She just laughed."

Along with a need for cleanliness and good order, OCPD also frequently manifests itself in hoarding, or collecting things. Mingled with his high-octane sexual drive, the disorder seems to have helped turn Williams's psyche into a witch's brew. It is hard to overstate the scale of the sexual obsessiveness that was characteristic of his crimes. The extraordinary cruelty displayed in the videos he made when he violated Comeau and Lloyd was matched only by his attention to detail as he elaborately orchestrated his documentation of their suffering. And of course, there was the immense collection of the spoils of his two and a half years of break-ins: 1,400 items of lingerie—possibly many more—a collection so big that twice he had to destroy some of it. And then there was his vast digital collection: an astonishing 3,000-plus photos of himself and his trophies, far more than he would ever be able to look at.

Williams told police that he had not had sex with his wife for years, and certainly one facet of his sexuality is that he was a chronic, lifelong masturbator with an unquenchable need for gratification. But also clear, and so much more unusual, is that he was addicted to his macabre photo-taking. He was asked why he had killed Comeau and Lloyd when he had allowed his two victims in Tweed to live. He replied that in both instances he feared that if he freed them, police would immediately connect the lengthy picture sessions to the Tweed attacks. Yet Williams, an extremely bright man, must have come to that realization long before he made preparations to slink into their homes armed with his cameras and other equipment—duct tape, rope, the disguise he wore to conceal his face. Some sex murderers kill their victims without initially intending to do so, often when they fight back and events spiral out of control. But by bringing his cameras along to the houses of Comeau and Lloyd, Williams had effectively sealed their fates ahead of time. He *had to have* his photos, just as he *had to have* his huge trove of stolen undergarments. As he told Laurie Massicotte, as long as he could get his photos, everything would be all right.

It's evident that Williams was in the grip of something resembling a sexual addiction, although it assuredly remained his conscious choice to do what he did. The largest question hanging over his crimes was one of timing: if he had been bottling up his urges for so many years without acting, as he claimed, what was the catalyst that sent him down the slope? In the Robert Louis Stevenson novel *Strange Case of Dr. Jekyll and Mr. Hyde*, it was a potion that transformed the good doctor into a fearsome monster. What might Williams's trigger have been?

During his confession, he was asked precisely that question by Smyth—what had made him commit such horrendous crimes? "Have you spent much time thinking about that?" he was asked.

"Yeah, but I don't know the answers, and I'm pretty sure the answers don't matter," Williams replied.

Smyth also asked Williams this: "If for whatever reason you didn't end up on our radar, so to speak, do you think it would've happened again?"

Williams replied: "I was hoping not, but I can't answer the question."

As for his apparent late start in life as a predator, at age forty-four, Williams couldn't explain that either. He conceded it was unusual and was not sure why he began when he did, but he insisted it was a relatively recent development. He told Smyth he thought his obsession with women's undergarments dated back to his twenties or thirties, but that for most of his adult life he had been able to rein it in.

The OPP officer who oversaw the investigation said he too had no clue as to what made Williams snap, and why he escalated so swiftly from thief to killer. "It was a very troubling case to investigate," Detective Inspector Chris Nicholas said outside the Belleville courtroom after Williams was convicted and sentenced. "I have no idea why he killed those two women. It's one thing to break into a house and take lingerie, but those women were killed needlessly. I don't think anyone could come up with an answer that will satisfy anybody."

During another segment of the confession, however—a blacked-out portion redacted from the court exhibit—Williams did provide some insight into his state of mind during his two-and-a-half-year rampage, without suggesting he had any excuse or explanation for what he did. "He said there were two things that had been causing him distress," said a source close to the investigation. "One was a medical problem for which he was taking some medication, though he didn't blame the medication. The other was the death of his cat."

People who knew Williams recognized that both factors were significant in his life, particularly his state of health, an arthritic condition that, not long before he took command of 8 Wing, had briefly threatened his career.

The cat was Curio, euthanized at age eighteen around the end of 2008, more than a year after Williams began the break-ins, and many months before his behavior sharply ramped up into sexual assault in September 2009. Curio was cherished by both Williams and Harriman, who had had her since she was a kitten, shortly before their marriage in Winnipeg in 1991, and was perhaps the child the couple never had. When she died, "both of them almost had tears in their eyes," recalls former neighbor

Shirley Fraser, who lived directly across the street from them in Orleans and often fed Curio when her owners were away. George White, who lived a few doors down, concurs. "It was their baby. Russ would sit out on the veranda with it on his lap. Her death was heartbreaking to them, but they kept it to themselves."

The black-and-white Curio was an indoor cat and a peculiarly bad-tempered one, Fraser says. Even when being fed by a benign neighbor she would wave a paw, growl and hiss. "The only people she got along with were Russ and Mary Elizabeth." At the time of his arrest, Williams had accumulated hundreds of photos of Curio, one of which served as the wallpaper on his BlackBerry. A pilot who knew Williams at the 8 Wing/CFB Trenton base recalls a mutual female friend commiserating about Curio's death. "And the conversation ended right there, very abruptly. Russ just said, 'What do you know about my cat?' and he just walked away."

Curio was soon replaced by Rosebud, adopted as a kitten from the local humane society, and also female and black and white (though much friendlier than Curio). Rosebud stayed with Harriman, and in his short post-confession note to his wife, Williams mentions the animal. But Curio, it seems, was hard to replace. "The striking thing about the interrogation was the clinical, matter-of-fact way he talked about the most horrendous conduct," says the source familiar with the investigation. "He'd say, 'And then I threw her down and then I raped her.' With other [killers] you'll see them stumbling over the first letter of the word, or they lower their head. With him it was as if he was describing a commonplace thing.

"But when he gets to his cat, he's different. He really mourned that cat. He mentions it on two or three occasions. None of this was offered as an excuse, it was more in passing. 'What were the kinds of things that happened to you at around that period of time?' So he told them. But as to why he is what he is, he doesn't know, and he doesn't know why he did what he did, and why it came on so late in life."

Also clear is that in the years prior to his arrest Williams was taking a strong combination of prescription drugs for arthritic pain in his back and joints. Farquhar recounts the time he visited the colonel at his Tweed cottage in July 2009, a couple of days before he took command of the 8 Wing base. "I saw approximately eight good-size prescription bottles in the bathroom, and I got the impression that some of it was painkillers, but there were many different labels. I wasn't snooping and I didn't examine the labels. It was just plainly evident on the bathroom counter, right next to the sink. As you were washing your hands, you could see them. And I thought, 'Gee, that's a lot.'"

Williams rarely talked about himself, and complained more rarely still. But he made no great effort to conceal his health problems. His next-door neighbor in Tweed, Monique Murdoch, has recounted him mentioning the pain he sometimes suffered, and his efforts to find the right combination of drugs to treat it.

Paul Ferguson, program director at Cool 100, Belleville's country radio station, remembers playing golf with Williams at the September 2009 annual wing commander's charity golf tournament. The colonel hit the first ball and it was an excellent shot, coming within five yards of the pin. He nonetheless appeared to be in some discomfort, Ferguson said afterward. "He didn't often use a driver. He said that if he used a driver all day long, his back would be ruined, so he hit with a hybrid club."

The cocktail of drugs Williams had been ingesting included prednisone, a corticosteroid used to treat inflammation and arthritis, among other ailments. And prednisone—an immuno-suppressant drug prescribed over decades to millions of patients—can also have adverse side effects, including insomnia, euphoria and, much more rarely, manic behavior.

Williams's arthritis had begun with inflamed tendons in his feet and the pain later extended to multiple joints and his back, according to a person familiar with his condition. And in the summer of 2007, a few months before his first acknowledged break-in, he began taking prednisone, initially ingesting a relatively high daily dosage, tapering off over the next two years to a lower one. As well, he was taking sulfasalazine, another anti-inflammatory agent.

It seems unlikely that either drug pushed Williams over the edge. Among those who have taken prednisone, by far the most common complaint is of extreme irritability, and occasionally even uncontrollable anger. Yet whatever deep-rooted rage may have lurked within Williams's psyche, it is clear that his two and a half years of lawbreaking were anything but uncontrolled. His burglaries, sex assaults and murders, some of which took place over periods of many hours, all seem to have been planned with a frightening precision.

His health problems nonetheless drew attention. And toward the end of 2008 they came under scrutiny by a panel of senior officers and medical personnel tasked with ensuring Williams still met Department of Defence rules about deployability. According to the source familiar with his medical condition and the drugs he was taking, he would need to undergo regular blood testing. Forced early retirement was a distinct possibility. Instead, however, he was deemed fit to serve, and soon after came his promotion to full colonel (approved by Lieutenant-General Angus Watt) and commander of 8 Wing.

Despite the smorgasbord of pills Farquahar glimpsed at Williams's home, it appears unlikely he was secretly taking any unauthorized medication. Under stringent military regulations, he was required to be 100 percent mentally alert when behind the controls of an airplane, as he was early in December 2009, in between the Comeau and Lloyd murders, when he piloted the plane from Cologne, Germany, back to Trenton. Under those rules, the military doctor known as the flight surgeon must be apprised of any medication ingested by the pilot, even an aspirin, and under the honor system, it's up to the pilot to tell the flight surgeon what, if anything, he has taken. Williams, whose whole life had essentially become a lie, was clearly capable of deceit. Nor, as wing commander of the base, did he have anyone looking over his shoulder. At the same time, however, the drugs he was taking were prescription drugs, and if they were not approved by a doctor on the air base, the physician who did prescribe them was compelled under protocol to inform the base.

After Williams's conviction, the military would not disclose anything about his medical condition and the drugs he had been taking, citing right-to-privacy constraints. But there was no mention of drug use in the detailed statement of facts that accompanied his guilty pleas. And while his health problems plainly caused him distress, it seems a stretch to suggest prescription drugs were the major catalyst that helped transform him into a serial sex killer. Certainly he himself suggested no such thing during his lengthy confession and nor, presumably, did he say as much to Edelson, who would have seized upon whatever extenuating circumstances he could during the eight months that separated Williams's arrest in February and his guilty pleas in October. A few days before the guilty plea, Edelson dispatched his client to Ottawa for a psychiatric examination by Dr. John Bradford, often consulted by defence lawyers, but evidently gleaned nothing useful.

There was another factor of possible relevance. In June 2007, a few months before Williams's first acknowledged break-in, there was wide media coverage of a former Revelstoke, B.C., RCMP officer, the married father of a young child, who was

jailed for a year for breaking into the homes of four female colleagues whose underwear he stole and soiled in much the same
way that Williams would later do. A huge cache of pornographic
pictures and videos was also found in the ex-officer's house. A sentencing report suggested the man's sexual arousal stemmed from
"creating real or imagined circumstances in which he can feel
sexually potent without fear of rejection or criticism." Might the
pathetic tale have contributed to Williams's decision to cross
the line that divides fantasy from lawbreaking?

It is possible that it did. The difficulty here is that we don't really
know when his life of crime began. Williams said he committed his
first burglary in September 2007, but there is no good reason to
believe that. While it seems increasingly improbable that he killed
anyone before Comeau and Lloyd, the police view of his sex-
related prowling is that it very likely began much earlier than he
was willing to concede. Whether the pattern began as voyeurism
or perhaps snooping around friends' homes, what is clear is that
the timeline of the break-ins he acknowledged committing corre-
sponds precisely to the detailed records he had hidden on his computer hard drive, and which he knew would be found. In other
words, he was admitting what he had to admit. There may well
have been many prior incidents for which there was no evidence.
Worth noting, for instance, is his very aggressive conduct during
that first admitted break-in, where he targeted the bedroom of a
twelve-year-old girl in Tweed whom he knew well, lingering there
for hours as he took photo after photo. Such confident behavior
suggests this was not his first home invasion.

But whenever the precise point of departure, the question
remains: what was the trigger? Something must have happened to
him, and clearly it did. But it was almost certainly not an external
event, such as the effect of the drugs, the loss of Curio, a dramatic

change in his relationship with his wife or any other single catalyst. Rather, in the collective opinion of the police, forensic psychiatrists and other justice system officials who took a role in the prosecution, there was a convergence of factors whose defining event was a conscious decision by Williams to indulge his long-suppressed instincts. He thus crossed the line into lawbreaking and took the first rapid steps up what criminal profilers call "the ladder."

"The ladder is a quick, dramatic escalation," says a police source who was part of the investigation. "What goes with intelligence is the ability to control your behavior, and he picked a time when he thought he was good. Maybe he didn't feel a lot of pressure at work and it was his biological clock ticking, he's in Tweed, his wife is in Ottawa and he says: 'Fuck it, now is the time.' Before that, maybe he didn't have that burning need, maybe he hadn't hit that threshold."

Among the many things that sets Williams apart from other serial killers and rapists, aside from his not being a psychopath, is the rigid self-discipline that had made him such a good soldier and a star athlete. And for much of his career, it appears, that same discipline enabled him to keep his sexual urges in check. But they built and kept building, until they finally uncoiled like a tightly wound spring, most likely at a point when his after-hours life was no longer under much scrutiny, as when he returned from Camp Mirage and began working the desk job at the Directorate of Air Requirements in Ottawa. And once he succeeded—and kept succeeding, concealed by a respectable veneer that placed him far above suspicion—his confidence surged. The lie he told at the roadblock, for example, when he foolishly said he was in a rush because he had a sick child to tend to, was unnecessary and surely a mark of hubris.

And there is one overarching reason why we can be reasonably confident that it was an internal trigger rather than any external event that launched Williams's descent into depravity and murder. As has been seen, he was deeply ashamed of his conduct, which is why his account of events is filled with exculpatory falsehoods and evasions, none of which made much difference to the criminal case against him because the evidence was so strong. Those lies had a single purpose: Williams was struggling to salvage from the situation what little he could, if only for the sake of his wife, and he did so by continually minimizing the preparation and planning he had put into his crimes, and by painting an almost casual picture of his dreadful deeds.

So if there had been a single event that had changed him, we would know about it—because Williams would have told us. He would have cited anything, anything at all, that might have helped explain or excuse what he did. But no such excuse was ever made, not in the initial confession and not in the many hours of subsequent police questioning. There was no potion, akin to Dr. Jekyll's mix, though it would have been more satisfying if there had been. In terms of his crimes' rapid acceleration, the most significant single tipping point, noted by Jim Van Allen, the former OPP profiler who aided the Ottawa police investigating the Orleans burglaries, may have occurred when Williams made the decision not just to break into women's homes but to be inside the house at the same time as they were.

And because his disorder lurked so deeply within him, it seems unfair to fault the Canadian Armed Forces for not detecting it. Conceivably there were shortfalls in his medical evaluation near the end of 2008, after which he was promoted. But no military screening or checks-and-balances system could have detected the sickness of a murderous human freak like Russ Williams, an exemplary soldier and commander who committed all his crimes while off-duty, wreaking such destruction and heartbreak, and who started so late in life. That's how unusual he is—rarely seen before and unlikely to surface again—and he is not a symptom of anything but himself. Most serial killers are losers: the recluse who lives in a basement, the schizophrenic who hears voices in his head, the resentful misfit who has failed in life and hates the world. Williams was a winner, a powerful high-achiever, and nothing like any of them. And neither did he want to get caught—an enduring myth about serial killers.

"Why did he do it? Because he's a bright, bright guy who's intelligent, intelligent guys get bored easily, and he's got this deviant thing," the police source says. "And while we on the outside look at his life and say, 'Wow, he's at the top of his heap, he's flown the prime minister, he's in charge of his own air base,' that wasn't enough for him. His dark side is deviant sexuality, it's his preoccupation, and he made the decision to act on it. That's all. He's a big boy."

In his cage at Kingston Penitentiary, or in some other place very similar, Williams will have the rest of his life to ask himself that same question: why? He told Smyth he didn't know, and that he suspected the answers, whatever they might be, made little difference to anything. There he was wrong. He holds a spot among Canada's very worst killers, and many people remain bewildered by him—not only by his particular brand of cruelty but by his willingness to betray everything he was supposed to represent, all for his own sexual gratification.

He's unlikely to provide any more answers than he already has. In large part his tailored confessions were seen by his inquisitors as his only means of salvaging any shred of control from his hopeless situation. But as well, they helped him unburden himself of some guilt. And when done, he told police he had no interest in further discussing his crimes with anyone, least of all the media. What could it possibly achieve? Williams is intelligent enough to know that however enormous his shame, he can never be forgiven and no parole board can ever set him free.

But he doesn't mind talking to other people casually—off the record, as it were. Two days after he pleaded guilty to all the charges, he told a guard at the detention center that had he known his plea and sentencing would be such an enormous news event, he would not have gone ahead with it. It was one more lie, and a very obvious one. He knew very well that if his crimes had gone to trial, all the horrific evidence would have come out anyway, along with a great deal more, including disclosure of his kiddie-porn collection. As well, his already substantial legal fees would have swelled by tens of thousands of dollars—costs he told Smyth he was particularly anxious to avoid. The remark nonetheless shows how painful the media onslaught was, and how acute his sense of humiliation.

Nor is any more light likely to be shed by the Ontario Provincial Police, despite their successful investigation and the copious amounts of evidence presented in court. When Williams was convicted, the OPP said that after the thirty-day appeal period, investigators would be willing to entertain questions. But then, when the thirty days elapsed, orders came from newly minted commissioner Chris Lewis, Fantino's recent successor: out of deference to the victims and their families, it had been resolved there would be no more discussion of the Russ Williams case by the police officers or anyone else involved, all of whom were ordered to comply. It looked to be a clumsy move, because most of the questions probably had good answers: whether the residents of Tweed were given sufficient warning about the twin sex attacks; why the agreed statement of facts omitted the unfortunate but significant incident when the Belleville policewoman drove up to Lloyd's house and then departed, as Williams skulked in the darkness; whether the various police forces investigating different crimes could have liaised differently; whether Williams was ever under police scrutiny before he was nabbed at the roadblock that night (from the outset, the OPP was adamant he was not, but doubts persisted).

All of this could probably have been addressed fairly easily. The other big, unstated reason for the police reticence, however, was the ever-familiar overconcern about investigative techniques being compromised. As well, Stephen Harper's federal government was anxious to see the last of a tragedy and scandal that had been so injurious to the armed forces, and pressure was felt from the Prime Minister's Office to make the story quickly vanish, according to OPP sources. And so it was decided to say almost nothing, leaving the impression that, once again, a big Canadian police force had circled its wagons and retreated into silence— even after scoring such a ringing victory.

Most of the hundreds of people directly affected by Russell Williams's betrayal—thousands, if the Canadian military is included—had doubtless already drawn their conclusions about who or what he is. And for most, there may be comfort in knowing he will never again prey upon the fellow Canadians he was sworn to protect. For many, too, there is justice in knowing he will spend the rest of his days in a nightmarishly claustrophobic environment that will bring him great distress. In the victim impact phase of the sentencing hearing in Belleville, Lloyd's mother, Roxanne, a pendant containing some of Jessica's ashes dangling from her neck, spoke for many as she described through her tears the experience of seeing her daughter in a coffin: "No amount of suffering Russell Williams will feel after today can compare with the suffering we have felt." And a young woman named Kirsten, one of Jessica Lloyd's best friends, also expressed what many were feeling. After Williams acceded to Kirsten's challenge to look her in the eye, she told the court: "I hope he rots."

Two weeks after Williams was dispatched to the penitentiary, Governor General David Johnston formally revoked his military commission, sealing his expulsion from the Canadian Armed Forces. Then, in December, the Department of National Defence announced that his two medals would be shredded, along with his commission scroll. And in the interim, the military would perform a curious act of exorcism.

The people who live along Cosy Cove Lane in Tweed, and on adjoining Charles Court, had long wearied of gawking tourists driving by for a glimpse of the house of horrors where Jessica Lloyd died, and that was, in a sense, the epicenter of events. No one expected the blue-gray cottage ever to be inhabited again—if and when it is leveled, next-door neighbor Larry Jones has said he might buy the land—but in the meantime, the property's status had for months been on hold, frozen by a judicial order stemming from Jane Doe's lawsuit against Williams and Harriman.

Then, one day in the third week of November, at around the same time that Williams was being given a medical examination that sealed his formal discharge from the military, a minivan pulled up outside number 62 Cosy Cove Lane. In it were four members of the 8 Wing base at Trenton, including two military police officers, who with Williams's permission unlocked the door and went inside. Ninety minutes later the van departed, loaded with all the fallen commander's military clothing and equipment: uniform, boots, shirts, headdress, books. When anyone leaves the armed forces, it is standard procedure to retrieve his or her gear, and if possible recycle it. And it may be that that's what happened to some of Williams's stuff.

But not the crisp blue uniform he had once worn so proudly, and not anything else that bore his name. In a building at the Trenton air base there is an incinerator used to dispose of secret or sensitive documents. In a move that had no precedent, Williams's uniform was dropped inside and burned. The homicidal ex-colonel's disgrace was complete.

ACKNOWLEDGMENTS

The first debt of gratitude is to those people who were willing to talk to me—either on the record or on condition of anonymity—in my effort to tell the story of Russell Williams. As well, none of this could have happened without the generosity of colleagues at the *Globe and Mail*, most of all investigative reporter Greg McArthur, whose hard work and talent was plundered. Special thanks, too, to reporters Colin Freeze, Tony Reinhart and Christie Blatchford and to the amazing folk who run our Editorial Research operation: take a bow Celia Donnelly, Rick Cash, Paula Wilson and, especially, Stephanie Chambers. Thanks also to the senior *Globe* management for cutting me loose for many months, particularly Deputy Editor Sylvia Stead, who instantly recognized the story for what it was. In Tweed, Lisa Ford became a great friend and ally, and in Trenton the debt is to Kathleen Rankine and Steve Bolton for their kindness in sharing their knowledge of all things military. At Random House, thanks to Anne Collins, editor Pamela Murray and the rest of the team there, as well as freelance editors John Sweet and Angelika Glover. Likewise to Charles Conrad and his people at Crown Publishing Group in New York. Last, not least, thanks to my best friend, Bob McKelvie, to Sheila Whyte, and to my agent, Helen Heller, for their constant support and insight.

Finally, it was of utmost importance to try to do justice to the memories of the two courageous women who were murdered by Williams, Corporal Marie-France Comeau and Jessica Lloyd, and to acknowledge the scores of others who were harmed. Any errors are my own, but I've tried to tell the truth and hope that in some small way it might help heal some of the wounds.

PHOTO CREDITS

All photos are copyright Timothy Appleby except where otherwise noted. Grateful acknowledgment is expressed to the following people and sources for permission to reprint these images.

The maps of Orleans and Tweed on page ix are copyright Brian Hughes/GetStock.com.

i
all images courtesy *The Globe and Mail*

ii
(bottom)
© George White

iv
(top left and right) courtesy *The Globe and Mail*

v
(top) courtesy *The Globe and Mail*

vi
(top and center) courtesy *The Globe and Mail*

vii
Court exhibits: handout

viii
(top)
© Kathleen Rankine

(center)
©Chris Mikula/Ottawa Citizen

(bottom)
©The Canadian Press/Nathan Denette

Every effort has been made to contact the copyright holders; in the event of an inadvertent omission or error, please notify the publisher.

INDEX